CW01024660

Nikon®

D800 & D800E
Digital **Field Guide**

Nikon®
D800 & D800E
Digital Field Guide

J. Dennis Thomas

WILEY

John Wiley & Sons, Inc.

Nikon® D800 & D800E Digital Field Guide

Published by
John Wiley & Sons, Inc.
10475 Crosspoint Boulevard
Indianapolis, IN 46256
www.wiley.com

ISBN: 978-1-118-16914-8

Manufactured in the United States of America

10 9 8 7 6 5 4 3 2 1

For general information on our other products and services or to obtain technical support, please contact our Customer Care Department within the U.S. at (877) 762-2974, outside the U.S. at (317) 572-3993 or fax (317) 572-4002.

Wiley publishes in a variety of print and electronic formats and by print-on-demand. Some material included with standard print versions of this book may not be included in e-books or in print-on-demand. If this book refers to media such as a CD or DVD that is not included in the version you purchased, you may download this material at http://booksupport.wiley.com. For more information about Wiley products, visit www.wiley.com.

Library of Congress Control Number: 2012939591

WILEY

About the Author

J. Dennis Thomas is a freelance photographer, author, and musician based out of Austin, Texas. He has nearly 25 years of experience behind the lenses of Nikon cameras. His work has been published in many regional, national, and international publications, including the magazines *Rolling Stone, SPIN, Country Weekly*, *Elle*, *W Magazine*, and *US Weekly*. His photography is syndicated by the internationally renowned agency Corbis Images. Thomas has written more than a dozen highly successful Digital Field Guides for Wiley Publishing and has more in the works.

Credits

Acquisitions Editor
Courtney Allen

Project Editor
Cricket Krengel

Technical Editor
Mike Hagen

Copy Editors
Kim Heusel, Scott Tullis

Editorial Director
Robyn Siesky

Business Manager
Amy Knies

Senior Marketing Manager
Sandy Smith

**Vice President and Executive Group
Publisher**
Richard Swadley

Vice President and Executive Publisher
Barry Pruett

Project Coordinator
Kristie Rees

Graphics and Production Specialists
Claudia Bell
Andrea Hornberger
Jennifer Mayberry

Quality Control Technician
Melissa Cossell

Proofreading and Indexing
Susan Hobbs
BIM Indexing & Proofreading Services

For Henrietta and Maddie.

Acknowledgments

Thanks to Connie for giving me a helping hand when I needed it.

Contents

CHAPTER 3
Setting up the Nikon D800　　　　65

APPENDIX C
How to Use the Gray Card and
Color Checker   259

Glossary   261

Index   269

Introduction

About the D800

With the release of the Nikon D800 and D800E Nikon once again astounded everyone by designing a camera that went far and beyond what anyone expected. When Nikon released the D700 it was basically a D3 packed into a smaller body. It was a low-light wunderkind and was an immediate success because it allowed photographers to get D3-type image quality in a compact package that cost much less than a D3.

It has been a long wait for the D800, and when Nikon announced its new flagship dSLR — the 16MP D4 — most of us expected the D800 to follow suit in true Nikon fashion. The D800 was expected to be a D4 repackaged in a smaller body. Well, Nikon turned the camera world on its head when it announced that the D800 was a camera with a whopping 36MP sensor, more resolution than any other dSLR camera on the market, nearing the resolution of medium format. Basically, Nikon took its flagship high-resolution camera; the D3X, and added 12 million more pixels, 1080p video, the new EXPEED 3 processor, a 91,000-pixel RGB metering sensor, an improved focus module (the Multi-CAM 3500), Color Matrix Metering III, a larger 3.2-inch screen (closer to film ratio), and a slew of new dedicated buttons for quicker control. What Nikon did, astonishingly, is take the $8000 D3X, make it smaller and better and do it all for $5000 *less* than the D3X.

In addition to the D800, Nikon also offers the D800E, which is essentially the same camera without an anti-aliasing filter, which offers protection against moiré patterns by introducing a slight blur to the image. Removing this filter from the camera allows the images to be a bit sharper.

The D800 was not necessarily what many Nikon fans were expecting — the D3X D4, and a D700, smashed all together with a few more megapixels to boot. However, it is definitely a camera that will be a very popular one.

About the Digital Field Guide

This guide isn't meant to replace the camera manual, but it is meant to give you an easier way to learn about what all the buttons and dials do and also provide tips on when to use certain features. This guide also provides insights into different types of photography as well, telling you what modes are most useful and offering advice on lighting and different subjects.

To be clear, this is not necessarily a guide for a working professional photographer; this guide is intended to help the semi-pro, advanced amateur, intermediate, and even newcomers to the world of dSLR photography.

CHAPTER 1

Exploring the Nikon D800

This first chapter covers the key components of the D800. These are the knobs, dials, buttons, switches, and more. High-level cameras aimed at more advanced photographers always have more controls on the external part of the camera. This makes shooting for professional and advanced photographers easier because there's no need to navigate through the menu system to access most of the features that are important to photographers.

The D800 will feel a little familiar to a previous D700 user, but the D800 has had some changes in button layout. More controls have been added to accommodate the newer and more varied features, as well as to make accessing some of the previous features that were available only in the menu system easier. Even if you're familiar with the layout of previous Nikon cameras, you'll want to give this section a read to discover the new buttons and features that have been added to the Nikon D800.

Knowing your camera inside and out helps you to capture better images more quickly.

D800 and D800E

This has been a widely discussed topic since the D800 and D800E was first announced, so therefore I want to cover this topic right from the beginning. What is the difference between the D800 and the D800E? For all practical purposes both cameras are *exactly* the same in function and feature except for one key difference: The D800 has an anti-aliasing filter, also known as an Optical Low Pass Filter, or OLPF for short, whereas the D800E has an OPLF without anti-aliasing properties. That's it. Everything else functions the same. The meters, the menu system, and the button layout are all the same.

An anti-aliasing filter has been installed in *every* Nikon dSLR since the D1. Anti-aliasing filters (for digital imaging purposes) are made to do one thing: subtly blur the image. This tiny amount of blurring gets rid of moiré (an almost rainbow type of artifact) on things with fine repetitive detail such as fabric, bird feathers, architectural patterns, and screens. This small amount of blurring hasn't been a problem because most cameras didn't have a resolution high enough to notice the difference in sharpness, even when zoomed into an image at 100%.

With the D800E, Nikon has left it up to the photographer to decide to forgo the anti-aliasing properties for the increased sharpness.

This leads to the question, which one is better? And here's the surprising answer: Neither one is better than the other. Both cameras are very capable for all subjects, but each camera has things that appeal to photographers who specialize in different areas of photography. So which camera is best for you? If you're a serious hobbyist or even a professional that shoots a wide variety of subjects, the D800 is the best for all-around use. If you shoot fashion, birds, or architecture exclusively, the D800 may also be the best choice for you because it will not show moiré, which will save you untold amounts of time in post-processing.

The D800E is a great choice for landscape and nature photographers because repeating patterns do not often occur in nature, and the risk of moiré is very minimal. If you're a high-end professional photographer shooting exclusively in the studio with complete control over your lighting, and you don't mind retouching the moiré (or maybe even have retouchers to do it for you) the D800E's extra sharpness may appeal to you as well.

Key Components of the D800

Start by exploring the various buttons and dials located on the exterior of the camera. These are the buttons that you'll find yourself using the most to control shooting while out in the field.

Knowing your camera is the key to being an on-the-ball photographer able to change settings with lightning quickness so that you never lose a shot. If you don't know your camera, you'll be fumbling around trying to find your settings while important things may be happening.

Top of the camera

A selection of the most important buttons is situated on the top side of the camera, most notably the On/Off switch and Shutter Release button as well as the Movie Record button.

▶ **On/Off switch.** This switch, located concentric to the Shutter Release button, is used to turn the camera on and off. Pull the switch to the right to turn the camera on. Push the switch all the way to the left to turn off the camera. This switch also has a spring-loaded function that, when you pull it all the way to the right, illuminates the top LCD (and the Speedlight LCD if one is attached). You can also set the spring-loaded feature to turn on the Info screen in Custom Settings menu (✐) f1.

▶ **Shutter Release button.** No doubt you're familiar with this button because it's probably the most important button on the camera. Halfway depress the button to activate the camera's autofocus and light meter. Fully depressing this button releases the shutter and a photograph is taken. When the camera has been idle and has "gone to sleep," lightly pressing the Shutter Release button wakes up the camera. When the image review is on, lightly pressing the Shutter Release button turns off the LCD and prepares the camera for another shot. Some professionals prefer to disengage the Shutter Release button for autofocus, using the AF-ON button to initiate focus (✐ a4) and the Shutter Release button for shooting only.

▶ **Movie Record button.** Located just behind the Shutter Release button slightly to the left, pressing this button when the camera is in Live View automatically starts recording video. Although this button made its appearance on the D5100, it was excluded from the D7000. Nikon brought it back for the D4 and D800 cameras. If you are familiar with the high-end Nikon cameras already, you may find that the button is in an awkward place because it resides in the spot that the Exposure Mode button has been since the D200.

▶ **MODE button.** Located just behind the Movie Record button is the MODE button (**MODE**). Pressing the button and rotating the Main Command dial on the back of the camera allows you to select exposure modes: P, S, A, and M, short for Programmed Auto (**P**), Shutter Priority (**S**), Aperture Priority (**A**), and Manual exposure (**M**). This button also doubles as the two-button format feature when pressed in combination with the Delete button (🗑) and held for approximately 2 seconds, released and pressed again. This *double press* feature helps prevent you from accidentally formatting your cards.

CROSS REF For a detailed description of all the exposure modes, see Chapter 2.

▶ **Exposure Compensation button.** Pressing the Exposure Compensation button (🔲) and rotating the Main Command dial allows you to adjust the exposure from the camera's auto and semi-auto exposure modes (P, A, and S) ± 5 EV in 1/3 stops. Turning the Main Command dial to the right decreases exposure; turning the dial to the left increases the exposure.

▶ **Accessory shoe.** Previously referred to as a hot shoe, this is where an accessory flash is attached to the camera body. The hot shoe has an electronic contact that tells the flash to fire when the shutter is released. A number of other electronic contacts allow the camera to communicate with the flash, enabling the automated features of a dedicated flash unit such as the SB-700. You can also use this as a cold shoe to mount accessories such as the ME-1 stereo microphone or the GP-1 GPS unit.

▶ **Bracketing button.** This is another button that the D800 has inherited from Nikon's top-level cameras, the D1, D2, D3, and D4 series. This allows you to set auto-bracketing without entering into the menu system. The BKT button (**BKT**) can be assigned to different bracketing functions in ✐ f8. You can select from the following:

  • **Bracketing.** Pressing **BKT** and rotating the Main Command dial allows you to choose the number of bracketed frames, the Sub-command dial changes the Exposure Value amount.

CROSS REF For more information on Bracketing types see Chapter 2 ✐ e5.

- **Multiple exposure.** Pressing **BKT** and rotating the Main Command dial turns on and off the multiple exposure feature. Rotating the Sub-command dial allows you to select the number of exposures.

- **HDR (High Dynamic Range).** Pressing **BKT** and rotating the Main Command dial turns the HDR function on and off. The Sub-command dial enables you to select the exposure range.

MODE button

Movie Record button

On/Off switch

Shutter Release button

Exposure Compensation button

LCD Control Panel

Release mode dial lock release

Image Quality button

White Balance button

ISO button

Bracketing button

Accessory shoe/hot-shoe

Image courtesy of Nikon, Inc.

1.1 Top-of-the-camera controls

▶ **ISO button.** This button provides easy access to the ISO settings. Simply press the ISO button **ISO** and rotate the Main Command dial right to increase the ISO and left to decrease the ISO. Rotating the Sub-command dial allows you to turn on or off the Auto-ISO setting.

► **White Balance button.** Press the WB button (**WB**) and rotate the Main Command dial to choose from factory white balance settings, Kelvin settings, or settings you can preset and save yourself. Rotating the Sub-command dial allows you to adjust the existing setting by adding a small amount of amber (left) or blue (right).

CROSS REF   For more information on white balance settings, see Chapter 2.

► **Image Quality/Image Size button.** When you push the Image Quality/Image Size button (**QUAL**), your choices are RAW, Fine (JPEG), Normal (JPEG), and Basic (JPEG). You can also shoot RAW and JPEG simultaneously with all the JPEG compression options available (RAW + Fine, RAW + Normal, or RAW + Basic). The dual card slots allow you to simultaneously record RAW and JPEG files to two separate cards.

► **Release mode dial lock release.** Press this button to unlock the release mode dial so that it can be rotated to change release modes.

Back of the camera

The back of the D800 has a slew of controls on it. This is where you find the Menu button (**MENU**) as well as the all-important 3.2-inch 912K dot LCD and all the playback buttons.

To the eye of a D300/s or D700 user the layout may look very familiar, but some significant changes have been made that will change your shooting style when switching over to a D800.

► **LCD monitor.** This is the most obvious feature on the back of the camera. This 3.2-inch, 921,000-dot liquid crystal display (LCD) is a minor improvement over the LCD on the D700. The LCD is where you view all your current camera settings and review your images after shooting; and it displays the video feed for Live View and video recording.

► **Viewfinder.** This is what you look through to compose your photographs. Light coming through the lens is reflected through a pentaprism, enabling you to see exactly what you're shooting. The rubber eyepiece around the viewfinder gives you a softer place to rest your eye and blocks any extra light from entering the viewfinder as you compose and shoot your images. One upgrade from the D700 is that you now have a 100% view of the frame as opposed to the 95% coverage of the D700. 100% viewfinder coverage makes it much more accurate when composing your images. The viewfinder eyepiece is removable and can be replaced with a magnified version to adjust to your vision.

▶ **Diopter adjustment control.** Just to the right of the viewfinder is the Diopter adjustment control. Use this control to adjust the viewfinder lens to suit your individual vision differences (not everyone's eyesight is the same). To adjust this, look through the viewfinder at the shooting information. Pull out the adjuster, just a bit, and rotate the adjustment control until the information in the viewfinder display looks sharp.

Diopter adjustment

Eyepiece shutter lever   Metering mode dial

Delete button   Viewfinder   AE-L/AF-L button

AF-ON button

Release mode dial

Playback button   Main Command dial

Menu button

Protect/Help/
Picture Control button   Multi-selector

Playback/
Zoom in button   Focus selector lock

Thumbnail/   Speaker
Zoom out button
                                                     Live View button/Live View selector
OK button

                                                     Memory card access lamp

LCD monitor   Info button

Ambient light sensor

Image courtesy of Nikon, Inc.

1.2 Back-of-the-camera controls

▶ **Eyepiece shutter lever.** Flipping this lever closes a metal shutter under the eyepiece glass. This is useful when shooting long exposures, Live View or movies to prevent stray light from entering the camera through the viewfinder. The shutter lever must also be closed to remove the viewfinder eyepiece to prevent dirt and debris from entering the camera.

▶ **Release Mode dial.** One of the most obvious changes to the back of the camera is that the release mode dial has been redesigned so that it's more easily read from the back of the camera. Rotating this dial allows you to select from six different release modes.

- **Single Frame.** When the Single Frame option (s) is selected, the camera takes only a single photo even if the Shutter Release button is held down. Releasing the button allows you to shoot another single frame. This is a good option for most subjects.

- **Continuous Low Speed.** When Continuous Low Speed release mode (CL) is set, you can press and hold the Shutter Release button and the camera will continue to take photographs until the Shutter Release button is released. CL is programmable from 1 to 4 fps (frames per second) in ⬙ d3 when in FX mode; in DX mode the camera can shoot up to 5 fps.

- **Continuous High Speed.** As with low speed, when Continuous High Speed release mode (CH) is set, you can press and hold the Shutter Release button and the camera will continue to take photographs until the Shutter Release button is released. CH allows you to fire off 4 fps in FX mode and 5 fps in DX mode. When using the optional MB-D12 with an EN-EL-18 or AA batteries, the frame rate is increased to 5 fps in FX mode and up to 6 fps in DX mode.

NOTE To achieve maximum fps, the shutter speed should be at least 1/125 second.

- **Quiet Shutter release.** In a typical shutter cycle the reflex mirror flips up, the shutter opens and closes, and the mirror flips down. All this happens with one press of the Shutter Release button. With Quiet Shutter release mode (**Q**), the mirror flips up, the shutter opens and closes, but the mirror remains locked in the upward position as long as the Shutter Release button is held down. This allows you to leave the quiet area where you can then return the mirror to ready position by letting go of the Shutter Release button. In reality **Q** makes the camera quieter only by 25% because you still hear the initial mirror slap and the shutter opening and closing (which is pretty quiet itself). Personally, I don't think this release mode quiets the camera substantially enough to bother using it. **Q** is a single release mode.

- **Self-timer mode.** The Self-timer mode (⟳) delays the shutter release when the Shutter Release button is pressed. This can be used to allow you to hop in the shot, or you can use it to allow the tripod to steady when doing long exposures. The length of the timer can be set in ⬙ c3.

- **Mirror Lockup.** The Mirror lockup (Mᴜᴘ) option locks up the mirror before releasing the shutter to reduce vibration from the mirror slap. This option is best used at slower shutter speeds on a tripod.

▶ **Playback button.** Pressing the Playback button (▶) activates the Playback mode and by default displays the most recently taken photograph; or, if you were reviewing images, the last photo you viewed. You can also view other pictures by pressing the multi-selector left (◀) or right (▶).

▶ **Delete button.** If you are reviewing your pictures and find some that you don't want to keep, you can delete them by pressing 🗑. To prevent accidentally deleting images, the camera displays a dialog box asking you to confirm that you want to erase the picture. Press 🗑 a second time to permanently erase the image. This also doubles as the "two-button" format when used in conjunction with **MODE**.

▶ **The AE-L/AF-L button.** Pressing the AE-L/AF-L button (AE-L/AF-L) locks the auto-exposure and autofocus settings, allowing you to recompose the image without changing the focus or exposure. This button can also be programmed to do a number of different things in ✐ f6.

▶ **Metering selector.** Concentric to AE-L/AF-L is the Metering selector. This allows you to quickly select a metering mode by simply rotating the dial. The choices are Spot metering (⬚), Matrix metering (▤), and Center-weighted metering (⬓).

CROSS REF Metering modes are covered in depth in Chapter 2.

▶ **AF-ON.** The AF-ON button (**AF-ON**) allows you to activate the camera's autofocus without half-pressing the Shutter Release button. Some photographers prefer using this method to the Shutter Release button. Personally, I stick with the old-fashioned way of using the half-press shutter release focus. I find that using two buttons rather than one takes more effort, but I wholeheartedly encourage you to try **AF-ON**. Quite a few photographers find this preferable for their shooting style. To use this button effectively set ✐ a4 to OFF and then set the camera to AF-C.

▶ **Main Command dial.** This dial is used to change a variety of settings depending on which button you are using in conjunction with it. By default, it is used to change the shutter speed when the camera is in **S** and **M**. It is also used to adjust exposure compensation and aperture when used in conjunction with ⬚, and change the flash mode when pressing the Flash mode button (⚡). If you zoom in during Playback mode, it scrolls through the image at the same magnification. When not in Playback mode, pressing the Protect/Help/Picture Control button (O—┓), the Main Command dial allows you to quickly change the Picture Controls.

▶ **Menu button.** Press **MENU** to access the D800 menu options. There are a number of different menus, including Playback (▶), Shooting (◻), Custom Settings (✎), and Retouch (☑). You can also choose between using the Recent Settings menu (☰), or the My Menu option. Use the multi-selector to choose the menu you want to view and press (⊙) to enter the specific menu screen.

▶ **Protect/Help/Picture Control button.** This button serves a number of different functions. When in Playback mode, pressing it as the Protect button (O—┓) locks the image from accidentally being deleted if 🗑 is pressed. In the Menu screen, pressing it as the Help button (**?**) gives you a synopsis of what that particular setting does. Pressing it as the Picture Control button (▣) when the camera is in Shooting mode allows you to change the Picture Controls by rotating the Main Command dial.

CAUTION Protected images are deleted when the memory card is formatted.

▶ **Playback/Zoom in button.** When reviewing your images, you can press the Zoom in button (🔍) to get a closer look at the details of your image. This is a handy feature for checking the sharpness and focus of your shot. When you are zoomed in, use the multi-selector to navigate around within the image. To view your other images at the same zoom ratio, you can rotate the Main Command dial. To return to full-frame playback, press the Zoom out button (🔍▦). You may have to press 🔍▦ multiple times, depending on how much you have zoomed in.

▶ **Thumbnail/Zoom out button.** In Playback mode, pressing 🔍▦ allows you to go from full-frame playback (or viewing the whole image) to viewing thumbnails. The thumbnails can be displayed as 4, 9, or 72 images on a page. You can also view images by calendar date. When you view the menu options, pressing 🔍▦ displays a help screen that explains the functions of that particular menu option. This button also allows you to zoom out after you have zoomed in on a particular image.

NOTE One important thing to notice when upgrading from a D300/s or a D700 is that 🔍 and 🔍▦ have been flip-flopped. 🔍▦ is now above 🔍. This can be initially annoying, especially when switching between the two cameras.

▶ **OK button.** When the D800 is in the Menu mode, you press ⊛ to select the highlighted menu item. Pressing ⊛ in Playback mode displays the Retouch menu options.

▶ **Multi-selector.** The multi-selector is another button that serves a few different purposes. In Playback mode, you use it to scroll through the photographs you've taken, and you can also use it to view image information such as histograms and shooting settings. When the D800 is in Single point or Dynamic area AF modes, you can use the multi-selector to change the active focus point. And you use the multi-selector to navigate through the menu options. In ✐ f2 you can set the multi-selector center button to do a few different functions: In Playback mode you can set it to Reset (select center focus point, which is my personal option), or highlight active focus point. In Playback mode, you can set it to show thumb-nails, view histograms (my personal setting), zoom in on the current image (low, medium, or high magnification), or choose slot and folder. ✐ f3 allows you to use the multi-selector to keep the auto-exposure meters active.

▶ **Focus Selector Lock.** This lever allows you to lock the focus multi-selector from changing the focus point.

▶ **Speaker.** This small speaker allows you hear sound playback from the video footage. It's not phenomenal, but it does its job.

▶ **Live View button/Live View selector.** Another change from the D700 is the addition of this switch that replaces the Focus Mode selector of the previous models. This is a much more convenient way to use the Live View and movie settings. Simply pressing the Live View button (Lv) activates the Live View option, and flipping the switch allows you to choose between shooting stills or video.

▶ **Memory card access lamp.** This light blinks when the memory card is in use. Under no circumstances should you remove the card when this light is on or blinking. You could damage your card or camera and lose any information in the camera's buffer.

▶ **Info button.** Pressing the Info button (info) displays the shooting information on the main LCD. Pressing it twice opens the information edit screen (⊟), which quickly allows you to change important settings without actually entering the menu system.

▶ **Ambient light sensor.** This allows the D800 to automatically control the LCD monitor brightness by assessing how bright the ambient light is.

Front of the camera

The front of the D800 (the lens facing you) is the business end of the camera. There are only a few features on this end of the camera (see Figure 1.3).

Built-in flash

AF-Assist illuminator

Sub-command dial

Preview button

Function button

Image courtesy of Nikon, Inc.
1.3 Front-of-the-camera controls

▶ **Built-in flash.** This is a handy feature that allows you to take sharp pictures in low-light situations. Although not as versatile as one of the external Nikon Speedlights, such as the SB-700 or SB-600, the built-in flash can be used very effectively and is great for snapshots. I highly recommend getting a flash diffuser if you plan on using the flash often. The best feature of the built-in flash is that it allows you to control off-camera Speedlights for more professional lighting results.

▶ **Sub-command dial.** This dial is used to change the aperture settings when in M and A. When pressing the WB button you can rotate this dial to fine-tune the white balance setting: right for blue, left for amber.

▶ **AF-assist illuminator.** This is an LED that shines on the subject to help the camera to focus when the lighting is dim. The AF-assist illuminator lights only when in Single-servo AF mode (AF-S) and the center AF point is selected. This is also lit when the camera is set to Red-Eye Reduction flash using the camera's built-in flash.

▶ **Preview button.** By default pressing the button stops down the lens aperture so you can judge the depth of field in real time before pressing the Shutter Release button. This button can also be programmed for other features in ⌀ f5. See Chapter 3 for all the options.

▶ **Function button.** The Function button (**Fn**) can also be programmed for a multitude of different functions in ⌀ f4.

CROSS REF See Chapter 3 for all the **Fn** options.

NOTE The Preview and **Fn** options can also be programmed in the Information Display Settings.

Left side of the camera

On the left side of the camera (the lens facing away from you) are some buttons that control the flash and the focus mode, as well as the lens release. The, output terminals, used to connect your camera to a computer or to an external source for viewing your images directly from the camera, are also located on the left side. Additionally, a stereo microphone input and a headphone jack are hidden under a rubber cover that helps keep out dust and moisture. There is also a button to control the flash output. Different lenses also have some options on this side of the lens body.

▶ **Flash pop-up button.** Pressing this button simply pops up the built-in flash. Gently pressing the built-in flash locks it back into place.

▶ **Flash mode/FEC button.** By pressing the Flash mode/FEC button (🔼) and rotating the Main Command dial you change the flash sync modes. Rotating the Sub-command dial allows you to dial in flash exposure compensation. You can dial in up to +1EV or down to –3EV in 1/3 stops.

Lens mounting mark

Flash mode/FEC button

Flash pop-up button

Built-in microphone

PC Sync port

10-pin terminal

Lens release button

Focus mode selector/
AF mode button

Image courtesy of Nikon, Inc.

1.4 Controls on the left side of the camera

CROSS REF The flash sync modes and exposure compensation are covered in depth in Chapter 5.

▶ **Microphone.** Just behind ⚡± is a small built-in microphone used for recording sound when shooting video.

▶ **PC sync port.** No, this isn't a port where you can sync your personal computer with your camera. PC stands for Prontor/Compur, which (to make a long story short) was a company that manufactured shutters and designed this terminal to sync electronic flash with the shutter. This is still the de facto wired syncing system for flashes, although most professionals prefer to go wireless these days.

▶ **10-pin remote terminal.** This is a Nikon standard port that allows you to plug in accessories to remotely control the camera. There are a number of different accessories such as the MC-22 and the MC-36 remote shutter releases. This terminal is also used to connect the GPS-1 unit or another type of GPS unit using the MC-35 adaptor.

▶ **Lens release button.** Pressing this button unlocks the lens and allows you to rotate it to remove it from the camera body.

▶ **Focus mode selector/AF mode button.** Flipping the switch allows you to select between manual and autofocus. Pressing the button in the center and rotating the Main Command dial allows you to switch between single-servo (AF-S) and continuous (AF-C), and rotating the Sub-command dial allows you to select AF modes. Which mode you can select differs depending on which shooting mode you are in.

CROSS REF AF modes are covered in depth in Chapter 2.

▶ **Lens mounting mark.** Most lenses have a white or red dot on them to help you line up your lens bayonet so that it can be rotated and locked into place properly. Use this mark to line up with the mounting mark on the lens.

▶ **External microphone input.** This allows you to connect an external microphone like the Nikon ME-1 stereo microphone for higher quality audio for your videos.

▶ **USB 3.0 port.** This is where you plug in the USB 3.0 cable supplied with the camera for downloading images straight from the camera or for tethered shooting. The USB 3.0 cable is backward-compatible and can be used with USB 2.0 ports, albeit with a reduced transfer rate.

▶ **HDMI output.** This terminal is for connecting your camera to an HDTV or HD monitor. This requires a type C mini-pin HDMI cable that's available at any electronics store.

▶ **Headphone output.** This allows you to plug in headphones so that you can accurately monitor the sound input while recording video.

External microphone input

USB 3.0 port

Headphone input

HDMI output

Image courtesy of Nikon, Inc.

1.5 Inputs on the left side of the camera

Right side of the camera

On the right side of the camera (the lens facing away from you) is the memory card slot cover. Sliding this door toward the back of the camera opens it so you can insert or remove your memory cards.

LCD Control Panel

The control panel on the top of the camera provides a wealth of information that's available with just a quick glance. Most of your important settings are shown here.

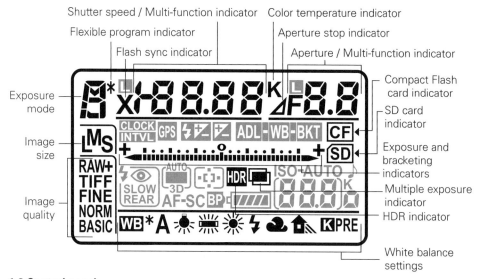

1.6 Control panel

▶ **Color temperature indicator.** When the WB is set to Kelvin, this K icon appears next to the color temperature number.

▶ **Shutter speed/Multi-function indicator.** By default this set of numbers shows you the shutter speed setting. This set of numbers also shows a myriad of other settings depending on which buttons are being pressed.

- **Exposure compensation value.** When pressing 🔲 and rotating the Main Command dial, the EV compensation number is shown.

- **FEC value.** Pressing 🔲 and rotating the Sub-command dial displays the FEC value.

- **WB fine-tuning.** Pressing **WB** and rotating the Sub-command dial fine-tunes the white balance setting. A is warmer, and B is cooler.

- **WB Preset number.** When using preset WB settings, the numbers appear here.

- **Color temperature.** When the WB is set to K, the panel displays the color temperature in the Kelvin scale when you press **WB**.

- **WB preset number.** When the WB is set to one of the preset numbers, pressing **WB** displays the preset number that is currently being used (d-1 – d-4).

- **Bracketing sequence.** When the D800 Auto-bracketing feature is activated, pressing **Fn** displays the number of shots in the bracketing sequence. This includes AE & flash, AE only, Flash only, WB, ADL, and Multiple exposure.

- **HDR Exposure differential.** When HDR is set to **BKT**, pressing the button displays the exposure differential.

- **Interval number.** When the D800 is set to interval photography, this displays how many exposures the camera is set to take.

- **Focal length (non-CPU lenses).** When the camera's **Fn** is set to choose a non-CPU lens number when pressed, the focal length of the non-CPU lens is shown. You must enter the lens data in the Setup menu.

▶ **Flash sync indicator.** This indicator appears as a small X. This comes on when you set your camera to the sync speed that is set in ✐ e1. This is available only when in **S** or **M**. To set the camera to the preset sync speed, dial the shutter speed down one setting past the longest shutter time, which is 30 seconds in **S** and bulb in **M**.

▶ **Flexible program indicator.** This appears as an asterisk next to the Exposure mode (**P***) when in **P**. This lets you know that you have changed the default auto exposure set by the camera to better suit your creative needs.

▶ **Exposure mode.** This tells you which exposure mode you are currently using: **P**, **S**, **A**, or **M**.

▶ **Image size.** When shooting JPEG or TIFF you can choose small, medium, or large file sizes. This indicates what size files are being recorded. When shooting RAW this area is blank.

▶ **Image quality.** This shows what image quality the D800 is set to shoot: RAW, TIFF, or JPEG compression Fine, Normal, or Basic.

▶ **White balance settings.** This displays the icon of the current WB setting. When fine-tuning has been applied to the default setting, an asterisk is shown next to WB icon as a reminder.

▶ **Exposure and bracketing indicators.** This is your light meter. When the bars are in the center, you are at the proper settings to get a good exposure; when the bars are to the right, you are overexposed; and when the bars are to the left, you are underexposing your image. The indicator appears when the camera is set to Π. When in P, 5, or R the indicator appears only when the current settings will cause an under- or overexposure. This also serves as your bracketing progress indicator when using auto-bracketing. If Exposure Compensation is applied this will be displayed in all Exposure modes indicating how much compensation is applied.

▶ **HDR indicator.** This lets you know when the HDR feature is activated.

▶ **Multiple exposure indicator.** When the Multiple exposure option is turned on, this icon is shown.

▶ **SD card indicator.** This is shown when an SD card is inserted.

▶ **CompactFlash card indicator.** This is shown when a CompactFlash card is inserted.

▶ **Aperture/Multi-function indicator.** At default settings, this displays the aperture at which the camera is set; or in the case of a non-CPU lens, this shows the number of stops of the lens, 1 being the widest, with the number going up as the aperture is stopped down. This indicator also displays other settings as follows:

    • **Auto-bracketing compensation increments.** This shows the increments of exposure at which your bracketing is set. When **BKT** is set to ADL bracketing, this displays the number of shots left in the sequence.

    • **Maximum aperture (non-CPU lenses).** When the non-CPU lens data is activated, the maximum aperture of the specified lens appears here.

▶ **Aperture stop indicator.** When using non-CPU lenses, you must use the aperture ring to adjust the aperture. When a non-CPU lens is mounted, this icon appears.

▶ **Flash Compensation indicator.** This icon is shown when flash compensation is applied to the built-in flash or an external Speedlight.

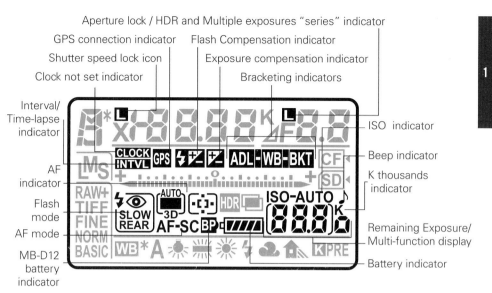

Aperture lock / HDR and Multiple exposures "series" indicator
GPS connection indicator   Flash Compensation indicator
Shutter speed lock icon   Exposure compensation indicator
Clock not set indicator   Bracketing indicators
Interval/Time-lapse indicator
AF indicator
Flash mode
AF mode
MB-D12 battery indicator
ISO indicator
Beep indicator
K thousands indicator
Remaining Exposure/Multi-function display
Battery indicator

1.7 Control panel

▶ **GPS Connection indicator.** When using an optional GP-1 or another GPS system, this indicator is shown. The icon remains lit if there is a good connection; if the GPS is searching for a signal, the icon blinks.

▶ **Shutter speed lock icon.** When the shutter speed is locked, this L icon appears next to the shutter speed setting.

▶ **Clock not set indicator.** When you first get your camera, this icon blinks until you set the information. An internal battery that gets its charge from the main battery powers the camera clock. You should never see this icon again unless you let your camera sit without a battery for 3 or 4 months.

▶ **Interval/Time-lapse indicator.** When your D800's intervalometer or time lapse setting is activated, this icon appears on the control panel.

▶ **AF-area Mode indicator.** This area displays the AF-area mode, if the camera is in Auto-area or 3D-tracking.

▶ **Flash modes.** This is where you find the information about your flash sync modes: Red-Eye Reduction, Slow Sync, Rear-Curtain Sync, or Slow and Rear-Curtain Sync in conjunction.

▶ **AF-Mode.** This area displays the focus mode the camera is set to: Single (AF-S) or Continuous (AF-C). If the camera is set to Manual focus nothing is shown here.

▶ **MB-D12 battery indicator.** When the camera is drawing power from the MB-D-12 battery, this BP icon appears next to the battery power level.

▶ **Battery indicator.** This shows the approximate power level of the battery in use.

▶ **Remaining exposure/Multi-function display.** By default this area shows how many exposures you have remaining on the memory card in use. This can also show a few other options:

- **Shots remaining in buffer.** When the Shutter Release button is half-pressed, the number of shots remaining before the buffer is full is shown.

- **ISO Sensitivity.** When ✐ d7 is set to ISO on or Easy ISO, the ISO setting is shown here.

- **Preset white balance indicator.** When pre-setting a white balance, this indicates whether the camera was successful in getting a reading. When Gd is shown, the setting was recorded successfully; if No Gd is shown, try again.

- **ADL Bracketing.** When ADL is set to **BKT**, this displays the bracketing amount of the HDR; rotating the Sub-command dial changes it.

- **Non-CPU lens number.** When the Non-CPU lens option is set to **Fn** or Preview button, when the button is pressed the lens number is shown here.

- **Capture mode indicator.** PC is shown when the camera is connected to a computer using Nikon Capture software.

▶ **K (thousands indicator).** This appears when the number of remaining exposures exceeds 1000. This is not to be confused with the K that may appear in the WB area, which is used to denote the Kelvin temperature.

▶ **Beep indicator.** This little musical note indicates that you have the AF confirmation beep activated. Note that the camera beeps only in Single AF mode.

▶ **ISO indicator.** When (ISO) is pressed and the ISO sensitivity is being displayed, the ISO indicator is shown. When the camera is set to Auto-ISO, this blinks ISO-Auto.

▶ **Aperture lock/HDR and multiple exposures series indicator.** When the aperture is locked, this L icon appears next to the aperture speed. This icon also appears if the camera is set to Series when using the HDR or Multiple exposure features.

▶ **Bracketing indicator.** This indicates when one of the bracketing features is engaged. For AE/Flash Bracketing, AE/Flash-BKT is shown; for AE bracketing, AE-BKT is shown; for Flash bracketing, Flash-BKT is shown; for white balance, WB-BKT is shown; and for Active D-Lighting, ADL-BKT is shown.

▶ **Exposure Compensation indicator.** The ⊞ icon appears if exposure compensation is applied in any of the semi-auto or auto exposure modes.

Viewfinder Display

When looking through the viewfinder, you see a lot of important information about the photo you are setting up (see Figure 1.8). Most of the information is also shown in the Information Display, but the Info Display is less handy when you are looking through the viewfinder composing a shot. Using the viewfinder display allows you to see what your settings are without taking your eye off of the scene.

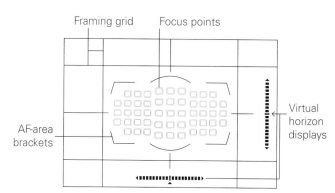

1.8 Viewfinder display

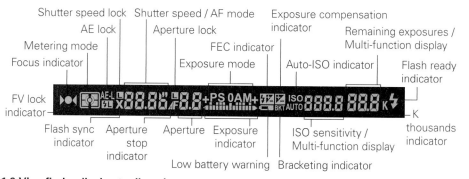

1.9 Viewfinder display toolbar close-up

▶ **Framing grid.** This option is shown when 🖉 d6 is set to On. The grid can help you line things up and keep your horizons straight.

▶ **Focus points.** The first things you're likely to notice when looking through the viewfinder are the small rectangles that appear directly in your field of view. These are the focus points. The active focus point lights up momentarily when the focus point is selected either manually or when the camera determines focus automatically. When in Auto-area AF mode (AF-A) it's possible for more than one focus point to be active.

▶ **AF-area brackets.** These show the limits of the AF points. Note that when shooting in 1.2X or DX mode, the focus points are closer to the edge of the frame, so you can focus on subjects nearer to the edge of the frame.

▶ **Virtual horizon display.** The virtual horizon tells whether the camera is level. To view this feature, **Fn** must be set to Virtual Horizon and pressed.

▶ **Focus indicator.** This is a green dot that lets you know whether the camera detects that the scene is in focus. When focus is achieved, the green dot lights up and stays lit, the indicator blinks while the camera is actively focusing, and if the camera is unable to achieve focus, it continues to blink. On either side of the dot there are two arrows that that indicate whether the focus falls in front of or behind the subject. The right arrow shows that the focus in front of the subject the left arrow shows that the focus is behind.

▶ **Metering mode.** This displays the metering mode currently in use, ▦ , ◉ , or ⊡ .

▶ **AE Lock.** This icon is displayed when the Auto Exposure is locked. AE-L is achieved by pressing ᴬᴱ-ᴸ or when the Shutter Release button is half-pressed and the focus is locked and 🖉 c1 to ON.

▶ **Shutter speed/AF Mode.** This area is where the current shutter speed is displayed. Smaller numbers are slower speeds and higher numbers are faster speeds. When the AF Mode button is pressed the AF modes are displayed here (AF-S or AF-C).

▶ **Aperture lock.** This icon is displayed next to the aperture setting if the aperture is locked. Aperture lock can be set in 🖉 f7.

▶ **Aperture.** This displays the aperture or f-stop setting. The smaller numbers are wider openings and larger numbers are narrower openings.

▶ **Exposure mode.** This displays your exposure mode setting: *P*, *S*, *A*, or *M*.

▶ **FEC indicator.** This icon appears when you adjust Flash Exposure Compensation (FEC). FEC is adjusted by pressing **⚡±** and rotating the Sub-command dial. Rotate right to add to the flash exposure and left to decrease the flash exposure.

▶ **Exposure compensation indicator.** This icon is displayed to remind you that exposure compensation has been applied to the exposure. While adjusting the settings, either the plus or minus is shown to indicate whether you are adding or decreasing exposure.

▶ **ISO sensitivity/multi-function display.** By default this is where you see the ISO sensitivity setting, but also displays a few other options.

  • **Preset white balance recording indicator.** When the camera is ready to record a white balance preset a blinking PRE icon is shown here.

  • **AF-area mode.** When the AF Mode button is pressed the AF-Area mode setting is displayed here. Rotating the Sub-command dial changes the settings between Single (S), Auto, Dynamic 9 points (d9), Dynamic 21 points (d21), Dynamic 51 points (d51), and 3D-Tracking (3d).

▶ **Remaining exposures/multi-function display.** By default this displays how many exposures are remaining on the currently active memory card. When the Shutter Release button is half-pressed, the number of shots remaining until the buffer is filled appears. When **±** or **⚡±** is pressed, the compensation amount is shown.

▶ **Flash read indicator.** This icon (**⚡**) is shown when the built-in flash or external Speedlight is fully charged and ready to fire.

▶ **FV (Flash Value) lock indicator.** This icon appears when the Preview button or **Fn** is assigned to lock the flash value.

▶ **Flash sync indicator.** This indicator is displayed as a small X. This is only available when in *S* or *M*. To set the camera to the preset sync speed, dial the shutter speed down one setting past the longest shutter time, which is 30 seconds in *S* and bulb in *M*. The Sync speed is set in ✐ e1.

▶ **Aperture stop indicator.** This is shown when a non-CPU lens is attached. If the non-CPU lens information is programmed into the camera the number the actual f-stop number is displayed, in no information is entered, the number of the aperture stop is displayed.

▶ **Exposure indicator.** This is your light meter. When the bars are in the center, you are at the proper settings to get a good exposure; when the bars are to the right, you are overexposed; when the bars are to the left, you are underexposing your image. This is displayed when the camera is set to M. When in P, S, or A this is displayed only when the current settings will cause an under- or overexposure or exposure compensation is dialed in.

▶ **Low battery warning.** This indicator appears when the battery is running low on charge. When the battery is fully depleted this icon blinks and the shutter release is disabled.

▶ **Bracketing indicator.** This icon is displayed only when the Auto-bracketing feature is in use. There are three types of bracketing to choose from: Autoexposure (AE), White Balance (WB), and Active D-Lighting (ADL).

▶ **Auto-ISO indicator.** This is displayed when using the D800's Auto-ISO feature. The Auto-ISO settings can be adjusted in the Shooting menu under ISO Sensitivity settings.

▶ **K thousands indicator.** This shows when you have more than 1000 shots remaining on the active memory card.

Information Display

The Information Display (Info Display for short) shows you just about every setting you have engaged on your camera. Simply pressing **info** brings the menu up on the LCD monitor (you can also program the On/Off switch to bring up the Info Display when pulled all the way to the right in ✐ f1). A lot of these features are also displayed on the LCD control panel and/or the viewfinder.

▶ **Exposure mode.** This tells you which exposure mode you are currently using: P, S, A, or M.

▶ **Flexible program indicator.** This is an asterisk that appears next to the Exposure mode when in P. This lets you know that you have changed the default auto exposure set by the camera to better suit your creative needs.

▶ **Flash sync indicator.** This indicator is displayed as a small X. This is only available when in S or M. To set the camera to the preset sync speed, dial the shutter speed down one setting past the longest shutter time, which is 30 seconds in S and bulb in M.

1

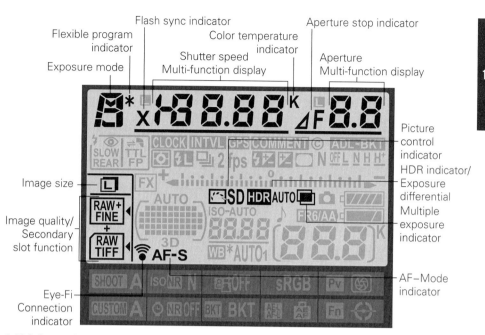

1.10 Information Display

▶ **Shutter speed/multi-function display.** By default this set of numbers shows you the shutter speed setting. This set of numbers also shows a myriad of other settings depending on which buttons are being pressed:

- **Exposure compensation value.** When pressing ☒ and rotating the Main Command dial, the EV compensation number is displayed.

- **FEC value.** Pressing ☒☒ and rotating the Sub-command dial displays the FEC value.

- **WB fine-tuning.** Pressing **WB** and rotating the Sub-command dial fine-tunes the white balance setting. A is warmer, and B is cooler.

- **Color temperature.** When the WB is set to K, the panel displays the color temperature in the Kelvin scale when you press **WB**.

- **WB preset number.** When the WB is set to one of the preset numbers, pressing **WB** displays the preset number that is currently being used (d-1 – d-4).

- **Bracketing sequence.** When the D800 Auto-bracketing feature is activated, pressing **Fn** displays the number of shots in the bracketing sequence. This includes AE & flash, AE only, Flash only, WB, ADL, and Multiple exposure.

- **Focal length (non-CPU lenses).** When the camera's **Fn** is set to choose a non-CPU lens number when pressed, the focal length of the non-CPU lens is displayed. You must enter the lens data in the Setup menu.

▶ **Color temperature indicator.** When this indicator is shown, the WB is set to Kelvin.

▶ **Aperture stop indicator.** When using non-CPU lenses you must use the aperture ring to adjust the aperture. When a non-CPU lens is mounted, this icon appears.

▶ **Aperture/Multi-function display.** At default settings this displays the aperture at which the camera is set; or in the case of a non-CPU lens, this shows the number of stops of the lens, 1 being the widest, with the number going up as the aperture is stopped down. This indicator also displays other settings as follows:

- **Auto-bracketing compensation increments.** This shows the increments of exposure at which your bracketing is set. When **BKT** is set to ADL bracketing, this displays the number of shots left in the sequence.

- **Maximum aperture (non-CPU lenses).** When the non-CPU lens data is activated, the maximum aperture of the specified lens appears here.

▶ **Picture control indicator.** This shows which Picture Control is set.

▶ **HDR indicator/ exposure differential.** This lets you know when the HDR feature is activated and what the exposure differential is set to. Note that HDR is unavailable when shooting in RAW.

▶ **Multiple exposure indicator.** When the Multiple exposure option is turned On, this icon is displayed.

▶ **AF-Mode indicator.** This area displays the focus mode the camera is set to Single (AF-S) or Continuous (AF-C). If the camera is set to Manual focus nothing is shown here.

▶ **Eye-Fi connection.** This icon is displayed only when an Eye-Fi card is inserted into the camera's SD memory port.

▶ **Image Quality/Secondary slot function.** There are two boxes in this section. The top one shows the image quality setting for the Primary memory card; the box below shows the function of the second slot. If it's set to Backup it will show the same Image Quality as the Primary slot. If it's set to Overflow, the box will be blank, but a small arrow will appear pointing from the top to the bottom. If the camera is set to record RAW on one card and JPEG on the other, the top displays RAW and the bottom JPEG. (Note that the QUAL settings must be set to RAW + JPEG or the camera defaults to Backup.)

▶ **Image size.** When shooting JPEG or TIFF you can choose small, medium, or large file sizes. This indicates what size files are being recorded. When shooting RAW this area is blank.

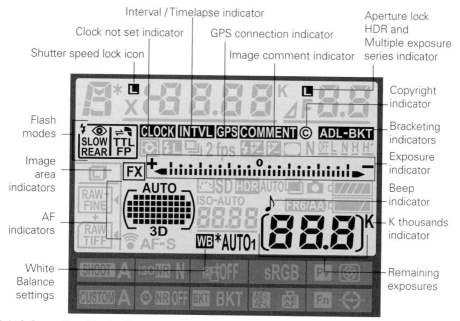

1.11 Information Display 2

▶ **Shutter speed lock icon.** When the shutter speed is locked, this L icon is displayed next to the shutter speed setting.

▶ **Clock not set indicator.** When you first get your camera, this icon blinks until you set the information. An internal battery that gets its charge from the main battery powers the camera clock. You should never see this icon again unless you let your camera sit without a battery for 3 or 4 months.

▶ **Interval/Time-lapse indicator.** When your D800's intervalometer or time lapse setting is activated, this icon appears in the Info Display.

▶ **GPS Connection indicator.** When using an optional GP-1 or another GPS system, this indicator is displayed. The icon remains lit if there is a good connection; if the GPS is searching for a signal, the icon blinks.

▶ **Image comment indicator.** In the Setup menu you can enter and attach comments to your images. If the Image Comment optionis enabled, you see this displayed.

▶ **Aperture Lock/HDR and Multiple exposure series indicator.** When the aperture is locked, this L icon is displayed next to the aperture speed. This icon also appears if the camera is set to Series when using the HDR or Multiple exposure features.

▶ **Copyright indicator.** Similar to the Image comment, in the Setup menu you can enter copyright information. You can enter the artist name and copyright holder. If you don't have a business name, you can just enter your name in the copyright field. This writes the information to the metadata. When the option is turned on, the copyright symbol (©) is displayed.

▶ **Bracketing indicator.** This indicates when one of the bracketing features is engaged. For AE/Flash Bracketing, AE/Flash-BKT is shown; for AE bracketing, AE-BKT is shown; for Flash bracketing, Flash-BKT is shown; for white balance, WB-BKT is shown; and for Active D-Lighting, ADL-BKT is shown.

▶ **Exposure indicator.** This is your light meter. When the bars are in the center, you are at the proper settings to get a good exposure; when the bars are to the right, you are overexposed; when the bars are to the left, you are underexposing your image. This is displayed when the camera is set to M. When in P, S, or A this is displayed only when the current settings will cause an under- or overexposure or exposure compensation is dialed in. This also serves as your Bracketing progress indicator when using auto bracketing.

CAUTION The exposure indicator default has been reversed from the default of all previous Nikons, including the pre-dSLR film cameras. If you want to switch back to Nikon's former default you can do so in ✎ f12.

▶ **Beep indicator.** This little musical note indicates that you have the AF confirmation beep activated. Note that the camera beeps only in Single AF mode.

▶ **K (thousands indicator).** This appears when the number of remaining exposures exceeds 1000. This is not to be confused with the K that may appear in the WB area, which is used to denote the Kelvin temperature.

▶ **Remaining exposures.** This number indicates the approximate amount of exposure you can store on your CF card. This display also shows the lens number of the saved non-CPU lens when that option is set to a function button. This also indicates that the camera is in the process of recording a time-lapse movie by displaying a succession of rotating lines.

▶ **White Balance setting.** This displays the icon of the current WB setting. When fine-tuning has been applied to the default setting, an asterisk is displayed next to the WB icon as a reminder.

▶ **AF indicators.** This display shows you the Autofocus area modes, as well as which focus point is selected.

▶ **Image area indicator.** This displays the selected image area: FX (36×24), 1.2X (30×20), DX (24×16), or 5:4 (30×24).

▶ **Flash modes.** This is where you find the information about your flash modes; flash sync modes are shown on the left. On the right the flash metering modes are displayed, and if an external Speedlight is attached, that also appears there.

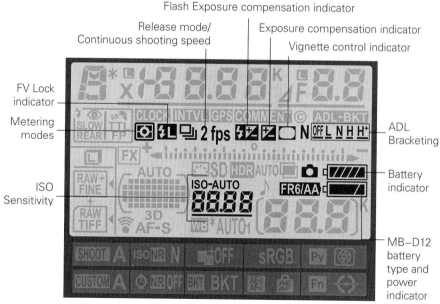

1.12 **Information Display 3**

▶ **Flash Value (FV) Lock indicator.** This icon is displayed if you have the **Fn** or the Preview button assigned to lock the Flash Value so you can meter the flash and recompose the image without changing the flash output value for the subject.

▶ **Release mode/continuous shooting speed.** These indicators display which Release mode your camera is set to. If the camera is set to CL or CH it also displays the max frames per second.

▶ **Flash Exposure Compensation indicator.** If you have adjusted your flash exposure, whether it be the built-in flash or an external Speedlight, this icon is shown 🔀.

▶ **Exposure Compensation indicator.** 🔀 is displayed if exposure compensation is applied in any of the semi-auto or auto exposure modes.

▶ **Vignette control indicator.** If you set your camera up for automatic vignette control, this icon is displayed. Beside it is a letter that tells you what the setting is: H (High) N (Normal), or L (Low).

▶ **ADL Bracketing amount.** If ADL Bracketing is applied, this option tells you which settings are chosen.

▶ **Battery indicator.** This shows the power level of the EN-EL15 battery in the camera.

▶ **MB-D12 Battery type and power indicator.** If you're using the optional MB-D12 grip, this displays the power level of the battery in it. It also shows the type of battery selected either the EN-EL15 or the EN-EL-18 (D4 battery), or the type of battery selected in ⌀ d11.

▶ **Metering modes.** This displays an icon showing your current metering mode: 🔳, 🔳, or 🔳.

Information Display Settings

Down at the bottom of the Information Display is a batch of setting displays, but what's different about these displays is that you can enter the Information Display and change these settings directly without entering the menu system, which can be a real timesaver. You can access the Info Display Settings by pressing **info** to bring up the Info Display and pressing it again to enter the Info Display Settings. You can then navigate through the settings using the multi-selector to highlight the setting you want, then press ⊛ or the multi-selector center button to enter the submenu to change the settings. All these settings were covered previously in the chapter. There are ten options:

1

▶ **Shooting Menu Bank**

▶ **High ISO Noise Reduction**

▶ **Active D-Lighting**

▶ **Color Space**

▶ **Preview button assignment**

▶ **Function button assignment**

▶ **AE-L/AF-L button assignment**

▶ **BKT button assignment**

▶ **Long Exposure Noise Reduction**

▶ **Custom Settings Bank**

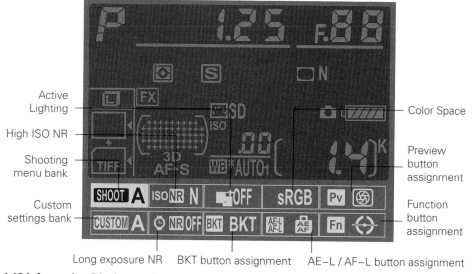

1.13 Information Display settings

CHAPTER 2

Nikon D800 Essentials

A fter you've acquainted yourself with all the buttons, dials, switches, and the changes to the aforementioned gadgets it's time to get familiarized with the essential operation of your camera.

Of course, if you've been using Nikon cameras for awhile, you may not need all of this information, but with the rapidly changing technology of digital photography today you might be surprised what you might have missed out on. The D800 has many new upgrades and features.

Knowing which modes and features to use in any given situation will allow you to get a good exposure no matter what.

Exposure Modes

The most important feature of your camera is the exposure modes. These modes allow you to control exactly how your camera controls the exposure settings.

Unlike some of the more entry-level cameras that Nikon offers, the D800 doesn't have scene modes, which means that you have some level of control of the exposure settings no matter which of the exposure modes is selected. In any shooting situation you can adjust the settings in a split second, which is exactly why most serious photographers use these modes as opposed to scene modes that lock you into the settings that the camera chooses.

You can easily switch among the four exposure modes by pressing the MODE button (**MODE**) and rotating the Main Command dial.

Programmed Auto

Programmed Auto mode (**P**) is an automatic exposure mode that frees you up from having to select the shutter speed or the aperture setting. This setting is handy when taking snapshots where you aren't concerned with having complete control over the exposure settings. Honestly, I find little use for this mode in professional photography, but as you will see it's not completely automatic, so you may find it useful.

P bases the exposure settings on a set of algorithms programmed in to the camera's firmware. The basic premise of the algorithm is to choose a shutter speed that's fast enough for handholding at the specified focal length while also maintaining an aperture that ensures enough depth of field to get everything in focus.

The camera uses the data supplied by the lens CPU to determine what the optimal settings are. Some of this data includes focal length and aperture range. For example, when you use a 24-70mm f/2.8 zoom lens, the camera keeps the aperture wide open until the shutter speed reaches about 1/40 second (just above minimum shutter speed to avoid camera shake). Upon reaching 1/40 second, the camera adjusts the aperture to increase depth of field. You can view the selected exposure settings in the viewfinder, the LCD control panel, and the Info display (**info**).

> **NOTE** When using Auto-ISO with **P** the camera tries to hold the shutter speed at the number specified in the Auto-ISO sensitivity settings.

Although **P** automatically selects the settings for you, you aren't locked into the settings. You can engage flexible program (**P***), which allows you to deviate from the camera's selected aperture and shutter speed. Use this feature by rotating the Main Command dial until the desired shutter speed or aperture is achieved. This allows you to choose a wider aperture/faster shutter speed when you rotate the dial to the right, or a smaller aperture/slower shutter speed when you rotate the dial to the left. With **P***, you can maintain the metered exposure while still having some control over the shutter speed and aperture settings.

A quick example of using **P*** would be if you're shooting a portrait, the camera has set the shutter speed at 1/60 second with an aperture of f/8, and you want a wider aperture to throw the background out of focus. By rotating the Main Command dial to the right, you can open the aperture up to f/4, which causes the shutter speed to increase to 1/250 second. This is what is known as an *equivalent exposure,* meaning you get the same exposure but the settings are different.

When **P*** is on, an asterisk appears next to the P on the LCD control panel. Rotate the Main Command dial until the asterisk disappears to return to the default Programmed Auto settings.

> **NOTE** **P** is not available when you use non-CPU lenses. When you're in **P** with a non-CPU lens attached, the camera automatically selects Aperture Priority mode (**A**). The P continues to appear on the LCD control panel, but **A** appears in the viewfinder display.

> **NOTE** In **P**, if there is not enough light to make a proper exposure, the camera displays Lo in place of the shutter speed setting.

Aperture Priority

Aperture Priority mode (**A**) is a semiautomatic exposure mode. You use this mode to select the aperture setting mostly for the purpose of controlling depth of field. Choosing the aperture to control depth of field is one of the most important aspects of photography and allows you to selectively control which areas of your image, from foreground to background, are in sharp focus and which areas are allowed to blur. Controlling depth of field enables you to draw the viewer's eye to a specific part of the image, which can make your images more dynamic and interesting to the viewer.

NOTE In *A*, if there is not enough light to make a proper exposure, the camera displays Lo in place of the shutter speed setting.

Shutter Priority

Shutter Priority mode (*S*) is another semiautomatic exposure mode. In this mode, you choose the shutter speed and the camera selects the aperture setting. *S* is used to control how the action is portrayed in the image. Faster shutter speeds to freeze movement or action or slow shutter speeds for static or slow-moving subjects or to allow motion blur from faster subjects.

CROSS REF For more information on how to effectively use your shutter speed for action shots, see Chapter 7.

NOTE In *S*, if there is not enough light to make a proper exposure, the camera displays Lo in place of the aperture setting.

Manual

When in the Manual mode (*M*) you set both the aperture and shutter speed settings. You can use the electronic analog exposure display on the D800 to determine the exposure needed, you can use a handheld light meter, or you can estimate the exposure.

CROSS REF For more info on the electronic analog exposure display, see Chapter 3.

You're probably wondering why you'd use *M* when you have the other modes. There are a few situations where you may want to set the exposure manually:

▶ **Complete control over exposure.** The camera decides the optimal exposure based on technical algorithms and an internal database of image information. What the camera decides is optimal is not necessarily what is optimal in your mind. You may want to underexpose to make your image dark and foreboding, or you may want to overexpose a bit to make the colors pop (making colors bright and contrasty). If your camera is set to *M*, you can choose the settings and place your image in whatever tonal range you want without having to fool with exposure compensation settings.

▶ **Studio flash.** When you're using studio strobes or external nondedicated flash units, you don't use the camera's metering system. When using external strobes, you need a flash meter or manual calculation to determine the proper exposure. Using ♍, you can quickly set the aperture and shutter speed to the proper exposure; just be sure not to set the shutter speed above the rated sync speed of 1/250 second.

▶ **Non-CPU lenses.** When you use older non-CPU lenses, the camera is automatically set to ♌ with the camera choosing the shutter speed. Switching to ♍ allows you to select both the shutter speed and aperture while using the camera's analog light meter that appears in the viewfinder display.

2

Metering Modes

Metering modes determine how the camera's light sensor collects and processes the information used to determine exposure. Each of these modes is useful for different types of lighting situations. The D800 has three metering modes — Matrix (▣), Center-weighted (▣), and Spot (▣) — to help you get the best exposure for your image. You can change the modes by using the Metering Mode dial directly to the right of the viewfinder.

Matrix

The Nikon D800 is using a brand-new metering system called 3D Color Matrix Metering III, or Matrix metering for short. The Matrix metering system takes measurements of the brightness, contrast, color, focus, distance of the scene, and runs the data through a series of algorithms that the camera firmware uses to determine the optimal exposure for the scene.

CROSS REF For more on lenses and lens specifications, see Chapter 4.

The D800 uses a newly designed 91,000-pixel RGB (Red, Green, Blue) to measure the intensity of the light and the color of a scene. The camera then compares the measurements to information from more than 30,000 images stored in its database. The D800 determines the exposure settings based on the findings from the comparison.

The Matrix metering system of the D800 performs several ways automatically, based on the type of Nikon lens that you use.

▶ **3D Color Matrix Metering III.** This is the default metering system that the camera employs when a G- or D-type lens is attached to the camera. Most lenses made since the early to mid-1990s are these types of lenses. The only difference between the G- and D-type lenses is there is no aperture ring on the G-type lens. When using the Matrix metering method, the camera decides the exposure setting largely based on the brightness and contrast of the overall scene and the colors of the subject matter as well as other data from the scene. It also takes into account the distance of the subject and which focus point is used, as well as the lens focal length to further decide which areas of the image need to get the proper exposure. For example, if you're using a wide-angle lens with a distant subject with a bright area at the top of the frame, the meter takes this into consideration when setting the exposure so that the sky and clouds don't lose critical detail.

▶ **Color Matrix Metering II.** This type of metering is used when a non-D- or G-type CPU lens is attached to the camera. Most AF lenses made from about 1986 to the early to mid-1990s fit into this category. The Matrix metering recognizes this and the camera uses only brightness, subject color, and focus information to determine the right exposure.

▶ **Color Matrix Metering.** This type of metering is engaged when a non-CPU lens is attached to the camera and when the focal length and maximum aperture are specified using the non-CPU data in the D800 Setup menu. The exposure is then calculated solely on the brightness of the scene and the subject color. If a non-CPU lens is attached and no lens information is entered, the camera's meter defaults to Center-weighted metering.

Matrix metering is suitable for use with most subjects given the large amount of image data in the Matrix metering database. The camera can make a fairly accurate assessment about what type of image you are shooting and adjust the exposure accordingly. Paired with Nikon's Active D-Lighting, your exposures will have good dynamic range throughout the entire image.

CROSS REF For more information on Active D-Lighting, see Chapter 3.

Center-weighted

When the camera's metering mode is switched to ⊡, the meter takes a light reading of the whole scene but bases the exposure settings mostly on the light falling on the center of the scene. The camera determines about 75% of the exposure from a circular pattern in the center of the frame and 25% from the area around the center.

By default, the circular pattern is 8mm in diameter, but you can choose to make the circle bigger or smaller depending on the subject. Your choices are 6, 8, 10, or 13mm and are found in the Custom Settings menu (✐) CSM b5.

> **NOTE** There is also a setting for Average, which takes a reading from the whole scene and averages out the exposure from the brightness levels. This option can often result in dull low-contrast images.

2

◉ works great when shooting photos where you know the main subject will be in the middle of the frame. This metering mode is useful when photographing a dark subject against a bright background, or a light subject against a dark background. It works especially well for portraits where you want to preserve the background detail while exposing correctly for the subject.

With Center-weighted metering, you can get consistent results without worrying about the adjustments in exposure settings that sometimes result when using Matrix metering.

CROSS REF You can change the Center-weighted circle diameter in ✐ b5, which I explain in more detail in Chapter 3.

Spot

In ⬚, the camera does just that: meters only a spot. This spot is only 3mm in diameter and only accounts for 2% of the frame. The spot is linked to the active focus point, which is good, so you can focus and meter your subject at the same time instead of metering the subject, pressing AE-L (Auto Exposure Lock), and then recomposing the photo. The D800 has 51 focus points, so it's like having 51 spot meters to choose from throughout the scene.

Choose Spot metering when the subject is the only thing in the frame that you want the camera to expose for. You select the spot meter to meter a precise area of light within the scene. This is not necessarily tied to the subject. For example, when you photograph a subject on a completely white or black background, you need not be concerned with preserving detail in the background; therefore, exposing just for the subject works perfectly.

NOTE When you use a non-CPU lens with Spot metering, the center spot is automatically selected.

Focus Modes

The Nikon D800 has three focus modes, two of which are AF modes: Continuous (C), Single (S), and Manual (M). Each of these modes is useful in its own way for different types of shooting conditions, from sports to portraits to still-life photographs. Nikon has changed this switch from previous models. You can switch from Manual to AF simply by flipping the switch. To switch between Single AF or Continuous AF press the button in the center of the switch and rotate the Main Command dial.

How the D800 autofocus works

The D800 has a completely new AF system, the Multi-CAM 3500FX with 51 focus points, 15 of which are cross-type sensor, which offer a better ability to detect contrast for focusing purposes.

Simplified, the Multi-CAM 3500FX AF works by reading contrast values from a sensor inside the camera's viewing system. As mentioned earlier, the D800 employs two sensor types: cross and horizontal. As you may have guessed, cross-type sensors are shaped like a cross while horizontal sensors are shaped like a horizontal line. You can think of them like plus and minus signs. Cross-type sensors are able to read the contrast horizontally and vertically. Horizontal sensors can only interpret contrast in one direction. (When the camera is positioned in portrait orientation, the horizontal sensors are positioned vertically.)

Cross-type sensors can evaluate for focus much more accurately than horizontal sensors, but horizontal sensors can do it a bit more quickly (provided that the contrast runs in the right direction). Cross-type sensors require more light to work properly so horizontal sensors are also included in the array to speed up the AF, especially in low-light situations.

Phase detection

The AF system on the D800 works by using *phase detection* using a sensor in the camera's body. Phase detection is achieved with a beam splitter that diverts light that is coming from the lens to two optical prisms that send the light as two separate images to the AF sensor in the D800. This creates a type of rangefinder where the base is the same as the diameter or aperture of the lens. The larger the length of the base, the easier it is for the rangefinder to determine whether the two images are in phase, or in focus. This is why lenses with wider apertures focus faster than lenses with smaller maximum apertures. This is also why the AF usually can't work with slower lenses coupled with a tele-converter, which reduces the effective aperture of the lens. The base length of the rangefinder images is simply too small to allow the AF system to determine the proper focusing distance. The AF sensor reads the contrast or phase difference between the two images that are being projected on it. This is the primary way that the D800 AF system works. This type of focus is also referred to as SIR-TTL, or Secondary Image Registration-Through the Lens, given the AF sensor relies on a secondary image, as opposed to the primary image, that is projected into the viewfinder from the reflex mirror.

Contrast detection

Contrast detection focus is only used by the D800 when using Live View mode and video. This is the same method smaller compact digital cameras use to focus. Contrast detection focus is slower and uses the image sensor itself to determine whether the subject is in focus. It is a relatively simple operation in which the sensor detects the contrast between different subjects in the scene. The camera does this by moving the lens elements until sufficient contrast is achieved between the pixels that lie under the selected focus point. With contrast detection, a greater area of the frame can be focused upon, which means you can set the focus area to anywhere within the scene.

Continuous

When the camera is set to Continuous AF (AF-C), the camera continues to focus as long as the Shutter Release button is pressed halfway (or the Autofocus-On [AF-ON] button is pressed). If the subject moves, the camera activates Predictive Focus Tracking. With Predictive Focus Tracking on, the camera tracks the subject to maintain focus and attempts to predict where the subject will be when the shutter is released. When in AF-C mode, the camera fires when the Shutter Release button is fully depressed whether the subject is in focus or not. This custom AF setting is known as Release Priority. Another option is Release + Focus. In this mode, you can take a picture whether or not the camera is in focus but the camera slows down the frame rate when there is low contrast or little light to allow the camera more time between shots to achieve focus. You can choose from Focus, Release, or Release + Focus Priority in ✐ a1. This is the AF-C mode you want to use when shooting sports or any subject that may be moving erratically. If you want to be sure that the scene is in focus before the shutter is released, you can change the setting to Focus Priority. When the Focus Priority option is selected, the camera continues to focus while the Shutter Release button is pressed but the shutter releases only when the subject is in focus. This may cause your frame rate to slow down.

Single

In Single AF, or AF-S mode (not to be confused with the lens designation), the camera focuses when the Shutter Release button is pressed halfway. When the camera achieves focus, the focus locks. The focus remains locked until the shutter is released or the Shutter Release button is no longer pressed. By default, the camera does not fire unless focus has been achieved (Focus Priority), but you can change this to Release Priority in ✐ a2. This allows you to take a photo whether the camera has achieved focus or not. I recommend sticking with Focus Priority for the AF-S, single servo mode and using Release Priority for AF-C, continuous servo. The AF-S mode is the best mode to use when shooting portraits, landscapes, or other photos where the subject is relatively static.

Using this mode helps ensure that you have fewer out-of-focus images.

Manual

When set to Ṁ, the AF system on the D800 is off. You achieve focus by rotating the focus ring of the lens until the subject appears sharp as you look through the view-finder. You can use the Manual focus setting when shooting still-life photographs or other nonmoving subjects, when you want total control of the focus, or simply when you are using a non-AF lens. You may want to note that the camera shutter releases regardless of whether the scene is in focus.

When using the Manual focus setting, the D800 offers a bit of assistance in the way of an electronic rangefinder. The rangefinder shows that you are in focus by displaying a green dot in the lower-left corner of the viewfinder.

Autofocus Area Modes

The D800 has four AF area modes to choose from: Single-point AF (☐), Dynamic-area AF (⊡), 3D-Tracking, and Auto-area AF (■). Each one is useful in different situations and can be modified to suit your needs for various shooting situations.

As discussed earlier in the chapter, the D800 employs an impressive 51 separate AF points. The 51 AF points can be used individually in [□] or they can be set to use in groups of 9, 21, or 51 when in [⊡].The D800 can also be set to employ 3D-tracking, which enables the camera to automatically switch focus points and maintain sharp focus on a moving subject as it crosses the frame. 3D-tracking is made possible by the camera recognizing color and light information and using it to track the subject.

Nikon's Scene Recognition System uses the 91K-pixel RGB sensor to recognize color and lighting patterns in order to determine the type of scene that you are photographing. This enables the AF to work faster than in previous Nikon dSLRs, and it also helps the D800 achieve more accurate exposure and white balance.

2

Single-area AF

□ is the easiest mode to use when you shoot slow-moving or completely still subjects. You can use the multi-selector right, or diagonally to choose one of the AF points. The camera only focuses on the subject if it is in the selected AF area. Once the point is selected, it can be locked by rotating the focus point lock switch right below the multi-selector.

By default, □ allows you to choose from any one of the 51 AF area points. Sometimes selecting from this many points can slow you down; this is why the D800 also allows you to change the number of selectable points to a more widely spaced array of 11 focus points. Anyone who has used a D200 will be immediately familiar with the 11-point pattern. You can choose the amount of focus points in ✐ a7.

Switching from 51 11 points can speed up your shooting process when using □. Using a smaller amount of focus points unfortunately give you less accuracy and it's often necessary to focus and recompose, which can cause you to lose important shots for fast-moving subjects.

Dynamic-area AF

[⊡] also allows you to select the AF point manually, but unlike □, the remaining unselected points remain active; this way, if the subject happens to move out of the selected focus area, the camera's highly sophisticated autofocus system can track it throughout the frame. You can set [⊡] to function with 9, 21, or 51 points by pressing the AF-mode button and rotating the Sub-command dial. Note that the camera must be set to continuous autofocus for this option to be selected.

When you set the focus mode to AF-S or Single AF (discussed earlier in the chapter), the mode operates exactly the same as if you were using [▫]. To take advantage of [⊡], the camera must be set to the AF-C, or Continuous AF mode.

CROSS REF For more information on the Custom Settings menu, see Chapter 3.

9 points

When your D800 is set to the 9-point option, you can select any one of the camera's 51 AF points to be the primary focus point. If your subject moves out of the selected point, the AF system uses the eight AF points immediately surrounding the selected point to achieve focus. Use this setting for more predictable sports such as baseball. Baseball players typically run in straight line and you don't need many points for AF coverage.

21 points

As with the 9-point area AF mode, you can select the primary focus point from any one of the 51 points. The camera then uses information from the surrounding 20 points if the subject moves away from the selected focus area. The 21-point area gives you a little more leeway with moving subjects because the active AF areas are in a larger pattern. This mode is good for shooting sports with more action such as soccer or football. Players are a bit more unpredictable and the larger coverage helps maintain focus when the player cuts left or right. However, the 21-point coverage isn't so large that the camera's AF doesn't tend to jump to other players.

51 points

The 51-point area AF mode gives you the widest area of active focus points. You can select the primary focus point the same way you do with the 9-point and 21-point options. The camera then keeps the surrounding 50 points active in case the subject leaves the selected focus area. This mode is best for situations where there is a lone subject against a plain background, such as a bird or even an airplane against a plain blue sky or a single person against a simple background.

NOTE When using [⊡] with 21 or 51 points you may notice that AF takes a little longer to work given the processor in the D800 has to sample more points.

51 points (3D-tracking)

This mode has all 51 AF points active. You select the primary AF point, but if the subject moves, the camera uses 3D-tracking to automatically select a new primary AF point. The camera achieves 3D-tracking by using distance and color information from the area immediately surrounding the focus point. The camera uses this information to determine what the subject is; if the subject moves, the camera selects a new focus point. This mode works very well for subjects moving unpredictably; however, you need to be sure that the subject and the background aren't similar in coloring. When photographing a subject that has a color that is similar to the background, the camera may lock focus on the wrong area, so use this mode carefully.

2

Auto-area AF

■ is exactly what it sounds like: The camera automatically determines the subject and chooses one or more AF points to lock focus. Due to the D800's Scene Recognition System, when it is used with Nikkor D- or G-type lenses, the camera is able to recognize human subjects. This means that the camera has a better chance of focusing where you want it than accidentally focusing on the background when shooting a portrait. When the camera is set to □, the active AF points light up in the viewfinder for about 1 second when the camera attains focus; when in Continuous AF mode, no AF points appear in the viewfinder.

> **TIP** You can view the selected AF point while reviewing the image on your LCD screen. To do this go to the Playback Menu, select Display mode, and select the Focus point under Basic photo info. Be sure to highlight Done and press the OK button (⊛) to lock in the setting. When the image is played back, the active focus points will be overlaid.

ISO Sensitivity

ISO, which stands for International Organization for Standardization, is the rating for the speed of film, or in digital terms, the sensitivity of the sensor. The ISO numbers are standardized, which allows you to be sure that when you shoot at ISO 100 you get the same exposure no matter what camera you are using.

The ISO for your camera determines how sensitive the image sensor is to the light that reaches it through the lens opening. Increasing or reducing the ISO affects the exposure by allowing you to use faster shutter speeds or smaller apertures (raising the ISO), or use slower shutter speeds or wider apertures (lowering the ISO).

You can set the ISO very quickly on the D800 by pressing and holding the ISO button and rotating the Main Command dial until the desired setting appears in the LCD control panel. As with other settings for controlling exposure, the ISO can be set in 1/3-, 1/2-, or 1-stop increments. You can choose the ISO increments in ✐ b1.

The D800 has a native ISO range of 100 to 6400. In addition to these standard ISO settings, the D800 also offers some settings that extend the available range of the ISO so you can shoot in very bright or very dark situations. These are labeled as L (low speed and H (high speed). By default, the options are set in 1/3-stop adjustments up to H1. The options are as follows:

▶ **L0.3, L0.7, and L1.0.** This gives you the option of shooting don to ISO 50 in 1/3 steps.

▶ **H0.3, H0.7, and H1.0.** These settings give you up to ISO 12,800 in 1/3 steps.

▶ **H2.** This setting isn't adjustable. You get one H2 setting, which is equivalent to ISO 25,600.

You can also set the ISO by going into the Shooting menu (◘) and choosing the ISO sensitivity settings option.

NOTE When ✐ b1 is set to half step, you have the option of selecting L0.5 or H0.5.

CAUTION Using the L and H settings will not produce optimal results. It can cause your images to have decreased contrast in L and increased amounts of digital noise in H.

Auto-ISO

Auto-ISO automatically adjusts the ISO settings for you in changing lighting situations. This frees you up from having to manually adjust the ISO as the lighting changes relieving you of the worry about one less setting.

Nikon has made the Auto-ISO feature available for a few years now, and I have been a big proponent of it. This setting has resulted in many more shots worth keeping when doing concert photography, and when I shoot in low light, I nearly always have this option enabled.

In true Nikon fashion, an amazing feature has been made even better. It is more intuitive, smarter, and quicker to access. To turn on Auto-ISO, simply press the ISO button (ISO) and rotate the Sub-command dial. Nikon has also added an Auto setting that selects the threshold for shutter speed versus ISO based on focal length, which is especially handy when using a zoom lens (which most people these days do).

Be sure to set the following options in ⬛ under the ISO sensitivity settings option:

▶ **Maximum sensitivity.** Choose an ISO setting that allows you to get an acceptable amount of noise in your image. If you're not concerned about noisy images, then you can set it all the way up to H2. If you need your images to have less noise, you can choose a lower ISO; the choices are 200 to H2 in 1/3 stops.

▶ **Minimum shutter speed.** This setting determines when the camera adjusts the ISO to a higher level. At the default, the camera bumps up the ISO when the shutter speed falls below 1/30 second. If you're using a longer lens or you're photographing moving subjects, you may need a faster shutter speed. In that case you can set the minimum shutter speed up to 1/4000 second. On the other hand, if you're not concerned about camera shake, or if you're using a tripod, you can set a shutter speed as slow as 1 second. When using the Auto setting the camera chooses the shutter speed based on the focal length of the lens (provided the lens has a CPU). When in Auto mode you can specify whether the camera gives priority to shutter speed or ISO sensitivity. Slower prioritizes Shutter speed and faster prioritizes ISO sensitivity.

NOTE The minimum shutter speed is only taken into account when using *P* or *S*.

Noise reduction

Noise, simply put, is randomly colored dots that appear in your image. Noise is caused by extraneous electrons that are produced as the image is being recorded. When light strikes the image sensor in your D800, electrons are produced. These electrons create an analog signal that is converted into a digital image by the analog-to-digital (A/D) converter in your camera (yes, digital cameras start with an analog signal). There are two specific causes of noise. The first is *heat-generated* or thermal noise. While the shutter is open and your camera records an image, the sensor starts to generate a small amount of heat. This heat frees electrons from the sensor, which in turn contaminate the electrons that have been created as a result of the light striking the photocells on your sensor. This contamination shows up as noise.

The second cause of digital noise is known as *high ISO noise*. Background electrical noise exists in any type of electronic device. For the most part, it's very miniscule and you never notice it. Cranking up the ISO amplifies the signals (photons of light) your sensor is receiving. Unfortunately, as these signals are amplified so is the background electrical noise. The higher your ISO, the more the background noise is amplified until it shows up as randomly colored specks.

Digital noise is composed of two elements: *chrominance* and *luminance*. Chrominance refers to the colored specks, and luminance refers to the size and shape of the noise.

Although the D800 has a very high signal-to-noise ratio, noise does exist. Noise starts appearing in images taken with the D800 when you shoot above ISO 800 or using long exposure times. For this reason, most camera manufacturers have built-in noise reduction (NR) features. The D800 has two types of NR: Long exposure NR and High ISO NR. Each one approaches the noise differently to help reduce it.

Long exposure NR

When Long exposure NR is turned on, the camera runs a noise-reduction algorithm to any shot taken with a long exposure (1 second or more). How this works is that the camera takes another exposure, this time with the shutter closed, and compares the noise from this dark image (called a dark frame) to the original one. The camera then applies the NR. The noise reduction takes about the same amount of time to process as the length of the shutter speed; therefore, expect double the time it takes to make one exposure. While the camera is applying NR, the LCD control panel blinks a message that says "Job nr." You cannot take additional images until this process is finished. If you switch the camera off before the NR is finished, no noise reduction is applied.

You can turn Long exposure NR on or off by accessing it in ◙.

High ISO NR

When this option is turned on, any image shot at ISO 800 or higher is run through the noise reduction algorithm.

This feature works by reducing the coloring in the chrominance of the noise and combining that with a bit of softening of the image to reduce the luminance noise. You can set how aggressively this effect is applied by choosing the High, Normal, or Low setting in ◙ in the High ISO NR option.

You may also want to be aware that High ISO NR slows down the processing of your images; therefore, the capacity of the buffer can be reduced, causing your frame rate to slow down when you're in Continuous shooting mode.

When the High ISO NR is set to "off," the camera still applies NR to images shot at ISO1600 and higher, although the amount of NR is less than when the camera is set to Low with NR on.

> **NOTE** When shooting in NEF (RAW), no actual noise reduction is applied to the image.

I choose not to use either of these in-camera NR features. In my opinion, even at the lowest setting, the camera is very aggressive in the NR, and for that reason, there is a loss of detail. For some people, this is a minor quibble and not very noticeable, but for me, I'd rather keep all the available detail in my images and apply noise reduction in post-processing. This way I can decide how much to reduce the chrominance and luminance rather than letting the camera do it.

> **NOTE** You can apply NR in Capture NX 2 or by using Photoshop's Adobe Camera Raw or some other image-editing software.

White Balance

Light, whether it is from sunlight, a light bulb, fluorescent light, or a flash, has its own specific color. This color is measured using the Kelvin scale. This measurement is also known as *color temperature*. The white balance (WB) allows you to adjust the camera so that your images can look natural no matter what the light source. Because white is the color that is most dramatically affected by the color temperature of the light source, this is what you base your settings on; hence the term *white balance*. The white balance can be changed in the Shooting menu or by pressing the WB button (**WB**) on the top of the camera and rotating the Main Command dial.

When dealing with different lighting sources, the color temperature of the source can have a drastic effect on the coloring of the subject. To adjust for the colorcast of the light source, the camera introduces a colorcast of the complete opposite color temperature. For example, to combat the green color of a fluorescent lamp, the camera introduces a slight magenta cast to neutralize the green.

The D800 has nine white balance settings:

▶ **Auto (⚙).** This setting is good for most circumstances. The camera takes a read-ing of the ambient light and makes an automatic adjustment. This setting also works well when you're using a Nikon CLS-compatible Speedlight because the color temperature is calculated to match the flash output. I recommend using this setting as opposed to the Flash (⚡) WB setting.

▶ **Incandescent (☀).** Use this setting when the lighting is from a standard house-hold light bulb.

▶ **Fluorescent (▦).** Use this setting when the lighting is coming from a fluorescent-type lamp. You can also adjust for different types of fluorescent lamps, including high-pressure sodium and mercury-vapor lamps. To make this adjustment, go to the Shooting menu and choose White Balance, then fluorescent. From there, use the multi-selector to choose one of the seven types of lamps.

▶ **Direct sunlight (☀).** Use this setting outdoors in the sunlight.

▶ **Flash (⚡).** Use this setting when using the built-in Speedlight, a hot-shoe Speedlight, or external strobes.

▶ **Cloudy(☁).** Use this setting under overcast skies.

▶ **Shade (☖).** Use this setting when you are in the shade of trees or a building or even under an overhang or a bridge — any place where the sun is out but is being blocked.

▶ **Choose color temp (Ⓚ).** This setting allows you to adjust the white balance to a particular color temperature that corresponds to the Kelvin scale. You can set it between 2500K (red) to 10,000K (blue).

▶ **Preset manual (PRE).** This setting allows you to choose a neutral object to mea-sure for the white balance. It's best to choose an object that is either white or light gray. There are some accessories that you can use to set the white bal-ance. One accessory is a gray card, which is included with this book. Simply put the gray card in the scene and balance off of it. Another accessory is the Expodisc. This attaches to the front of your lens like a filter; you then point the lens at the light source and set your WB. This setting is best used under difficult lighting situations, such as when there are two light sources lighting the scene (mixed lighting). I usually use this setting when photographing with my studio strobes.

Figures 2.1 and 2.2 show the difference that the white balance settings can make to your image.

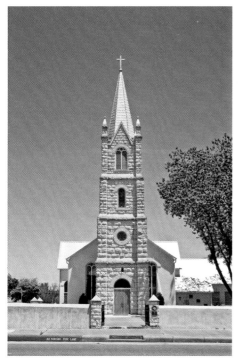 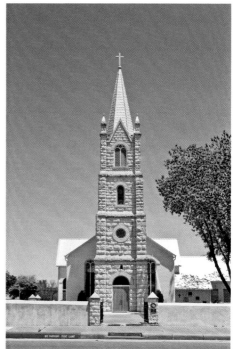

2.1 Auto   **2.2 Sunlight**

Picture Controls

The Nikon Picture Controls have become a standard feature on all Nikon dSLRs. Picture Controls allow you to quickly adjust your image settings, including sharpening, contrast, brightness, saturation, and hue based on your shooting needs. Picture Controls are standard among all Nikon cameras, which is great for photographers who shoot with more than one Nikon camera and do batch processing to their images. It allows both cameras to record the images the same so global image correction can be applied without differences in color, tone, saturation, and sharpening.

Picture Controls can also be saved to one of the memory cards and imported into Nikon's image-editing software, Capture NX 2 or View NX 2. You can then apply the settings to RAW images. You can also save and share these Picture Control files with other Nikon users, either by importing them to Nikon software or loading them directly to another camera.

The D800 comes with six standard Picture Controls already loaded on the camera, and you can custom modify up to nine Picture Control settings in-camera.

Original Picture Controls

Right out of the box the D800 comes with six Picture Controls installed:

▶ **SD (⊞SD).** This is the Standard setting. This applies slight sharpening and a small boost of contrast and saturation. It is recommended for most shooting situations.

▶ **NL (⊞NL).** This is the Neutral setting. This setting applies a small amount of sharpening and no other modifications to the image. This setting is preferable if you do extensive post-processing to your images.

▶ **VI (⊞VI).** This is the Vivid setting. This setting gives your images a fair amount of sharpening, and the contrast and saturation are boosted highly, resulting in brightly colored images. This setting is recommended for printing directly from the camera or memory card as well as for shooting landscapes. Personally, I think this mode is a little too saturated and often results in unnatural color tones. This mode is not ideal for portrait situations, as skin tones are not typically reproduced with accuracy.

▶ **MC (⊞MC).** This is the Monochrome setting. As the name implies, this option makes the images monochrome. This doesn't simply mean black and white; you can also simulate photo filters and toned images such as sepia, cyanotype, and more. The settings for sharpening, contrast, and brightness can also be adjusted.

▶ **PT (⊞PT).** This is the setting for Portraits. It gives you just a small amount of sharpening, which gives the skin a smoother appearance. The colors are muted just a bit to help with achieving realistic skin tones.

▶ **LS (⊞LS).** This is the Landscape setting. This is very close to the Vivid Picture Control with a little more boost added to the blues and greens.

Custom Picture Controls

Original Picture Controls can be customized to fit your personal preferences. You can adjust the settings to your liking, giving the images more sharpening and less contrast or myriad other options.

NOTE Although you can adjust the Original Picture Controls, you cannot save over them, so there is no need to worry about losing them.

There are a few customizations to choose from:

▶ **Quick adjust.** This option works with ⊡SD, ⊡VI, ⊡PT, and ⊡LS. It exaggerates or de-emphasizes the effect of the Picture Control in use. Quick adjust can be set from ±2.

▶ **Sharpness.** This controls the apparent sharpness of your images. You can adjust this setting from 0 to 9, with 9 being the highest level of sharpness. You can also set this to Auto (A) to allow the camera's imaging processor to decide how much sharpening to apply.

▶ **Contrast.** This setting controls the amount of contrast your images are given. In photos of scenes with high contrast (sunny days), you may want to adjust the contrast down; in low-contrast scenes, you may want to add some contrast by adjusting the settings up. You can set this from ±3 or to A.

▶ **Brightness.** This adds or subtracts from the overall brightness of your image. You can choose 0 (default) + or −.

▶ **Saturation.** This setting controls how vivid or bright the colors in your images are. You can set this between ±3 or to A. This option is not available in ⊡MC.

> **NOTE** The Brightness and Saturation option is unavailable when Active D-Lighting is turned on.

▶ **Hue.** This setting controls how your colors look. You can choose ±3. Positive numbers make the reds look more orange, the blues look more purple, and the greens look more blue. Choosing a negative number causes the reds to look more purple, the greens to look more yellow, and the blues to look more green. This setting is not available in ⊡MC. I highly recommend leaving this in the default setting of 0.

▶ **Filter Effects.** This setting is only available when you set your D800 to ⊡MC. The monochrome filters approximate the types of filters traditionally used with black-and-white film. These filters increase contrast and create special effects. The options are:

  • **Yellow.** Adds a low level of contrast. It causes the sky to appear slightly darker than normal and anything yellow to appear lighter. It is also used to optimize contrast for brighter skin tones.

  • **Orange.** Adds a medium amount of contrast. The sky will appear darker, giving greater separation between the clouds. Orange objects appear light gray.

- **Red.** Adds a great amount of contrast, drastically darkening the sky while allowing the clouds to remain white. Red objects appear lighter than normal.

- **Green.** Darkens the sky and lightens any green plant life. This color filter can be used for portraits as it softens skin tones.

▶ **Toning.** Toning adds a color tint to your monochrome (black-and-white) images. Toning options are:

- **B&W.** The black-and-white option simulates the traditional black-and-white film prints done in a darkroom. The camera records the image in black, white, and shades of gray. This mode is suitable when the color of the subject is not important. You can use it for artistic purposes or, as with the sepia mode, to give your image an antique or vintage look (see Figure 2.3).

- **Sepia.** The sepia color option duplicates a photographic toning process that is done in a traditional darkroom using silver-based black-and-white prints. Sepia toning a photographic image requires replacing the silver in the emulsion of the photo paper with a different silver compound, thus changing the color, or *tone*, of the photograph. Antique photographs were generally treated to this type of toning; therefore, the sepia color option gives the image an antique look. The images have a reddish-brown look to them. You may want to use this option when trying to convey a feeling of antiquity or nostalgia to your photograph. This option works well with portraits as well as still-life and architecture images. You can also adjust the saturation of the toning from 1 to 7, with 4 being the default and the middle ground (see Figure 2.4).

- **Cyanotype.** The cyanotype is another old photographic printing process; in fact, it's one of the oldest. When the image is exposed to the light, the chemicals that make up the cyanotype turn deep blue. This method was used to create the first blueprints and was later adapted to photography. The images taken while in this setting are in shades of cyan. Because cyan is considered to be a cool color, this mode is also referred to as cool. You can use this mode to make very interesting and artistic images. You can also adjust the saturation of the toning from 1 to 7, with 4 being the default setting (see Figure 2.5).

- **Color toning.** You can also choose to add colors to your monochrome images. Although this is similar to the Sepia and Cyanotype toning options, this type of toning isn't based on traditional photographic processes. It is simply adding a colorcast to a black-and-white image. There are seven color options you can choose from: red, yellow, green, blue-green, blue, purple-blue, and red-purple. As with Sepia and Cyanotype, you can adjust the saturation of these toning colors (see Figure 2.6).

2.3 Black and white

2.4 Sepia

2

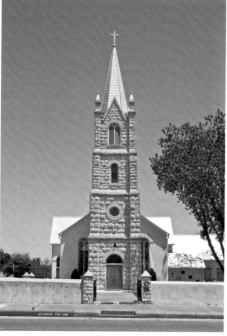

2.5 Cyanotype

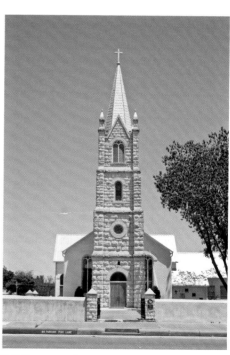

2.6 Green toning

To customize an Original Picture Control, follow these steps:

1. **Go to the Set Picture Control option in ☐ and press the multi-selector right (▶).**

2. **Choose the Picture Control you want to adjust and press ▶.** For small adjustments choose ⊞NL or ⊞SD option. To make larger changes to color and sharpness, choose ⊞VI mode. To make adjustments to monochrome images, choose ⊞MC.

3. **Press the multi-selector up (▲) or down (▼) to highlight the setting you want to adjust (sharpening, contrast, brightness, and so on).** When the setting is highlighted, press the multi-selector left (◀) or ▶ to adjust the settings. Repeat this step until you've adjusted the settings to your preferences.

4. **Press ⊛ to save the settings.**

NOTE To return the Picture Control to the default setting, follow the preceding Steps 1 and 2 and press the Delete button (🗑). A dialog box appears asking for confirmation. Select Yes to return to default or No to continue to use the Picture Control with the current settings.

NOTE When the Original Picture Control settings have been altered, an asterisk is displayed with the Picture Control setting (⊞SD*, ⊞VI*, and so on).

To save a Custom Picture Control, follow these steps:

1. **Go to the Manage Picture Control option in ☐ and press ▶.**

2. **Press ▲ or ▼ to select Save/edit and press ▶.**

3. **Choose the Picture Control to edit and press ▶.**

4. **Press ▲ or ▼ to highlight the setting you want to adjust (sharpening, contrast, brightness, and so on).** When the setting is highlighted, press ◀ or ▶ to adjust the settings. Repeat this step until you've adjusted the settings to your preferences.

5. **Press ⊛ to save the settings.**

6. **Use the multi-selector to highlight the Custom Picture Control you want to save to and press ▶.** You can store up to nine Custom Picture Controls; they are labeled C-1 through C-9.

7. **When the Rename Menu appears, press the Zoom in (🔍) button and press ◄ or ► to move the cursor to any of the 19 spaces in the name area of the dialog box.** New Picture Controls are automatically named with the Original Picture Control name and a two-digit number (for example, STANDARD _02 or VIVID_03).

8. **Press the multi-selector (without pressing the Zoom) to select letters in the keyboard area of the dialog box.** Press the multi-selector center button to set the selected letter and press 🗑 to erase the selected letter in the Name area. After you type the name you want, press ⊛ to save it. The Custom Picture Control is then saved to the Picture Control menu and can be accessed through the Set Picture Control option in the Shooting menu.

> **NOTE** To return the Picture Control to the default setting, follow the preceding Steps 1 through 3 and press 🗑. A dialog box appears asking for confirmation; select Yes to return to default or No to continue to use the Picture Control with the current settings.

Your Custom Picture Controls can be renamed or deleted at any time by using the Manage Picture Control option in the Shooting menu. You can also save the Custom Picture Control to your memory card so that you can import the file to Capture NX 2 or View NX 2.

To save a Custom Picture Control to the memory card, follow these steps:

1. **Go to the Manage Picture Control option in 📷 and press ►**.
2. **Press ▲ or ▼ to highlight the Load/save option and press ►.**
3. **Press ▲ or ▼ to highlight the Copy to card option and press ►.**
4. **Press ▲ or ▼ to select the Custom Picture Control to copy and press ►.**
5. **Select a destination on the memory card to copy the Picture Control file to.** There are 99 slots in which to store Picture Control files. The Custom Picture Controls are saved to the Primary memory card.
6. **After you choose the destination, press ►.** A message appears that the file is then stored to your CF or SD card.

After you copy your Custom Picture Control file to your card, you can then import the file to the Nikon software by mounting the memory card to your computer by your usual means (card reader or USB camera connection). See the software user's manual for instructions on importing to the specific program.

You can also upload Picture Controls to your camera from users that have saved their settings to a CF or SD card. Follow these steps:

1. **Go to the Manage Picture Control option in ▢ and press ▶.**

2. **Press ▲ or ▼ to highlight the Load/save option and press ▶.**

3. **Press ▲ or ▼ to highlight the Copy to camera option, and press ▶.**

4. **Select the Picture Control to copy and press ⊛ or ▶ to confirm.** The camera displays the Picture Control settings.

5. **Press ⊛.** The camera automatically displays the Save As menu.

6. **Select an empty slot to save to (C-1 through C-9).**

7. **Rename the file, if necessary, and press ⊛.**

JPEG

JPEG, which stands for Joint Photographic Experts Group, is a method of compressing photographic files and also the name of the file format that supports this type of compression. The JPEG is the most common type of file used to save images on digital cameras. Due to the small size of the file that is created and the relatively good image quality it produces, JPEG has become the default file format for most digital cameras.

The JPEG compression format came into being because of the immense file sizes that digital images produce. Photographic files contain millions upon millions of separate colors and each individual color is assigned a number, which causes the files to contain vast amounts of data, therefore making the file size quite large. In the early days of digital imaging, the huge file sizes and relatively small storage capacity of computers made it almost impossible for most people to store images. For people to efficiently store images, a file that could be compressed without losing too much of the image data during reconstruction was needed. Enter the Joint Photographic Experts Group. This group of experts came in and designed what is now affectionately know as the JPEG.

JPEG compression is a very complicated process involving many mathematical equations, but it can be explained quite simply. The first thing the JPEG process does is break down the image into 8 × 8-pixel blocks. The RGB color information in each 8 × 8 block is then treated to a color space transform where the RGB values are changed to represent luminance and chrominance values. The luminance value describes the brightness of the color while the chrominance value describes the hue.

Once the luminance and chrominance values have been established, the data is run through what is known as the Discrete Cosine Transform (DCT). This is the basis of the compression algorithm. What the DCT does is take the information about the 8 × 8 block of pixels and assigns it an average number because, for the most part, the changes in the luminance and chrominance values will not be very drastic in such a small part of the image.

The next step in the process is *quantizing* the coefficient numbers that were derived from the luminance and chrominance values by the DCT. Quantizing is basically the process of rounding off the numbers. This is where the file compression comes in. How much the file is compressed depends on the *quantization matrix*. The quantization matrix defines how much the information is compressed by dividing the coefficients by a quantizing factor. The larger the number of the quantizing factor, the higher the quality (therefore, the less compression). This is basically what is going on in Photoshop when you save as JPEG and the program asks you to set the quality; you are simply defining the quantizing factor.

Once the numbers are quantized, they are run through a binary encoder that converts the numbers to the ones and zeros computers love so well. You now have a compressed file that is on average about one-fourth of the size of an uncompressed file.

The one important consideration with JPEG compression is that it is what's known as a *lossy* compression. When the quantizing is put in effect, rounding off the numbers necessarily loses information. For the most part, this loss of information is imperceptible to the human eye. A bigger issue to consider with JPEGs comes from what is known as *generation loss*. Every time a JPEG is opened and resaved, a small amount of detail is lost. After multiple openings and savings, the image's quality starts to deteriorate, as less and less information is available. Eventually the image may start to look pixilated or jagged (this is known as a JPEG artifact). Obviously, this can be a problem, but the JPEG would have to be opened and resaved many hundreds of times before you'd notice a drop in image quality as long you save at high-quality settings.

Image Size

When saving to JPEG or TIFF format, the D800 allows you to choose an image size. Reducing the image size is like reducing the resolution on your camera; it allows you to fit more images on your card. The size you choose depends on what your output is going to be. If you know you will be printing your images at a large size, then you definitely want to record large JPEGs. If you're going to print at a smaller size (8 × 10 or 5 × 7), you can get away with recording at the Medium or Small setting. Image size is expressed in pixel dimensions. When set to FX format, the large JPEG setting records your images at 7360 × 4912 pixels; this gives you a file that is equivalent to 36.3 megapixels. Medium size gives you an image of 5520 × 3680 pixels, which is in effect the same as a 20 megapixel camera. The small size gives you a dimension of 3680 × 2456 pixels, which gives you about a 9-megapixel image.

You can quickly change the image size by pressing the QUAL button (**QUAL**) and rotating the Sub-command dial on the front of the camera. You can also change the image size in ▣ by selecting the image size menu option.

> **NOTE** You can only change image size when using the JPEG file format. RAW files are always recorded at the largest size.

Image Quality

For JPEGs, other than the size setting, which changes the pixel dimension, you have the Quality setting, which is the setting that decides how much of a compression ratio is applied to your JPEG image. Your choices are Fine, Normal, and Basic. JPEG Fine files are compressed to approximately 1:4, Normal are compressed to about 1:8, and Basic are compressed to about 1:16. To change the image quality setting, simply press **QUAL** and rotate the Main Command dial. Doing this scrolls you through all the file-type options available including RAW, Fine (JPEG), Normal (JPEG), and Basic (JPEG). You will also be able to shoot RAW and JPEG simultaneously with all of the JPEG compression options available (RAW + Fine, RAW + Normal, or RAW + Basic).

NEF (RAW)

Nikon's RAW files are referred to as NEF in Nikon literature. NEF stands for Nikon Electronic File. RAW files contain all the image data acquired by the camera's sensor. When a JPEG is created, the camera applies different settings to the image, such as WB, sharpness, noise reduction, and so on. When the JPEG is saved, the rest of the unused image data is discarded to help reduce file size. With a RAW file, this image data is saved so it can be used more extensively in post-processing. In some ways the RAW file is like a *digital negative*, in which the RAW files are used in the same way as a traditional photographic negative; that is, you take the RAW information and process it to create your final image.

Although some of the same settings are tagged to the RAW file (WB, sharpening, saturation, and so on), these settings aren't fixed and applied as in the JPEG file. This way, when you import the RAW file into your favorite RAW converter you can make changes to these settings with no detrimental effects.

Capturing your images in RAW allows you to be more flexible when post-processing your images and generally gives you more control over the quality of the images.

The D800 offers a few options for saving NEF (RAW) files. They include compression and bit depth. Like JPEGs, RAW files can be compressed to save space so that you can fit more images on your CF or SD card. You can also choose to save the RAW file with more bit depth, which can give you more available colors in your image file.

Type

Under the NEF (RAW) recording option in the Shooting menu, you can choose the type of compression you want to apply to the NEF (RAW) file or you can choose none at all. Keep in mind that with the D800 you can save a NEF file in 12-bit or 14-bit, which affects the number of files you can capture.

You have three options:

▶ **Lossless compressed.** Unlike JPEG compression, this algorithm loses no data information when the file is closed and stored. When the file is opened, the algorithm reverses the compression scheme and the exact same data that was saved is retrieved. This is the camera's default setting for storing RAW files. You will get a file size that is approximately 15 to 40% of the size of an uncompressed RAW file.

▶ **Compressed.** Similar to JPEG compression, with this algorithm some of the image data is lost when these types of files are compressed. The complex algorithms they use to create these files actually run two different compression schemes to the same file. Because your eyes perceive changes in the darker areas of images more than in the lighter areas, the image data for the shadow areas are compressed using a lossless compression while the midtones and lighter areas are compressed using a lossy method. This compression scheme has very little impact on the image data and allows you to be sure that you retain all your shadow detail. Using this compression scheme, your file size will be about 30 to 60% of the size of an uncompressed file.

▶ **Uncompressed.** Simply put, these files are stored just as they are captured. There is no compression or degradation in quality from the original.

Bit depth

Bit depth is how many separate colors your sensor can record. The term *bit depth* is derived from digital terminology. A bit is the smallest unit of data; it is expressed in digital language as either a 1 or a 0. Most digital images saved as JPEG or TIFF are recorded in 8 bits or 1 byte per channel (each primary color being a separate color: Red, Green, and Blue [RGB]), resulting in a 24-bit image. For each 8 bits there are 256 possible colors; multiply this by 3 channels and you get over 16 million colors, which is plenty enough information to create a realistic-looking digital image. By default, the D800 records its RAW files using a bit depth of 12 bits per channel, giving you a 36-bit image. What this means is that your sensor can recognize far more shades of color, which gives you a smoother gradation in tones, allowing the color transitions to be much smoother. In addition to the 12-bit setting, the D800 also offers the option of recording your NEF (RAW) files at 14 bits per channel, which gives you even more color information to work with when processing your images.

All this comes with a cost: the higher the bit depth, the more information contained in the file. This makes your files bigger, especially when the camera is shooting 14-bit NEF (RAW) files, which can result in larger files. When shooting at 14 bits, the camera has much more image data to contend with, so your top frame rate is reduced just a bit.

I find that for most general applications, shooting NEF (RAW) files at 12 bits is more than enough color information. I only switch to 14 bits when shooting portraits or in low light. This helps me get much smoother transitions from the shadow areas to the highlights.

NOTE The Nikon D800 uses a 14-bit A/D converter, so its theoretical maximum dynamic range is 14 stops. High bit depth really only helps minimize image posterization because actual dynamic range is limited by noise levels. A high bit-depth image does not necessarily mean that the image contains more colors; it just means it has the capacity to store more color data.

RAW versus JPEG

This issue has caused quite a controversy in the digital imaging world, with some people saying that RAW is the only way to go to have more flexibility in processing images, and others saying if you get it right in-camera then you don't need to use RAW images. For what it's worth, both factions are right in their own way.

Choosing between RAW and JPEG basically comes down to the final output or what you're using the images for. Remember that you don't have to choose one file format and stick with it. You can change the settings to suit your needs as you see fit, or you can even choose to record both RAW and JPEG simultaneously.

Some reasons to shoot JPEGs include:

▶ **Small file size.** JPEGs are much smaller in size than RAW files; therefore, you can fit many more of them on your CF or SD card and later on your hard drive. If space limitations are a problem, shooting JPEG allows you to get more images in less space.

▶ **Printing straight from camera.** Some people like to print their images straight from the camera or CF or SD card. RAW files can't be printed without first being converted to JPEG.

▶ **Continuous shooting.** Given JPEG files are smaller than RAW files, they don't fill up the camera's buffer as quickly, allowing you longer bursts without the frame rate slowing down.

▶ **Less post-processing.** If you're confident in your ability to get the image exactly as you want it at capture, you can save yourself time by not having to process the image in a RAW converter and save straight to JPEG.

▶ **Snapshot quality.** If you're just shooting snapshots of family events or if you only plan to post your images on the Internet, saving as JPEG will be fine.

Some reasons to shoot RAW files include:

▶ **16-bit images.** The D800 can capture RAW images in 12- or 14-bit. When converting the file using a RAW converter such as Adobe Camera Raw (ACR) or Capture NX 2, you can save your images with 16-bit color information. When the information is written to JPEG in the camera, the JPEG is saved as an 8-bit file. This gives you the option of working with more colors in post-processing. This can be extremely helpful when you're trying to save an under- or overexposed image. Bit depth is discussed in more detail earlier in the chapter.

▶ **White balance.** Although the WB that the camera was set to is tagged in the RAW file, it isn't fixed in the image data. Oftentimes, the camera can record a WB that isn't quite correct. This isn't always noticeable by looking at the image on the LCD screen. Changing the WB on a JPEG image can cause posterization and usually doesn't yield the best results. Because you have the RAW image data on hand, changing the WB settings doesn't degrade the image at all.

continued

> *continued*
>
> ▶ **Sharpening and Saturation.** As with WB, these settings are tagged in the RAW file but not applied to the actual image data. You can add sharpening and saturation (or other options, depending on your software).
>
> ▶ **Image Quality.** Because the RAW file is an unfinished file it allows you the flexibility to make many changes in the details of the image without any degradation to the quality of the image.

TIFF

You can also record to TIFF or Tagged Image File Format. This is an uncompressed file format similar to JPEG in that the image data such as white balance and exposure settings are fixed when the file is saved. Because there is no compression there's much more image data retained. TIFF files can also be recorded in Small, Medium, and Large formats. TIFF files are very large and offer no appreciable value over the NEF format, so I suggest sticking with RAW format. The only time I find it's necessary to shoot a TIFF file is for direct straight-from-the-camera upload to a publishing company or client.

CHAPTER 3

Setting up the Nikon D800

The Nikon D800 is one of the most customizable cameras on the market. You can assign buttons to different functions that you find yourself using frequently. The My Menu feature allows you to create personal menu options so that you quickly find the options for settings you use most often.

Most options in the Menu system are used to change things that don't need to be changed very often or quickly.

Press the Menu button (**MENU**) on the back of the camera to access the menus and use the multi-selector to scroll through the toolbar on the right side of the LCD.

Setting up your camera effectively allows you to focus on your art.

Playback Menu

The Playback Menu is where you manage the images stored on your memory card and also where you control how the images are displayed and what image information is displayed during review. There are ten options available from the Playback Menu that are explained in the following sections.

Delete

This option allows you to delete selected images from your memory card or to delete all of the images at once.

To delete selected images, follow these steps:

1. **Press the multi-selector right (▶), highlight Selected (default), and press ▶ again.** The camera displays an image selection screen.

2. **Press the multi-selector up (▲) or down (▼) to set the image for deletion; more than one image can be selected.** You can also use the Zoom in button (🔍) to review the image close up before deleting. When the image is selected for deletion it shows a small trash-can icon (🗑) in the right-hand corner.

3. **Press the OK button (⊙) to erase the selected images.** The camera asks you for confirmation before deleting the images.

4. **Select Yes then press ⊙ to delete.** To cancel the deletion, highlight No (default), then press ⊙.

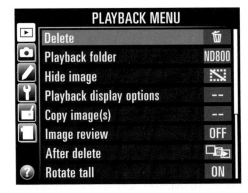

3.1 The Playback menu — shown in two parts

3.2 Selecting images to delete

To delete all images, use the multi-selector to highlight All, and then press ⊛. Select Yes when asked to confirm the deletion, and then press ⊛ to delete. To cancel deletion, highlight No (default), then press ⊛.

Playback folder

The Nikon D800 automatically creates folders in which to store your images. The main folder that the camera creates is called DCIM, and within this folder the camera creates a subfolder to store the images; the first subfolder the camera creates is titled 100ND800. After shooting 999 images the camera automatically creates another folder, 101ND800, and so on. If you have used the memory card in another camera and have not formatted it, there will be additional folders on the card (ND700, ND3S, and so on).

The current folder can be changed using the Active folder option in the Shooting menu. You have three folder choices.

► **ND800.** This is the default setting. The camera only plays back images from folders that were created by the D800 and ignores folders from other cameras that may be on the memory cards.

► **All.** This option plays back images from all folders that are on the memory cards whether they were created by the D800 or not.

► **Current.** This option displays images only from the folder to which the camera is currently saving. This feature is useful when you have multiple folders from different sessions. Using this setting allows you to preview only the most current images.

Hide Image

This option is used to hide images so that they can't be viewed during playback. When the images are hidden they are also protected from being deleted. To select images to be hidden, press ▶, highlight select/set (default), and then press ▶. Use the multi-selector to highlight the thumbnail images you wish to hide. Then press ⊛.

To allow the hidden images to be displayed highlight Deselect all, the camera then asks you for confirmation before revealing the images. Select Yes then press ⊛ to display during playback. To cancel and continue hiding the images, highlight No (default) then press ⊛.

Playback display options

There is quite a bit of image information that is available for you to see when you are reviewing images, and the Playback display options settings allow you to customize that information. Enter the Playback display options menu by pressing ▶. Then use the multi-selector to highlight the option you want to set. When the option is high-lighted press ▶ or ⊛ to set the display feature. The feature is set when a check mark appears in the box to the left of the setting. Be sure to scroll up to Done and press ⊛ to set. If this step is not done, the information does not appear in the display.

The Playback display options options are Basic photo info and Additional photo info. Basic photo info offers one option — Focus point. When this option is set, the focus point that was used will be overlaid on the image to be reviewed. No focus point is displayed if the camera did not achieve focus or if Continuous AF was used in conjunc-tion with Auto-area AF.

The Additional photo info menu option offers four choices:

▶ **None (image only).** As indicated this shows the image only. No info at all.

▶ **Highlights.** When this option is activated any highlights that are blown out will blink. If this happens you may want to apply some exposure compensation or adjust your exposure to be sure to capture highlight detail. You can also view the highlight information in each separate color channel (RGB) by pressing the Thumbnail button (◔❖) and pressing ◀ or ▶.

▶ **RGB Histogram.** When this option is turned on you can view the separate histo-grams for the Red, Green, and Blue channels along with a standard luminance histogram. The highlights are also displayed in this option, and as with the stan-dard highlights option you can choose to view the highlights in each separate channel by pressing ◔❖ and pressing ◀ or ▶.

▶ **Shooting Data.** This option allows you to review the shooting data (metering, exposure, lens focal length, etc.).

▶ **Overview.** This option shows a thumbnail version of the image with the Luminosity histogram and general shooting data: shutter speed, aperture, ISO, etc...

Copy image(s)

This option allows you to copy images from the SD card to the CF card and vice versa. To do this:

1. **Choose the Select source option from the menu.** Press ▶ to view the options. Use ▲ or ▼ to highlight CF card slot or SD card slot. Press ☉ or the multi-selector center button when ready.

2. **Choose the Select image(s) option from the menu and press ▶ to view the options.** The menu displays a list of the available folders on the card. Select the folder you want to copy from and press ▶. This brings up the Default image selection submenu.

3. **From the Default image selection submenu select one of the three options.** These options determine which images (if any) are selected by default. Once you determine which selection method you want to use press ☉ to display thumbnails of all the images on the card. Use the multi-selector to browse the images. When an image is highlighted press the multi-selector center button to set or unset the image for copying. When the image is selected for transfer a check mark appears in the upper left corner of the thumbnail. You can use ⚲ to take a closer look at the highlighted image. Press ☉ when you are finished making your selections. There are three options:

   ▶ **Deselect all.** This option selects no images for transfer. Manually select any images you want to copy.

   ▶ **Select all images.** This selects all images for transfer. Manually deselect any images you don't want to copy.

   ▶ **Select protected images.** This selects only images that have been protected by pressing the Protect button (○┐). You can manually select or deselect any other images.

4. **Choose the Select destination folder option from the menu and press ▶ to view the options.** You can select by folder number by using the multi-selector. Or you can choose Select Folder from list and use the multi-selector to highlight an existing folder.

CAUTION Images will not be copied if there isn't enough space on the destination card.

5. **Select Copy image(s), press ☉, then select Yes.**

If an image with the same filename is in the destination folder you are required to enter information on what you want to do with the images in a dialog box. The following are your options:

▶ **Replace existing image.** This option overwrites the image on the destination card with the image from the source card.

▶ **Replace all.** This option replaces all images from the source disk with images with the same name on the destination disk. Use this option in if you're positive you don't want to lose any images that may be different yet have the same file-name (this can happen if the Custom Settings menu (✐) d5 File Number Sequence is set to Off or Reset).

▶ **Skip.** This option skips copying that single image and continues on with the rest, and the dialog box appears again if there is another issue with the filenames.

▶ **Cancel.** This cancels any further image copying.

NOTE If the image is protected the copy will also be protected. If you have set up the image as a DPOF that image will *not* be copied. Hidden images are exempt from being copied.

Image review

This option allows you to choose whether the image is shown on the LCD immediately after the image is taken. When this option is turned off (default), the image can be viewed by pressing ▶. This allows you a chance to preview the image to check the exposure, framing, and sharpness. There are times, however, when you may not want the images to be displayed. For example, when shooting sports at a rapid frame rate you may not need to check every shot. Turning this option off conserves battery power because the LCD is actually the biggest drain on your battery. When shooting events with a lot of quickly changing action such as a concert you want to turn this option off. I found that when trying to move focus points and the images are being previewed, instead of moving the focus point the camera is scrolling through the image's data.

All in all, it's best to turn the feature off and use ▶ unless you absolutely need to look at every image you shoot.

After delete

This allows you to choose which image is displayed after you delete an image during playback. The options are:

▶ **Show next.** This is the default setting. The next image taken is displayed after the selected image is deleted. If the image deleted is the last image, the previous image is displayed.

▶ **Show previous.** After the selected image is deleted the one taken before it is displayed. If the first image is deleted the following image is displayed.

▶ **Continue as before.** This option allows you to continue in the order that you were browsing the images. If you were scrolling through as shot, the next image is displayed (Show next). If you were scrolling through in reverse order the previous image is shown (Show previous).

Rotate tall

The D800 has a built-in sensor that can tell whether the camera was rotated while the image was taken. This setting rotates images that are shot in portrait orientation to be displayed upright on the LCD screen. I usually turn this option off because the portrait orientation image appears substantially smaller when displayed upright on the LCD.

The options are:

▶ **On.** The camera automatically rotates the image to be viewed while holding the camera in the standard upright position. When this option is turned on (and the Auto image rotation setting is set to On in the Setup menu), the camera orientation is recorded for use in image-editing software.

▶ **Off (default).** When the auto-rotating function is turned off, images taken in portrait orientation are displayed on the LCD sideways in landscape orientation.

Slide show

This allows you to display a slide show of images from the current active folder. You can use this to review the images that you have shot without having to use the multi-selector. This is also a good way to show friends or clients your images. You can connect the camera to an HD TV to view the slide show on a big screen. There are three options to choose from:

▶ **Start.** This simply starts the slide show. It plays back both still images and movies.

▶ **Image type.** This allows you to select what kind of files are played back. You can select Still images and movies, Still images only, or Movies only.

▶ **Frame interval.** This option allows you to select how long the still images are displayed. The options are 2, 3, 5, or 10 seconds.

While the slide show is in progress, you can use the multi-selector to skip forward or back (◀ or ▶) and view shooting info or histograms (▲ or ▼). You can also press the

Menu button (MENU) to return to the Playback Menu, press ▶ to end the slide show, or press the Shutter Release button lightly to return to the Shooting mode.

Pressing ⊛ while the slide show is in progress pauses the slide show and offers you options for restarting the slide show, changing the frame rate, or exiting the slide show. Press ▲ or ▼ to make your selection, and then press ⊛.

Print set (DPOF)

DPOF stands for Digital Print Order Format. This option allows you to select images to be printed directly from the camera. This can be used with Pict-bridge-compatible printers or DPOF-compatible devices such as a photo kiosk at your local photo printing shop. This is a handy feature if you don't have a printer at home and want to get prints made quickly, or if you do have a printer and want to print your photos without down-loading them to your computer.

CAUTION	DPOF can only be made with JPEG or TIFF files and not RAW files. If you shoot RAW you can use the RAW editing features in the Retouch menu to create a JPEG copy.

To create a print set:

1. **Use the multi-selector to choose the Print set (DPOF) option and then press ▶ to enter the menu.**

2. **Use the multi-selector to highlight Select/set and press ▶ to view thumbnails.** You can press ⊕ to view a larger preview of the selected image.

3. **Press ▶ or ◀ to highlight an image to print and press ▲ or ▼ when the desired image is highlighted to set the image and choose the number of prints you want of that specific image.** You can choose from 1 to 99. The number of prints and a small printer icon appear on the thumbnail. Continue this procedure until you have selected all of the images that you want to print. Press ▼ to reduce the number of prints and to remove it from the print set.

4. **Press ⊛.** A menu appears with three options:

   • **Done (default).** Press ⊛ to save and print the images as they are.

   • **Data imprint.** Press ▶ to set. A small check mark appears in the box next to the menu option. When this option is set, the shutter speed and aperture setting appear on the print.

- **Date imprint.** Press ▶ to set. A small check mark appears in the box next to the menu option. When this option is set, the date the image was taken appears on the print.

5. **If you choose to set the imprint options, be sure to return to the Done option and press ⊛ to complete the print set.**

Shooting Menu

The shooting controls that you find yourself using most often have dedicated buttons to access them. These are controls such as ISO, QUAL, and WB. These features can also be set in the Shooting menu. There are also other settings here that are used quite often such as Picture Controls, Active D-Lighting, and Noise Reduction.

Shooting menu bank

The Shooting menu bank allows you to store combinations of settings for use during different shooting scenarios. If you shoot a variety of subjects and you change your settings depending on the subject, you can save your shooting settings so you can pull up the settings quickly rather than changing them all separately. For example, when you shoot landscapes, you may want to shoot RAW images at 14-bit with your white balance set to Daylight and the Picture Control set to Vivid; but when you shoot portraits, you like to shoot Large JPEG images with the white balance set to Auto and the Picture Control set to Standard. You can save these groups of settings to separate banks and recall them when shooting that particular type of subject. This can save you time because you don't have to change your settings every time you change your subject matter.

The Shooting menu banks store the Shooting settings such as image quality, Picture Controls, Noise Reduction settings, and others. Be careful not to confuse the Shooting menu bank with the Custom Settings bank, which stores any changes made to the Custom Settings Menu (this is covered later in the chapter).

Each of these banks operates separately from one another so any changes you make while in Bank A will not affect any of the other banks. One thing you need to remember is that any changes you make while in a shooting bank will be saved. If you are shooting in Bank B and you change the Noise Reduction setting, that setting will be saved until you change back. The Shooting menu bank does not reset when the camera is turned off. So if you modify certain settings be sure to change them back after you finish shooting or you may find yourself using the wrong settings.

You have four banks available where you can save your settings: A, B, C, and D. Each of these banks can be renamed with a custom designation so you can easily remember which bank is for what subject. To rename the bank, follow these steps:

1. **Press MENU and use the multi-selector to select the Shooting menu.**

2. **Select Shooting menu bank from the list of options.**

3. **Use the multi-selector to choose the bank to rename and to choose from A, B, C, or D, and then press ▶.** This displays the text entry screen, where you can choose up to 20 characters to name your Shooting menu bank.

4. **Enter the text.** Using the multi-selector you can scroll around within the set of letters, numbers, and punctuation marks. There are several buttons you can use to maneuver in the text entry screen.

   • Use the multi-selector center button to insert the letter that is highlighted.

   • Press ⊞ and press ◄ or ▶ to move the cursor within the text box. You can use it to add spaces or to overwrite another character.

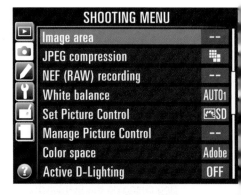

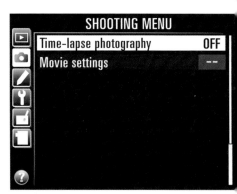

3.3 The Shooting menu shown in three sections so you can see all the available options.

   • To erase a character you have inserted move the cursor over the top of the character and press 🗑.

5. **Once you've entered your text, press ⊛ to save the changes.**

The only way to check to see which Shooting menu bank you're using is to check the Shooting menu or check the Info Display by pressing the Info button (**info**). You can also change the Shooting menu in the Info edit (**⊞**) screen.

3.4 Text entry screen

> **NOTE** Remember the text entry screen. You will use it for various functions including changing the filename, naming Custom Picture Controls, and Custom Shooting menu banks.

Extended Menu Banks

This is a brand-new feature on the D800. When you select On it allows you to include the exposure mode and shutter speed when in Shutter Priority mode (**S**) or Manual modes (**M**) or exposure mode and aperture setting when using Aperture Priority Auto mode (**A**) or **M** in your Shooting menu banks.

Storage folder

As discussed earlier, the D800 automatically creates folders in which to store your images. The camera creates a folder named ND800 then stores the images in subfolders starting with folder 100. You can choose to change the folder that the camera is saving to. You can choose from 100 up to 999. You can use this option to separate different subjects into different folders. I separate my photos into different folders when I shoot concerts and festivals to make it easier to sort through the images later. If there are five bands I start out using folder 101, then 102 for the second act, and so on. If you are travelling you could save your images from each destination to separate folders. These are just a couple of different examples of how this feature can be used.

When selecting the active folder you can choose a new folder number or you can select a folder that has already been created. When you format your memory card, all preexisting folders are deleted and the camera creates a folder with whatever number the active folder is set to. So if you set it to folder 105, the camera creates folder 105ND800 when the card is formatted. It does not start from the beginning with a folder 100. If you want to start with folder 100 you need to be sure to change the active folder back to 100 then format your card.

To change the Storage folder:

1. **From the Shooting menu, use the multi-selector to choose Storage folder and press ▶ to highlight Select folder number.**

2. **Press ◀ or ▶ to select a digit and ▲ or ▼ to change the number.** Existing folders display an icon that tells you whether the folder is empty, has images in it, or is full. Folders that have 999 images cannot be used.

3. **Press ☉ or the multi-selector center button to save changes.**

File naming

When image files are created, the D800 automatically assigns a filename. The default filenames start with DSC_ followed by a four-digit number and the file extension (DSC_0123.jpg) when using the sRGB color space. When using the Adobe RBG color space, the filenames start with _DSC followed by a four-digit number and the file extension (_DSC0123.jpg).

This menu option allows you to customize the filename by replacing the DSC prefix with any three letters of your choice. For example, I customize mine so that the filename reads JDT_0123.jpg.

To customize the filename:

1. **Highlight the File naming option in the Shooting menu. Press ▶ to enter the menu.** The menu shows a preview of the filename (sRGB: DSC_1234/ Adobe RGB: _DSC1234).

2. **Press ▶ to enter a new prefix within the text entry screen.** This text entry screen doesn't have lowercase letters or any punctuation marks because the file naming convention only allows for files to be named using capital letters and the numbers 0-9.

3. **Use the multi-selector to choose the letters and/or numbers.** Press ☉ when you finish.

Primary slot selection

This menu option allows you to choose the primary card slot to which your images are saved. You can choose the CF card slot or the SD card slot. I generally choose the CF card slot because CF cards are much more durable than SD cards.

Secondary slot function

This determines the function of your secondary card slot. You have three items to choose from:

▶ **Overflow.** If this option is selected when the Primary card is full the camera automatically switches to the secondary card. If the Primary card is replaced with a blank card the camera automatically switches back to writing to the Primary card. This is the option I usually choose.

▶ **Backup.** When this option is selected the camera automatically writes two copies of the images, one to the Primary card and one to the Secondary card.

▶ **RAW primary/JPEG secondary.** When this option is selected and the Image Quality is set to RAW + JPEG, RAW files are saved to the Primary card and JEPGs to the Secondary card.

> **NOTE** When two card are inserted into the camera you can select one of them to be dedicated to video in the Movie Settings ➜ Destination option in the Shooting menu.

Image quality

This menu option allows you to change the image quality of the file. You can choose from these options:

▶ **NEF (RAW).** This option saves the images in RAW format. You can adjust the RAW recording settings in the NEF (RAW) recording option in the Shooting menu.

▶ **TIFF (RGB).** This option saves the images in an 8-bits per channel TIFF format.

▶ **JPEG fine.** This option saves the images in JPEG with minimal compression of about 1:4.

▶ **JPEG normal.** This option saves the images in JPEG with standard compression of about 1:8.

▶ **JPEG basic.** This option saves the images in JPEG with high compression of about 1:16.

▶ **NEF (RAW) + JPEG fine.** This option saves two copies of the same image, one in RAW and one in JPEG with minimal compression.

▶ **NEF (RAW) + JPEG normal.** This option saves two copies of the same image, one in RAW and one in JPEG with standard compression.

▶ **NEF (RAW) + JPEG basic.** This option saves two copies of the same image, one in RAW and one in JPEG with high compression.

These settings can also be changed by pressing the QUAL button (**QUAL**) and rotating the Main Command dial to choose the file type and compression setting. The setting can be viewed on the LCD control panel on the top of the camera.

CROSS REF For more detailed information on image quality, compression, and file formats, see Chapter 2.

Image size

This allows you to choose the size of the TIFF and JPEG files. The choices are Small, Medium, and Large. The pixel sizes of the images vary depending on what Image Area you have selected FX, DX, 1.2, or 5:4 mode (this is covered in the next section). Change the image size depending on the intended output of the file.

▶ **FX (36X24)**

 • **Large.** This setting gives you a full-resolution image of 7360 × 4912 pixels or 36.2 megapixels.

 • **Medium.** This setting gives you a resolution of 5520 × 3680 pixels or 20.3 megapixels.

 • **Small.** This setting gives your images a resolution of 3680 × 2456 pixels or 9 megapixels.

CROSS REF For more detailed information on image size, see Chapter 2.

NOTE Image size for JPEG and TIFF can also be changed by pressing **QUAL** and rotating the Sub-command dial. The settings are shown on the LCD control panel on the top of the camera.

▶ **1.2X (30X20)**

 • **Large.** This setting gives you a full-resolution image of 6144 × 4080 pixels or 25 megapixels.

- **Medium.** This setting gives you a resolution of 4608 × 3056 pixels or 14 megapixels.

- **Small.** This setting gives your images a resolution of 3072 × 2040 pixels or 6.3 megapixels.

▶ **DX (24X16)**

- **Large.** This setting gives you a full-resolution image of 4800 × 3200 pixels or 15.3 megapixels.

- **Medium.** This setting gives you a resolution of 3600 × 2400 pixels or 8.7 megapixels.

- **Small.** This setting gives your images a resolution of 2400 × 1600 pixels or 3.8 megapixels.

▶ **5:4 (30X24)**

- **Large.** This setting gives you a full-resolution image of 6144 × 4912 pixels or 30 megapixels.

- **Medium.** This setting gives you a resolution of 4608 × 3680 pixels or 16.6 megapixels.

- **Small.** This setting gives your images a resolution of 3072 × 2456 pixels or 7.5 megapixels.

Image area

If you switched over from a Nikon DX format dSLR such as the D300s or D7000, you have likely invested some money in DX lenses. Nikon has enabled you to use these DX lenses on the D800 by allowing you to switch between FX and DX formats. The huge resolution of the D800 allows you to use DX lenses and still have a high image resolution near that of the D7000, which is much higher than the 5MP DX crop of the D700 and D3/s cameras. There are two choices: Auto DX crop and choose image area.

▶ **Auto DX crop.** This allows the camera to recognize when a Nikkor DX lens is attached and automatically switches the camera into DX mode. This is only guaranteed to work with Nikkor DX lenses. With some third-party DX lenses the camera may not recognize that the lens is DX. You can turn this option on or off. If you have Nikkor DX lenses that you want to use along with your FX lenses you should keep this option on. If you're using third-party DX lenses, you can safely turn this off. If you have both third-party and Nikkor lenses then, again, I suggest turning this on (just be sure to switch to DX when using non-Nikon lenses).

▶ **Choose image area.** This allows you to manually choose between FX and DX. Select FX format (36 × 24) for full-frame, 1.2X (30 × 20), DX format (24 × 16) for APS-C sensor size, or 5:4 (30 × 24).

FX, DX, and 1.2 modes provide a standard 2:3 aspect ratio. The 5:4 option is standard for shooting 8 × 10 aspect images, which may be preferred when shooting headshots or portraits.

> **CAUTION** For more detailed information on using DX lenses see Chapter 4.

JPEG compression

This menu allows you to set the amount of compression applied to the images when recorded in the JPEG file format. The options are:

▶ **Size priority.** With this option the JPEG images are compressed to a relatively uniform size. Image quality can vary depending on the amount of image information in the scene you photographed. To keep the file sizes similar, some images must be compressed more than others.

▶ **Optimal quality.** This option provides the best compression algorithm. The file sizes vary with the information contained in the scene recorded. Use this mode when image quality is a priority.

(NEF) RAW recording

This option is for setting the amount of compression applied to RAW files. This menu is also where you choose the bit depth of the RAW file. Use the Type submenu (accessed from the RAW recording menu) to choose the compression. The options are:

▶ **Lossless compressed.** This is the default setting. The RAW files are compressed reducing the file size from 20-40 percent with no apparent loss of image quality.

▶ **Compressed.** The RAW file is compressed by 40-50 percent. There is some file information lost.

▶ **Uncompressed.** The RAW file is saved to the card exactly as it was recorded. There is no compression. The file sizes are *very* large.

Use the NEF (RAW) bit depth submenu to choose the bit depth of the RAW file; there are two options:

▶ **12 bit.** This records the RAW file with 12 bits of color information.

▶ **14 bit.** This records the RAW file with 14 bits of color information. The file size is significantly larger, but there is much more color information for smoother color transitions in your images.

CROSS REF For more detailed information on RAW compression and bit depth, see Chapter 2.

White balance

You can change the white balance options using this menu option, which allows you to fine-tune your settings with more precision. It also gives you a few more options than when using the dedicated WB button located on the top of the camera. You can select a WB setting from the standard settings (auto, incandescent, fluorescent, direct sunlight, flash, cloudy, shade) or you can choose to set the WB according to color temperature by selecting a Kelvin temperature, you can choose between 2500 K to 10,000 K. A third option is to select from a preset WB that you have set.

CROSS REF For detailed information on white balance settings and color temperature, see Chapter 2.

Using standard WB settings

To select one of the standard settings, choose the White balance option from the Shooting menu, then use the multi-selector to highlight the preferred setting, and then press ▶ or the multi-selector center button. This displays a new screen giving you the option to fine-tune the standard setting. Displayed on this screen is a grid that allows you to adjust the color tint of the WB setting selected. The hori-

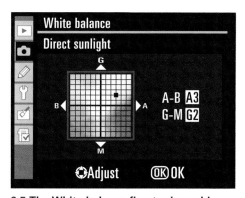

3.5 The White balance fine-tuning grid

zontal axis of the grid allows you to adjust the color from amber to blue, making the image warmer or cooler while the vertical axis of the grid allows you to change the tint by adding a magenta or green cast to the image. Using the multi-selector you can choose a setting from 1 to 6 in either direction; additionally, you can add points along the horizontal and vertical axes simultaneously. For example you can add 4 points of amber to give it a warmer tone and also add 2 points of green shifting the amber tone more toward yellow.

Choosing the fluorescent setting displays some additional menu options: You can choose among seven non-incandescent lighting types. This is handy if you know what specific type of fixture is being used. For example, I was shooting a night football game recently. I had the camera set to Auto WB, but I was getting very different colors from shot to shot and none of them looked right.

Because I wasn't shooting RAW, I needed to get more consistent shots. I knew that most outdoor sporting arenas used mercury-vapor lights to light the field at night. I selected the fluorescent WB setting from the Shooting menu and chose the #7 option, High temp. mercury vapor. I took a few shots and noticed I was still getting a sickly greenish cast so I went back to the fine-tuning option and added 2 points of magenta to cancel out the green colorcast. This gave me an accurate and consistent color.

The seven settings are:

▶ **Sodium-vapor.** These are the types of lights often found in streetlights and parking lots. They emit a distinct deep yellow color.

▶ **Warm-white fluorescent.** These types of lamps give a white light with a bit of an amber cast to add some warmth to the scene. These lights burn at around 3000 K similar to an incandescent bulb.

▶ **White fluorescent.** These lights cast a very neutral white light at around 5200 K.

▶ **Cool white fluorescent.** As the name suggests this type of lamp is a bit cooler than a white fluorescent lamp and has a color temperature of 4200 K.

▶ **Day white fluorescent.** This lamp approximates sunlight at about 5500 K.

▶ **Daylight fluorescent.** This type of lamp gives you about the same color as daylight. This lamp burns at about 6300 K.

▶ **High temp. mercury-vapor.** These lights vary in temperature depending on the manufacturer and usually run between 4200 and 5200 K.

NOTE Sunlight and Daylight are quite different color temperatures. Sunlight is light directly from the sun and is about 5500 K. Daylight is the combination of sunlight and skylight and has a color temperature of about 6300 K.

Choosing a color temperature

Using the K white balance option you can choose a specific color temperature, assuming that you know the actual color temperature. Some light bulbs and fluorescent lamps are calibrated to put out light at a specific color temperature, for example full-spectrum light bulbs burn at a color temperature of 5000 K.

As with the other settings you get the option of fine-tuning the setting using the grid.

Preset white balance

Preset white balance allows you to make and store up to five custom white balance settings. You can use this option when shooting in mixed lighting, for example, in a room with an incandescent light bulb and sunlight coming in through the window, or when the camera's auto white balance isn't quite getting the correct color.

10,000 —
9,000 —
8,000 —
7,000 —
6,000 —
5,000 —
4,000 —
3,000 —
2,000 —
1,000 —

3.6 Kelvin color temperature scale

3

You can set a custom white balance in two ways; direct measurement, this is when you take reading from a neutral colored object (a gray card works the best for this) under the light source or copy from existing photograph, this allows you to choose a WB setting directly from an image that is stored on your memory card.

The camera can store up to four presets that are labeled d-1 through d-4.

CROSS REF   See Appendix B for instructions on using the included gray card to preset the white balance.

To manually preset the white balance, simply press the WB button (**WB**), rotate the Main Command dial to PRE, and then rotate the Sub-command dial to the desired preset number (d-1 – d4). Release **WB** momentarily, then press and hold it for 2 seconds until PRE begins flash on the Control Panel and the Viewfinder Display. Then aim the camera at a neutral subject and take a photo. If the preset was successful, GD flashes in the viewfinder. If No GD flashes in the viewfinder, you need to shoot another photo. A good amount of light is required to get a proper white balance setting.

The D800 also allows you to add a comment to any of the presets. You can use this to remember the details of your WB setting. For example, if you have a set of photographic lights in your studio you can set the WB for these particular lights and enter "photo lights" into the comment section. You can enter up to 36 characters (including spaces). To enter a comment on a WB preset:

1. Press MENU and use the multi-selector to choose White Balance from the Shooting menu.

2. Select Preset manual from the White balance menu and press the multi-selector button ▶ to view the preset choices.

3. Use the multi-selector to highlight one of the presets. You can choose from d-1 – d-4.

4. Press the multi-selector center button. The preset menu is displayed.

5. Use the multi-selector to highlight Edit comment and press ▶. This displays the text entry screen discussed earlier in the chapter.

6. Enter your text and press ⊛ to save the comment.

Copy white balance from existing photograph

As mentioned previously, you can also copy the white balance setting from any photo that is saved on the memory card that's inserted into your camera. Follow these steps:

> TIP If you have particular settings that you like, you should consider saving the images on a memory card. This way you can always have your favorite WB presets saved so you don't accidentally erase them from the camera.

1. Press MENU and use the multi-selector to choose White Balance from the Shooting menu.

2. Select Preset manual from the White balance menu and press ▶ to view the preset choices.

3. Use the multi-selector to highlight d-1, d-2, d-3, or d-4 and press the multi-selector center button. This displays a menu.

4. Use the multi-selector to highlight Select image and press ▶. The LCD displays thumbnails of the images saved to your memory card. This is similar to the Delete and DPOF thumbnail display. Use the multi-selector directional buttons to scroll through the images. You can zoom in on the highlighted image by pressing ⊕.

5. Press the multi-selector center button to set the image to the selected preset (d-1, d-2, and so on) and press ⊛ to save the setting. Once you've

selected the image, the thumbnail is shown in the setting area. You can also go up to the fine-tune option for adjustments, enter a comment, or protect the setting as with the Manual preset option.

Once your presets are in order you can quickly choose among them by following these easy steps:

1. **Press WB located on top of the camera.**

2. **Rotate the Main Command dial until PRE appears on the LCD control panel.**

3. **Continue to press WB and rotate the Sub-command dial.** The top right of the LCD control panel displays the preset options from d-1 – d-4.

Set Picture Control

Nikon includes Picture Controls in the D800. These controls allow you to choose how the images are processed and they can also be used in Nikon's Nikon View and Nikon Capture NX 2 image-editing software. Picture Controls allow you to get the same results when using different cameras that are compatible with the Nikon Picture Control System.

All of these Picture Controls can be adjusted to suit your specific needs or tastes. In the color modes — SD (⊠SD), NL (⊠NL), VI (⊠VI), PT (⊠PT), LS (⊠LS) — you can adjust the sharpening, contrast, brightness, hue, and saturation. In MC (⊠MC) mode you can adjust the filter effects and toning. After the Picture Controls are adjusted you can save them for later use. You can do this in the Manage Picture Control option described in the next section.

CROSS REF For detailed information on customizing and saving Picture Controls, see Chapter 2.

NOTE When saving to NEF the Picture Controls are imbedded into the metadata. Only Nikon's software can use these settings. When opening RAW files using a third-party program such as Adobe Camera RAW in Photoshop, the Picture Controls are not used.

Manage Picture Control

This menu is where you can edit, save, and rename your Custom Picture Controls. There are four menu options:

▶ **Save/edit.** In this menu, you choose a Picture Control, make adjustments to it, then save it. You can rename the Picture Control to help you remember what adjustments were made or to remind you of what the Custom Picture Control is to be used for. For example, I have one named ultra-VIVID, which has the contrast, sharpening, and saturation boosted as high as it can go. I sometimes use this setting when I want crazy, oversaturated, unrealistic-looking images for abstract shots or light trails.

▶ **Rename.** This menu allows you to rename any of your Custom Picture Controls. You cannot, however, rename the standard Nikon Picture Controls.

▶ **Delete.** This menu gives you the option of erasing any Custom Picture Controls you have saved. This menu only includes controls you have saved or may have downloaded from an outside source. The standard Nikon Picture Controls cannot be deleted.

▶ **Load/save.** This menu allows you to upload Custom Picture Controls to your camera from your memory card, delete any Picture Controls saved to your memory card, or you can save a Custom Picture Control to your memory card to export to Nikon View or Capture NX 2 or to another camera that is compatible with Nikon Picture Control.

CROSS REF For detailed information on creating and managing Picture Controls see Chapter 2.

The D800 also allows you to view a grid graph that shows you how each of the Picture Controls relates to each other in terms of contrast and saturation. Each Picture Control is displayed on the graph represented by a square icon with the letter of the Picture Control to which it corresponds. Custom Picture Controls are denoted by the number of the custom slot to which it has been saved. Standard Picture Controls that have been modified are displayed with an asterisk next to the letter. Picture Controls that have been set with one or more auto settings are displayed in green with lines extending from the icon to show you that the settings will change depending on the images.

To view the Picture Control grid select the Picture Control option from the Shooting Menu. Press ⊛ and the

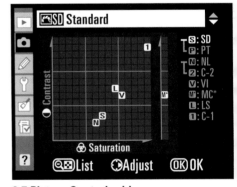

3.7 Picture Control grid

Picture Control list is displayed. Press the Thumbnail/Zoom out button (⊞) to view the grid. Once the Picture Control grid appears you can use the multi-selector to scroll though the different Picture Control settings. After you highlight a setting you can press ▶ to adjust the settings or press ⊛ to set the Picture Control. Press **MENU** to exit back to the Shooting menu or tap the Shutter Release button to ready the camera for shooting.

Color space

Color space simply describes the range of colors, also known as the gamut, that a device can reproduce. You have two choices of color spaces with the D800: sRGB and Adobe RGB. The color space you choose depends on what the final output of your images will be.

▶ **sRGB.** This is a narrow color space, meaning that it deals with fewer colors and also less-saturated colors than the larger Adobe RGB color space. The sRGB color space is designed to mimic the colors that can be reproduced on most low-end monitors.

▶ **Adobe RGB.** This color space has a much broader color spectrum than is available with sRGB. The Adobe gamut was designed for dealing with the color spectrum that can be reproduced with most high-end printing equipment.

This leads to the question of which color space you should use. If you take pictures, download them straight to your computer, and typically only view them on your monitor or upload them for viewing on the Web, then sRGB is fine. The sRGB color space is also useful when printing directly from the camera or memory card with no post-processing.

If you are going to have your photos printed professionally or you intend to do a bit of post-processing to your images, using the Adobe RGB color space is recommended. This allows you to have subtler control over the colors than is possible using a narrower color space like sRGB.

For the most part, I capture my images using the Adobe RGB color space. I then do my post-processing and make a decision on the output. Anything that I know I will be posting to the web I convert to sRGB; anything destined for my printer is saved as Adobe RGB. I usually end up with two identical images saved with two different color spaces. Because most web browsers don't recognize the Adobe RGB color space, any images saved as Adobe RGB and posted on the Internet usually appear dull and flat.

Active D-Lighting

Active D-Lighting is a setting that is designed to help ensure that you retain highlight detail when shooting in a high-contrast situation, such as shooting a picture in direct bright sunlight, which can cause dark shadows and bright highlight areas. Active D-Lighting basically tells your camera to underexpose the image a bit; this underexposure helps keep the highlights from becoming blown out and losing detail. The D800 also uses a subtle adjustment to avoid losing any detail in the shadow area that the underexposure may cause.

Using Active D-Lighting changes all of the Picture Control brightness and contrast settings to Auto; adjusting the brightness and contrast is how Active D-Lighting keeps detail in the shadow areas.

Active D-Lighting has six settings: Auto, Extra high, High, Normal, Low, and Off.

> **CAUTION** Using the Extra high or High setting can cause excessive noise or banding to appear in the shadow areas.

From my experiences using Active D-Lighting I find that it works, but it can be subtle in the changes that it makes when using the lower settings. For general shooting I recommend setting Active D-Lighting to Auto. I prefer to shoot in RAW and although the settings are saved to the metadata for use with Nikon software, I would rather do the adjustment myself in Photoshop so I turn this feature off.

When using Active D-Lighting some extra time has to be taken to process the images. Your buffer will fill up faster when shooting continuously, so expect shorter burst rates.

High Dynamic Range (HDR)

Although this term has become synonymous with overprocessed hyper-realistic imagery, in fact HDR is really just a tool to make your images look more like they do to the human eye. Nikon's built-in HDR takes two shots and combines them using in-camera processing to expand the shadow and the highlight detail. Once you select the HDR mode from the Shooting menu you have some options to select:

▶ **HDR mode.** This is where you turn the HDR on and off. There are three options.

- **On (series).** This allows you to shoot HDR continuously. On previous cameras the HDR setting only took one HDR shot and then had to be reset for the next shot.

- **On (single photo).** This setting is as described previously. The camera takes one HDR image and then resets back to default photos.

- **Off.** This disables the HDR setting.

▶ **Exposure differential.** This option is used to set the difference between the exposures of the two images that are to be merged. You have four options:

- **Auto.** In this mode, the camera meter assesses the scene and automatically adjusts the exposure difference of the two images. I've found that this option works best, especially with the D800's new 91K pixel RGB metering sensor.

- **1EV.** This gives a 1-stop difference between exposures, which is a pretty safe setting for most HDR shots.

- **2EV.** This is a 2-stop difference, which is pretty substantial. There should be a good amount of contrast in the scene when selecting this option.

- **3EV.** This option provides 3 stops of exposure difference and should only be used in the most extreme contrast situations. Possibly a bright sunlit day at high noon would be the best time to use this setting.

▶ **Smoothing.** This option controls how the two images are blended together. There are these options: High, Normal, and Low. Higher options provide smoother blending, but I find that Normal works the best for most applications especially when using the Auto setting.

> **NOTE** When the camera is combining the images, the Job HDR will flash in the control panel and the LCD and no photos can be taken until the HDR is finished being processed.

Vignette control

Some lenses, especially wide-angle lens, have a tendency to *vignette* or darken near the edges of the frame. This problem is more common on cameras with FX sensors than it is with DX cameras. The problem is due to the extremely oblique angle at which the light enters the lens. Vignetting is more pronounced when using wide apertures; therefore, reducing the aperture size also reduces the amount of vignetting that occurs.

Although vignetting can be corrected in post-processing Nikon includes a vignette control feature that lightens the edges to make the exposure more uniform.

There are four Vignette control options: High, Normal, Low, and Off. I have tried this feature numerous times, and it still tends to leave a vignette even on the High setting. I usually leave this option off because there are much better ways to control vignetting using image-editing software such as Lightroom or Adobe Camera RAW. Nikon even notes in the manual that this setting may cause fogging or noise on the edges of the frame when shooting JPEG or TIFF, and Custom Picture Controls may not function as desired; just more reasons to leave this option off.

Auto distortion control

As with vignetting, there is some distortion that occurs in accordance with lens design. Each lens has its own specific distortion characteristics and Nikon has built-in software that automatically corrects lens distortion based on the specific lens used. Note that this feature only works with Nikkor D and G lenses. Nikkor Perspective Control and fisheye lenses do not work with this feature because of the lens design. Nikon also warns that this feature is not guaranteed to work with third-party lenses.

Long exp. NR

This menu option allows you to turn on noise reduction (NR) for exposures of 1 second or longer. When this option is on, after taking a long exposure photo the camera runs a noise-reduction algorithm that reduces the amount of noise in your image to produce a smoother result. This adds processing time and slows your frame rate. Again, this is a setting I leave off preferring to do my own noise reduction using other software in post-processing.

High ISO NR

This allows you to choose how much noise reduction (NR) is applied to images that are taken at high ISO settings (Nikon doesn't specify at what setting this starts; it's probably somewhere around ISO 800). There are four settings:

▶ **High.** This setting applies fairly aggressive NR. A fair amount of image detail can be lost when this setting is applied.

▶ **Normal.** This is the default setting. Some image detail may be lost when using this setting.

▶ **Low.** A small amount of NR is applied when this option is selected. Most of the image detail is preserved when using this setting.

▶ **Off.** When this setting is selected, NR is only applied to images at ISO 1600 or higher, but it less NR than the Low setting.

ISO sensitivity settings

This menu option allows you to set the ISO. This is the same as pressing the ISO button (ISO) and rotating the Main Command dial. You can also change the ISO settings in the Info Settings display. The options go from ISO 50 (Lo1) on up to ISO 25,600 (Hi2). The standard settings are ISO 100 to ISO 6400. It's recommended that you stick with the standard settings rather than the Lo and Hi settings. The Lo settings give slightly higher contrast and the Hi settings cause excessive noise.

> **NOTE** Pressing the ISO button (ISO) and rotating the Sub-command dial turns the Auto-ISO setting on and off.

You also use this menu to set the Auto ISO parameters.

> **CROSS REF** For more information on ISO settings, Auto-ISO, and noise reduction, see Chapter 2.

3

Multiple exposure

This allows you to record multiple exposures in one image. You can record from two to ten shots in a single image. This is an easy way to get off-the-wall multiple images without using image-editing software like Photoshop. Select Multiple exposure mode from the menu then (just like the HDR menu) choose from these three settings:

▶ **On (series).** This allows you to shoot multiple exposures continuously. On previous cameras the multiple exposure setting only took the amount of images selected for one multiple exposure and then had to be reset for the next shot.

▶ **On (single photo).** The camera takes enough shots to create the multiple exposure and then resets back to default photos.

▶ **Off.** This disables the Multiple exposure setting.

To use this feature, follow these steps:

1. **Press ▶ to select the mode: On (series) or On (single photo).**
2. **Select the Number of shots menu option and press ▶.**

3. **Press ▲ or ▼ to set the number of shots and press ⊛ when the number of shots selected is correct.**

4. **Select the Auto gain option and press ▶.**

5. **Set the gain, and then press ⊛.** Using auto gain enables the camera to adjust the exposure according to the number of images in the multiple exposures. This is the recommended setting for most applications. Setting the gain to Off does not adjust the exposure values and can result in an overexposed image. The Gain-off setting is recommend only in low-light situations.

6. **Use the multi-selector to highlight Done and press ⊛.** This step is very important. If you do not select Done, the camera will not be in Multiple exposure mode.

7. **Take your pictures.** Single burst mode is recommended.

Interval timer shooting

This allows you to set your camera to shoot a specified number of still photos at pre-determined intervals throughout a set period of time. You can use this interesting feature to record the slow movements of plants or animals, such as a flower opening or a snail crawling. Another option is to set up your camera with a wide-angle lens and record the movement of the sun or moon across the sky.

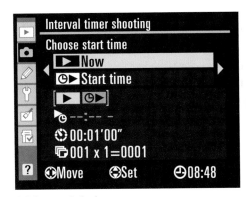

3.8 Interval timing menu screen

Naturally, you need a tripod to do this type of photography, and I suggest that you use Nikon's EH-5b AC power supply to be sure that your camera battery doesn't die in the middle of your shooting. At the very least an MB-D12 battery grip should be used with an extra battery.

After you record your series of images you can use image-editing software to combine the images and create an animated GIF file.

You can set:

▶ **Starting time.** The camera can be set to start 3 seconds after the settings have been completed (Now) or you can set to start photographing at a predetermined time in the future.

- ▶ **Interval.** This determines how much time is elapsed between each shot. You can set Hours, Minutes, and Seconds.

- ▶ **Number of intervals.** This sets how many times you want photos to be shot.

- ▶ **Shots per interval.** This sets how many shots are taken at each interval.

- ▶ **On or Off.** This starts or stops the camera from shooting with the current settings.

Time-lapse photography

The time-lapse photography option is very similar to the interval timer shooting except that it automatically joins the photos together as a video, creating a time-lapse movie file.

The time-lapse movie is filmed using the current Movie settings that are selected (covered in the next section). For consistency it's recommended that you use M and take the white balance setting off of Auto. You can check the framing using (Lv). Be sure the selector is set to the movie option before pressing Lv to frame. You need to use a tripod or have the camera set on something stable. Additionally, there are a few things that need to be set before you begin shooting.

3

> **NOTE** Shooting in Manual focus is recommended for the most consistent results.

- ▶ **Interval.** This sets the time between video clips. Note that you can't choose an interval longer than 10 minutes. The interval needs to be longer than any expected shutter speed.

- ▶ **Shooting time.** This sets the allotted amount of time that the time-lapse covers. It can be no longer than 7 hours and 59 minutes.

Just underneath the Interval and Shooting time setting is what appears to be another setting, but is actually an approximation of the length of the final time-lapse movie. It s calculated by dividing the number of shots by the frame rate.

Movie settings

The movie settings options on the D800 allow you to adjust the size, frame rate, and quality of the videos you record. There are a number of different options to choose from.

> **CROSS REF** In depth information about recording video is discussed in Chapter 6.

▶ **Frame size / frame rate.** This option is where you set the size of the HD video and select the frame rate that is appropriate for your output. These are the options:

- **1920 × 1080; 30fps** (1080 30)
- **1920 × 1080; 25fps** (1080 25)
- **1920 × 1080; 24fps** (1080 24)
- **1280 × 720; 60fps** (720 60)
- **1280 × 720; 50fps** (720 50)
- **1280 × 720; 30fps** (720 30)
- **1280 × 720; 25fps** (720 25)

▶ **Movie quality.** There are two options, High quality and Normal. The difference between the two options is the maximum bit rate at which the videos are recorded.

CROSS REF   Bit rate is covered more in depth in Chapter 6.

▶ **Microphone.** This allows you to adjust the volume of the recording using the built-in microphone or an external microphone. There are three easy options.

- **Auto.** This simple option automatically adjusts the volume level so that the audio levels don't clip. This works well enough for most general video usage.

- **Manual Sensitivity.** This option allows you to set the microphone to record at a specified volume. This option is best for recording sound in a controlled environment.

- **Destination.** This allows you to select which memory card the video is recorded to. If you only have one memory card inserted, the camera will default to that card no matter which one you select.

Custom Settings Menu

The Custom Settings menu (✐) is where you really start getting into customizing your D800 to shoot to your personal preferences. You can also choose four banks in which to store your settings for different shooting situations, similar to the Shooting menu banks. Basically this is where you make the camera yours. There are dozens of options that you can turn off or turn on to make shooting easier for you. This is probably the most powerful menu in the camera.

Custom settings bank

Like the Shooting menu banks, this option allows you to save your custom settings to four banks for easy recall. Simply select a bank — A, B, C, or D — then change any of the custom settings to the option of your choice. The changed settings are stored until you choose to reset custom settings (described in the next section).

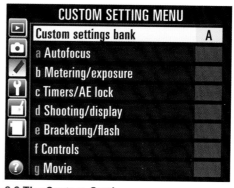

3.9 The Custom Settings menu

You can also add a descriptive name to your Custom settings bank to help you remember what your Custom settings bank is to be used for. While in the Custom settings bank menu, simply press 🗑 to bring up the text entry screen.

The active Custom settings bank is shown in the Shooting info display on the main LCD when **Info** is pressed. You can quickly switch between Custom settings banks by using the Info Menu Settings (covered in Ch 2).

Custom settings menu a - Autofocus

The 🖉 a submenu controls how the camera performs its autofocus (AF) functions. Because focus is a very critical operation, this is a very important menu.

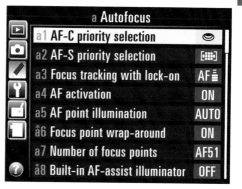

3.10 Custom settings menu a — shown in two sections so all options are visible

a1 – AF-C priority selection

This chooses how the camera AF functions when in Continuous autofocus (AF-C) mode. You can choose from three modes:

▶ **Release.** This is the default setting. It allows the camera to take a photo whenever the Shutter Release button is pressed regardless of whether the camera has achieved focus or not. This setting is best used for fast action shots of for when it's imperative to get the shot whether it's in sharp focus or not.

▶ **Release + focus.** This allows the camera to take pictures when the subject is not in focus, but slows the frame rate to allow the camera more time to focus on the subject. You can use this for action shots when you want to be sure that the subject is in focus and the frame rate is not important. You wouldn't want to use this option when attempting to take sequential shots at a high frame rate.

▶ **Focus.** This allows the camera to take photos only when the camera achieves focus and the focus indicator (green dot in the lower-left corner of the viewfinder) is lit. This is the best setting to for slow-moving subjects where you want to be absolutely sure that your subject will be in focus.

a2 – AF-S priority selection

This sets how the camera AF functions when in single autofocus (AF-S) mode. You can choose from these two settings.

▶ **Release.** This is the default setting. It allows the camera to take a photo whenever the Shutter Release button is pressed regardless of whether the camera has achieved focus or not.

▶ **Focus.** This allows the camera to take photos only when the camera achieves focus and the focus indicator (green dot in the lower-left corner of the viewfinder) is displayed.

a3 – Focus tracking with lock-on

When photographing in busy environments, such as sporting events or weddings, things can often cross your path resulting in the camera refocusing on the wrong subject. Focus tracking lock-on allows the camera to hold focus for a time before switching to a different focus point. This helps stop the camera from switching focus to an unwanted subject passing through your field of view.

In previous models there were three settings: Long, Normal, and Short. The D800 adds a numbering system of 1-5, adding number 2 between Short and Normal, and 4 between, Normal and Long.

You can also set the focus tracking lock-on to off, which allows your camera to quickly maintain focus on a rapidly moving subject. Normal is the default setting.

a4 – AF activation

By default the camera's AF system is activated by half-pressing the Shutter Release button or by pressing the AF-ON button (**AF-ON**). This option allows you to set the D800 so that the AF is activated only when pressing **AF-ON**. If the camera is set to

AF-ON, half-pressing the Shutter Release button only activates the camera's metering system. This is a personal preference, and I like to use the Shutter Release button to engage the AF.

▶ **Shutter/AF-ON.** This allows you to engage the camera's AF system either by half-pressing the Shutter Release button or by using **AF-ON** (either on the camera body or on the MB-D10 grip).

▶ **AF-ON only.** With this option turned on the camera's AF system is activated only by pressing **AF-ON**. Half-pressing the Shutter Release button only activates the D800 metering system.

a5 – AF point illumination

This menu option allows you to choose whether the active AF point is highlighted in red momentarily in the viewfinder when focus is achieved. When the viewfinder grid is turned on the grid is also highlighted in red. When choosing Auto, which is the default, the focus point is lit only to establish contrast from the background when it is dark. When set to On, the active AF point is highlighted even when the background is bright. When set to Off, the active AF point is not highlighted in red but appears black.

a6 – Focus point wrap-around

When using the multi-selector to choose your AF point, this setting allows you to be able to keep pressing the multi-selector in the same direction and wrap around to the opposite side or stop at the edge of the focus point frame (no wrap). Personally, I like to set mine to wrap to allow me to quickly switch to the other side of the frame if I need to when shooting in a fast-paced environment.

a7 – Number of focus points

This option allows you to choose the number of available focus points from which you can choose when using AF. You can set 51 points, which allows you to choose all of the D800's available focus points. You can also set it to 11 points, which allows you to choose from only 11 focus points similar to the D200 and D2 series cameras. Use the 11-point option to select your focus points much more quickly than using 51 points. The 51-point option allows you to more accurately choose where in the frame the camera will focus.

a8 – Built-in AF-assist illuminator

The AF-assist illuminator lights up when there isn't enough light for the camera to focus properly (when using the viewfinder only). In certain instances, you may want to turn this option off, such as when shooting faraway subjects in dim settings (concerts or plays). When set to On, the AF-assist illuminator lights up in a low-light situation only when in AF-S mode and Auto-area AF is chosen. When in Single point mode or Dynamic area AF is chosen, the center AF point must be active.

When set to Off, the AF-assist illuminator does not light at all.

Custom settings menu b − Metering/exposure

This is where you change the settings that control exposure and metering. These settings allow you to adjust the exposure, ISO, and exposure compensation adjustment in increments. Setting the increments to 1/3 stops allows you to fine-tune the settings with more accuracy than setting them to 1/2 or 1 full stop. There are six options to choose from.

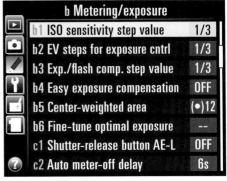

3.11 Custom settings menu b − Metering/exposure

b1 − ISO sensitivity step value

This is where you control whether the ISO is set in 1/3-, 1/2-, or 1-stop increments. Setting the ISO using smaller steps allows you to fine-tune your sensitivity with more precision allowing you more control over keeping high ISO noise to a minimum.

b2 − EV steps for exposure cntrl

This determines how the increments for shutter speed, aperture, and auto bracketing are set. The choices here are also 1/3, 1/2, or 1 stop. Choosing a smaller increment gives a much less drastic change in exposure and allows you to get a more exact exposure in critical situations.

b3 − Exp./flash comp. step value

This allows you to choose whether the exposure compensation is set in 1/3-, 1/2-, or 1-stop increments. Again, choosing a lower increment setting allows you to fine-tune to the exposure more precisely.

b4 − Easy exposure compensation

By default, to set the exposure compensation you must first press ☒ and use the Main Command dial to add or subtract from the selected exposure. If you tend to use exposure compensation frequently, you can save yourself some time by using this option to set Easy exposure compensation. When this function is set to On, it's not necessary to press ☒ to adjust exposure compensation. Simply rotate the Main Command dial when in Aperture Priority mode **A** or the Sub-command dial when in Shutter Priority mode **S** or either dial when in Programmed Auto (**P**) to adjust the exposure compensation. The exposure compensation is then applied when you rotate the appropriate command dial until the exposure compensation indicator disappears from the LCD control panel.

If you choose to use Easy exposure compensation, probably the best setting to use is the On (Auto reset) setting. This allows you to adjust your exposure compensation while shooting, but returns the exposure compensation to default (0) when the camera is turned off or when the camera's exposure meter turns off. If you've ever accidentally left exposure compensation adjusted and ended up with wrongly exposed images the next time you used your camera, you will appreciate this helpful feature.

When set to Off, exposure compensation is applied normally by pressing ☒ and rotating the Main Command dial.

b5 – Center-weighted area

This menu allows you to choose the size of your center-weighted metering area. You can choose from four sizes: 8, 12, 15, or 20mm. You also have the option of setting the meter to Average.

Choose the area size depending how much of the center of the frame you want the camera to meter for. The camera determines the exposure by basing 75 percent of the exposure on the circle.

Average uses the whole frame to assess the exposure and can lead to flat, low-contrast images.

CROSS REF For more information on center-weighted metering, see Chapter 2.

b6 – Fine-tune optimal exposure

If your camera's metering system consistently over- or underexposes your images, you can adjust it to apply a small amount of exposure compensation for every shot. You can apply a different amount of exposure fine-tuning for each of the metering modes: Matrix (▨), Center-weighted (▣), and Spot (⊡).

You can set the EV ±1 stop in 1/6-stop increments.

> **CAUTION** When Fine-tune optimal exposure is on, there is no warning indicator that tells you that exposure compensation is being applied.

Custom settings menu c – Timers/AE lock

This small submenu controls the D800's various timers and also the Auto-exposure lock setting. There are four options.

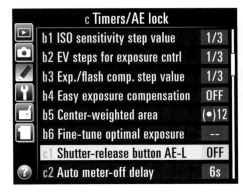

c1 – Shutter-release button AE-L

Set to default (Off), the camera only locks exposure when the AE-L/AF-L button (AE-L/AF-L) is pressed. When set to On, the auto-exposure settings are locked when the camera's Shutter Release button is half-pressed.

c2 – Auto meter-off delay

This menu option is used to determine how long the camera's exposure meter is active before turning off when no other actions are being performed. You can choose 4, 6, 10, or 30 seconds; or 1, 5, 10, or 30 minutes. You can also specify for the meter to remain on at all times while the camera is on (no limit).

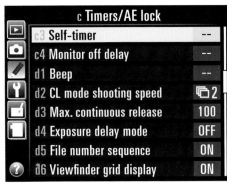

3.12 Custom settings menu c

c3 – Self-timer

This setting puts a delay on when the shutter is released after the Shutter Release button is pressed. This is handy when you want to do a self-portrait and you need some time to get yourself into the frame. The self-timer (⟳) can also be employed to reduce camera shake caused by pressing the Shutter Release button on long exposures.

There are three settings that you can adjust.

▶ **Self-timer delay.** You can set the delay at 2, 5, 10, or 20 seconds.

▶ **Number of shots.** You can press ▲ or ▼ to set the camera to take up to nine photos.

▶ **Interval between shots.** When ☉ is set to more than one shot use this option to select the interval between shots by pressing ▲ or ▼. The interval can be set to 0.5, 1, 2, or 3 seconds.

c4 – Monitor off delay

This controls how long the LCD monitor remains on when no buttons are being pushed. Because the LCD monitor is the main source of power consumption for any digital camera, choosing a shorter delay time is usually preferable.

▶ **Playback –** 4s, 10s (default), 20s, 1min, 5min, 10min

▶ **Menu –** 4s, 10s, 20s, 1min(default), 5min, 10min

▶ **Information display –** 4s, 10s (default), 20s, 1min, 5min, 10min

▶ **Image review –** 2s, 4s (default), 10s, 20s, 1min, 5min, 10min

▶ **Live view –** 5min, 10min (default), 15min, 20min, 30min, No Limit

Custom settings menu d – Shooting/display

The ✐ d submenu is where you make changes to some of the minor shooting and display details.

d1 – Beep

When this option is on, the camera emits a beep when the self-timer is counting down or when the AF locks in Single focus mode. You can choose 3, 2, 1, or Off and high or low pitch. Although the beep can be kind of useful when in self-timer mode, it's an annoying option especially if you are photographing in a relatively quiet area. The beep will not sound when using Live View or when shooting in Quiet mode (**Q**).

d2 – CL mode shooting speed

This allows you to set the maximum frame rate in the Continuous Low shooting mode (CL). You can set the frame rate between 1 and 5 fps. This setting limits your burst rate for shooting slower-moving action. This is a handy option to use when you don't necessarily need the highest frame rate, such as when shooting action that isn't moving very fast but also isn't moving slow. I have this set to 3 fps, which is about half of the frame rate I get when using the MB-D12 battery grip with AA batteries or an EN-EL-18 in DX mode.

d3 – Max. continuous release

This option sets the maximum number of images that can be captured in a single burst when the camera is set to cʟ or Continuous High shooting mode (cʜ). You can set this anywhere from 1 to 100. Setting this option doesn't necessarily mean that your camera is going to capture 100 frames at the full frame rate speed. When shooting continuously, especially at a high frame rate, the camera's buffer gets full and the camera's frame rate slows down or even stops while the buffer transfers data to the memory card. How fast the buffer fills up depends on the image size, compression, and the speed of your memory card. With the

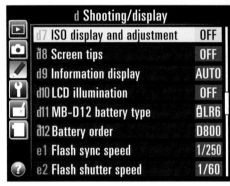

3.13 Custom settings menu d — shown on two screens so all options are visible

D800's large file sizes I find it very beneficial to use a faster card to achieve the maximum frame rate for extended periods.

d4 – Exposure delay mode

Turning this option on causes the shutter to open 1, 2, or 3 seconds after the Shutter Release button is pressed and the reflex mirror has been raised. This option is for shooting long exposures with a tripod where camera shake from pressing the Shutter Release button and mirror slap vibration can cause the image to be blurry. It's best to use a longer delay when using longer lenses.

d5 – File number sequence

The D800 names files by sequentially numbering them. This option controls how the sequence is handled. When set to Off, the file numbers reset to 0001 when a new folder is created, a new memory card is inserted, or the existing memory card is formatted. When set to On, the camera continues to count up from the last number until the file number reaches 9999. The camera then returns to 0001 and counts up from there. When this is set to Reset the camera starts at 0001 when the current folder is empty. If the current folder has images the camera starts at one number higher than the last image in the folder.

d6 – Viewfinder grid display

This handy option displays a grid in the viewfinder to assist you with composition of the photograph. I find this option to be very helpful especially when composing landscape and architectural photos.

d7 – ISO display and adjustment

There are three options for this setting. Selecting Show ISO shows the ISO setting instead of the remaining number of frames on the control panel. Selecting Show ISO/ Easy ISO shows the ISO setting in place of the remaining exposures number. This setting also allows you to quickly change the ISO setting by rotating the Sub-command dial when using **S** or **P** modes or the Main Command dial when in **S** mode. The default setting is Show frame count, which shows how many remaining exposures you have on the active memory card.

d8 – Screen tips

When this option is turned on the camera displays descriptions of the menu options available when using the Information display. The menu options in the display are pretty self-evident as to what they are so I have this option turned off. If you're unsure of any menu option pressing the Help (**?**) button displays a screen that describes the function.

d9 – Information Display

This controls how the shooting info display on the LCD panel is colored. When set to Auto (default), the camera automatically sets it to White on Black or Black on White to maintain contrast with the background. The setting is automatically determined by the amount of light coming in through the lens. You can also choose for the information to be displayed consistently no matter how dark or light the scene is. You can choose B (black lettering on a light background) or W (white lettering on a dark background).

d10 – LCD illumination

When this option is set to Off (default), the LCD control panel on the camera (and on a Speedlight if attached) is lit only when the power switch is turned all the way to the right engaging the momentary switch. When set to On, the LCD control panel is lit as long as the camera's exposure meter is active, which can be quite a drain on the batteries (especially for the Speedlight).

d11 – MB-D12 battery type

When using the optional MB-D12 battery pack with AA batteries, use this option to specify what type of batteries are being used to ensure optimal performance. Your choices are:

▶ **LR6 (AA alkaline).** These are standard everyday AA batteries. I don't recommend their use as they don't last very long when used with the D800.

▶ **HR6 (AA Ni-Mh).** These are standard nickel metal hydride re-chargeable batteries available at most electronics stores. I recommend buying several sets of these. Make sure they are rated at least 2500 MaH for longer battery life.

▶ **FR6 (AA Lithium).** These lightweight batteries are not rechargeable but last up to seven times longer than standard alkaline batteries. These batteries cost about as much as a good set of rechargeable batteries.

> **NOTE** When using an EN-EL15 or EN-EL18 battery, selecting this option is unnecessary.

d12 – Battery order

This option is used to set which order the batteries are used when the optional MB-D12 battery grip is attached. Choose MB-D12 to use the battery grip first, or choose D800 to use the camera battery first. If you're using the MB-D12 with AA batteries or an EN-EL15 or EN-EL18 battery to achieve a faster frame rate you need to be sure that the battery order is set to use MB-D12 first. If you're using AA batteries in the MB-D12 only as a backup, set this option to use the camera battery first.

Custom settings menu e – Bracketing/flash

This submenu is where you set the controls for the built-in Speedlight. Some of these options also affect external Speedlights. This menu is also where the controls for Bracketing images are located. There are seven choices.

e1 – Flash sync speed

This is where you determine what shutter speed your camera uses to sync with the Speedlight. You can set the sync speed between 1/60 and 1/250 second. When using an external Speedlight, you can also set the sync to 1/250 (Auto FP) or 1/320 (Auto FP); this allows you to use faster shutter speeds to maintain wider apertures in bright situations if needed.

CROSS REF For more information on sync speed and Auto FP, see Chapter 5.

e2 – Flash shutter speed

This option lets you decide the slowest shutter speed that is allowed when you do flash photography using Front-curtain sync or Red-Eye Reduction mode when the camera is in P or A exposure mode. You can choose from 1/60 second all the way down to 30 seconds.

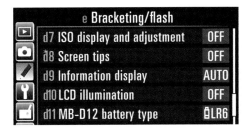

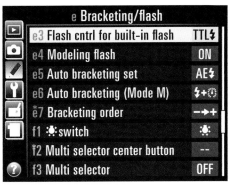

3.14 Custom Settings menu e

When the camera is set to **S** or the flash is set to any combination of Slow sync, this setting is ignored.

e3 – Flash cntrl for built-in flash

This submenu has other submenus nested within it. Essentially, this option controls how your built-in flash operates. The four submenus are

▶ **TTL.** This is the fully auto flash mode. Minor adjustments can be made using FEC (Flash Exposure Compensation).

▶ **Manual.** You choose the power output in this mode. You can choose from Full power all the way down to 1/128 power.

▶ **Repeating flash.** This mode fires a specified number of flashes.

▶ **Commander mode.** Use this setting to control a number of off-camera CLS-compatible Speedlights.

CROSS REF For more information on flash photography, see Chapter 5.

e4 – Modeling flash

When using the built-in flash or an external Speedlight, pressing the Depth of Field preview button fires a series of low-power flashes that allow you to preview what the effect of the flash is going to be on your subject. When using CLS and Advanced Wireless Lighting with multiple Speedlights, pressing the button causes all of the Speedlights to emit a modeling flash. You can set this to On or Off. I prefer Off because the Preview button is easily pressed accidentally.

e5 – Auto bracketing set

This option allows you to choose how the camera brackets when Auto-bracketing is turned on. You can choose for the camera to bracket AE and flash, AE only, Flash only, or ADL, or WB bracketing. WB bracketing is not available when the image quality is set to record RAW images.

e6 – Auto bracketing (Mode M)

This determines which settings the camera changes to adjust the exposure when using Auto-bracketing in Manual exposure mode. The options are:

▶ **Flash/speed.** The camera varies the shutter speed and flash output (when set to AE + flash), or the shutter speed only (when set to AE only).

▶ **Flash/speed/aperture.** The camera varies the shutter speed, aperture, and flash output (when set to AE + flash), or the shutter speed and aperture (when set to AE only).

▶ **Flash/aperture.** The camera varies the aperture and flash level (when set to AE + flash), or the aperture only (when set to AE only).

▶ **Flash only.** The camera varies the flash level only (when set to AE + flash).

NOTE ✐ e5 must be set to AE + Flash or AE for these options to take effect.

e7 - Bracketing order

This determines the sequence in which the bracketed exposures are taken. When set to default (N), the camera first takes the metered exposure, the underexposures next, then the overexposures. When set to Under → MTR → over, the camera starts with the lowest exposure, increasing the exposure as the sequence progresses. This is the setting I prefer as it follows a more natural progression.

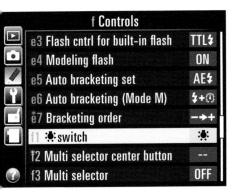

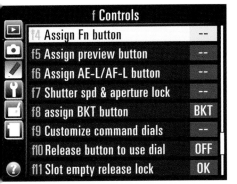

3.15 Custom settings menu f

Custom settings menu f – Controls

This submenu allows you to customize some of the functions of the different buttons and dials of your D800. There are ten options.

f1 switch

The on-off switch can be rotated past the on setting that acts as a momentary switch. You can use this option to light the LCD control panel (LCD backlight) or you can light the LCD control panel and display the info screen on the rear LCD monitor (Both).

f2 – Multi selector center button

This allows you to set specific options for pressing the center button of the multi-selector. The options vary depending on whether the camera is in Shooting or Playback mode.

Shooting mode

In Shooting mode, the options are as follows:

▶ **RESET.** This allows you to automatically select the center focus point by pressing the center button of the multi-selector. This is my preferred setting.

▶ **Highlight active focus point.** This causes the active focus point to light up in the viewfinder when the center button of the multi-selector is pressed.

▶ **Not used.** The center button has no effect when in Shooting mode.

Playback mode

In Playback mode the options are as follows:

► **Thumbnail on/off.** This allows you to switch between full-frame Playback and Thumbnail view by pressing the center button of the multi-selector.

► **View histogram.** This option displays the histogram of the current image selected when the center button of the multi-selector is pressed. This is the setting I prefer.

► **Zoom on/off.** Pressing the center button of the multi-selector allows you to automatically zoom in to the selected image to check focus. You can choose Low, Medium, or High magnification.

► **Choose slot and folder.** Pressing the center button of the multi-selector displays the list of folders currently on the flash card. You can then choose a folder to play back images from.

Live View

For Live View the options are:

► **RESET.** This resets the focus point to the center.

► **Zoom on/off.** This allows you to instantly zoom in on the Live View. You can also choose the initial magnification from Low, Medium, or High.

► **Not used.** Pressing the center button has no effect.

f3 – Multi selector

This allows you to set the multi-selector to turn on the exposure meter when pressed. By default, the meter will not turn on when the multi-selector is pressed in Shooting mode.

f4 – Assign Fn button

This button chooses what functions the Function button (**Fn**) performs when pressed. Be aware that not all options are available depending on which particular setting is chosen. You can choose from two **Fn** options: Fn button press and Fn button + command dials. You can also access this setting using the Quick Settings menu. The options are:

► **Preview.** Just in case you want to use the Depth of Field preview button for another function you can reassign it to this button. This option closes down the aperture so you can see in real time what effect the aperture will have on the image's depth of field. This function is cancelled when you select a function for Fn button + command dials. If you choose this setting for button press only, the function for Fn button + command dials will be deactivated.

▶ **FV lock.** This allows you to use the **Fn** to fire a preflash to determine flash exposure, the can then recompose the frame and the flash will expose for the original subject as long as you continue to hold the **Fn** button down. This function is cancelled when you select a function for Fn. button + command dials. If you choose this setting for button press only, the function for Fn. button + command dials will be deactivated.

▶ **AE/AF Lock.** The focus and exposure lock when the button is pressed and held.

▶ **AE lock only.** The exposure locks when the button is pressed and held. Focus continues to function normally.

▶ **AE lock (reset on release).** The exposure locks when the button is pressed. The exposure remains locked until the shutter is released, the **Fn** is pressed again, or the exposure meter turns off. This function is cancelled when you select a function for Fn button + command dials. If you choose this setting for button press only, the function for Fn button + command dials will be deactivated.

▶ **AE Lock (hold).** The exposure locks until the button is pressed a second time or the exposure meter is turned off.

▶ **AF Lock only.** The focus locks while the button is pressed and held. The AE continues as normal.

▶ **AF-ON.** This activates the cameras AF system. This works best when ✐ a4 is set to AF-ON only.

▶ **Flash off.** With this option the built-in flash (if popped up) or an additional Speedlight will not fire when the shutter is released as long as **Fn** is pressed. This allows you to quickly take available-light photos without having to turn off the flash. This is quite handy especially when shooting weddings and events.

▶ **Bracketing burst.** The camera fires a burst of shots when the Shutter Release button is pressed and held while in Single shot mode when Auto-bracketing is turned on. The number of shots fired depends on the Auto-bracketing settings. When in Continuous shooting mode, the camera continues to run through the bracketing sequence as long as the Shutter Release button is held down.

▶ **Matrix metering.** Allows you to automatically use Matrix metering no matter what the metering mode dial is set to.

▶ **Center-weighted.** Allows you to automatically use Center-weighted metering no matter what the metering mode dial is set to.

▶ **Spot metering.** Allows you to automatically use ⊡ no matter what the metering mode dial is set to.

▶ **Playback.** This allows the **Fn** to display the playback review, which can be handy when using a heavy lens and you want to keep both hands on the camera.

▶ **Access top item in My Menu.** This brings up the top item set in the My Menu option. You can use this to quickly access your most used menu option. This function is cancelled when you select a function for Fn. button + command dials. If you choose this setting for button press only, the function for Fn. button + command dials will be deactivated.

▶ **+ NEF(RAW).** Pressing the **Fn** when this is activated and the camera is set to record JPEG allows the camera to simultaneously record a RAW file and a JPEG. Pressing the button again allows the camera to return to recording only JPEGs. This function is cancelled when you select a function for Fn. button + command dials. If you choose this setting for button press only, the function for Fn. button + command dials will be deactivated.

▶ **Virtual Horizon.** When this option is selected pressing **Fn** shows the pitch and roll virtual horizon bars in the viewfinder.

▶ **None.** The default setting. No function is performed when the button is pressed.

A second subset in this menu is Fn. + command dials. This allows you to use **Fn** in combination with the Main Command or Sub-command dial to perform certain functions. The options are:

▶ **Choose image area.** Press **Fn** and rotate either command dial to choose between FX and DX settings.

▶ **Shutter spd and aperture lock.** Press **Fn** and rotate the Main Command dial to lock the shutter speed when in **5** or **M**. Press **Fn** and rotate the Sub-command dial when using **A** or **M**. To unlock, press **Fn** and rotate the appropriate dial again. You can use this setting to be sure you don't accidentally change your settings in a situation where you need a specific setting, such as when photographing a sporting event where you need a fast aperture or a portrait where you might want to keep the aperture wide open.

▶ **1 step spd/aperture.** When **Fn** is pressed, the aperture and shutter speed are changed in 1-stop intervals.

▶ **Choose non-CPU lens number.** Press **Fn** and rotate the Main Command dial to choose one of your presets for a non-CPU lens.

▶ **Active D-Lighting.** This allows you to quickly adjust the active D-Lighting settings by pressing the button and rotating the command dials.

▶ **None.** No functions are performed.

f5 – Assign preview button

This allows you to assign a function to the Depth of Field preview button. The choices are exactly the same as that of **Fn** as described in the previous section.

f6 – Assign AE-L/AF-L button

This allows you to assign a function to ⚏. The button press choices are exactly the same as that of **Fn** and Preview buttons with the addition of an AF-ON setting and the subtraction of the 1 stp/spd/aperture and ADL settings. The AE-L/AF-L + command dials only offer three choices.

▶ **Choose image area.** This allows you to press the button and use the Sub-command dial to select the image area. This option has a sub-menu that allows you to select which image area option you want. You can choose them all or turn off certain ones.

▶ **Shutter spd and aperture lock.** This allows you to press (⚏) and lock the shutter speed by rotating the Main Command dial when in **M** and **R**, unfortunately rotating the Main Command dial while pressing ⚏ can only be done with two hands so you can't do it on the fly. Pressing ⚏ and rotating the Sub-command dial allows you to lock the aperture setting when in **M** and **R**. In **P**, this option has no effect.

▶ **Choose non-CPU lens number.** This allows you to use the Sub-command dial to select the lens info that you have stored in the non-CPU lens option (in the Setup (**Y**) menu).

f7 – Shutter spd & aperture lock

This option allows you to lock your exposure settings to avoid accidentally changing them. You can lock the shutter speed when using **S**, and the aperture when using **R**. When in **M** you can lock the aperture only, the shutter speed only, or both simultaneously. When using **P**, this feature is disabled.

f8 – Assign BKT button

This option allows you to customize the BKT button (**BKT**). You have three options.

▶ **BKT.** This is the default function for this button. Press the button and rotate the Main Command dial to choose the number of shots and the Sub-command dial to choose the increment.

▶ **Multiple exposure.** This option allows you to access the Multiple exposure feature directly by pressing **BKT** instead of going through the menus. The Sub-command dial allows you to select the number of exposures. The Main Command dial allows you to set it to single or series. When the multiple exposure icon appears in the control panel, single mode is selected, when the multiple exposure icon and the aperture lock icon are displayed in the control panel then you are in series mode.

▶ **HDR.** This option allows you to set the HDR options. You can set the exposure differential using the Sub-command dial. Rotating the Main Command dial allows you to select single or series. When HDR appears in the control panel, single mode is selected, when HDR and the aperture lock icon are displayed in the control panel, then you are in series mode. Note that HDR mode isn't available in RAW or RAW+JPEG mode.

f9 – Customize command dials

This menu allows you to control how the Main Command and Sub-command dials function. The options are:

▶ **Reverse rotation.** This causes the settings to be controlled in reverse of what is normal. For example, by default, rotating the Sub-command dial right makes your aperture smaller. Reversing the dials gives you a larger aperture when rotating the dial to the right.

▶ **Change main/sub.** This switches functions of the Main Command dial to the front and the Sub-command dial to the rear of the camera.

▶ **Aperture setting.** This allows you to change the aperture only using the aperture ring of the lens. Note that most newer lenses have electronically controlled apertures (Nikkor G lenses) and do not have an aperture ring. When used with a lens without an aperture ring the Sub-command dial controls the aperture by default.

▶ **Menus and playback.** This allows you to use the command dials to scroll the menus and images in much the same fashion the multi-selector is used. In Playback mode, the Main Command dial is used to scroll through the preview images and the Sub-command dial is used to view the shooting information and/or histograms. When in Menu mode, the Main Command dial functions the same as pressing ▲ or ▼, and the Sub-command dial operates the same as pressing ◀ or ▶.

f10 – Release button to use dial

When changing the Shooting mode, exposure compensation, Flash mode, AF Mode, WB, QUAL, BKT, or ISO, you must press and hold the corresponding button and rotate the Main Command dial to make changes. This setting allows you to press and release the button, make changes using the command dials, then press the button again to set the value.

f11 – Slot empty release lock

This setting controls whether the shutter will release when no memory card is present in the camera. When set to Enable release, the shutter fires and an image that is displayed in the monitor the image will be temporarily saved. When set to Release locked, the shutter will not fire. If you happen to be using Camera Control Pro 2 shooting tethered directly to your computer, the camera shutter will release no matter what this option is set to.

f12 – Reverse indicators

This allows you to reverse the indicators on the electronic light meter displayed in the viewfinder and on the LCD control panel on the top of the camera. For some, the default setting showing the overexposure on the left and the underexposure on the right is counterintuitive. Reversing these makes more sense to some people (including me). This option also reverses the display for the Auto Bracketing feature.

f13 – Assign MB-D12 AF-ON

This allows you to customize the button on the optional MB-D12 vertical grip. There are eight options:

▶ **AF-ON.** This option allows you to initiate the autofocus without half-pressing the Shutter Release button.

▶ **FV lock.** This allows you to use **Fn** to fire a preflash to determine flash exposure, the then recompose the frame and the flash exposes for the original subject as long as you continue to hold **Fn** down. This function is cancelled when you select a function for Fn. button + command dials. If you choose this setting for button press only, the function for Fn. button + command dials will be deactivated.

▶ **AE/AF Lock.** The focus and exposure lock when the button is pressed and held.

▶ **AE lock only.** The exposure locks when the button is pressed and held. Focus continues to function normally.

▶ **AE lock (reset on release).** The exposure locks when the button is pressed. The exposure remains locked until the shutter is released, **Fn** is pressed again, or the exposure meter turns off. This function is cancelled when you select a function for Fn. button + command dials. If you choose this setting for button press only, the function for Fn. button + command dials will be deactivated.

▶ **AE Lock (hold).** The exposure locks until the button is pressed a second time or the exposure meter is turned off.

▶ **AF Lock only.** The focus locks while the button is pressed and held. The AE continues as normal.

▶ **Same as Fn. Button.** This sets **AF-ON** on the MB-D12 to perform the same task as **Fn**.

Custom settings menu g – Movie

This is a brand-new menu that deals with settings solely for the video features. It mostly deals with customizing button assignments.

g1 – Assign Fn button

This option allows you to customize what **Fn** does when in Live View Movie mode. There are four options:

3.16 Custom settings menu g

▶ **Power aperture (open).** This automatically opens the aperture when the button is pressed. This is best used in conjunction with 🖉 g2 set to Power aperture (closed).

▶ **Index marking.** Pressing the button places an index mark at that position in the video. Index marks are used when editing videos.

▶ **View photo shooting info.** Setting this option allows you to view the shooting info, including shutter speed, aperture, frame rate, and so on. Pressing the button again allows you to return to the standard movie recording scene.

▶ **None.** Pressing the button does nothing.

g2 – Assign preview button

Similar to **Fn** this allows you to select the options for the Preview button.

▶ **Power aperture (closed).** This automatically closes the aperture when the button pressed. This is best used in conjunction with ✐ g1 set to Power aperture (open).

▶ **Index marking.** Pressing the button places an index mark at that position in the video. Index marks are used when editing videos.

▶ **View photo shooting info.** Setting this option allows you to view the shooting info, including shutter speed, aperture, frame rate, and so on. Pressing the button again allows you to return to the standard movie recording scene.

▶ **None.** Pressing the button does nothing.

> **NOTE** Power aperture is only available in **A** and **M** and is unavailable while shooting or while the shooting info is displayed.

g3 – Assign AE-L/AF-L button

This allows you to set the options for the AE-L/AF-L (⚷) button. It has a couple of the same options as ✐ g1 and g2, but mostly deals with auto-exposure settings.

▶ **Index marking.** Pressing the button places an index mark at that position in the video. Index marks are used when editing videos.

▶ **View photo shooting info.** Setting this option allows you to view the shooting info including shutter speed, aperture, frame rate, and so on. Pressing the button again allows you to return to the standard movie recording scene.

▶ **AE/AF Lock.** The focus and exposure lock when the button is pressed and held.

▶ **AE lock only.** The exposure locks when the button is pressed and held. Focus continues to function normally.

▶ **AE Lock (hold).** The exposure locks until the button is pressed a second time or the exposure meter is turned off.

▶ **AF Lock only.** The focus locks while the button is pressed and held. The AE continues as normal.

▶ **None.** Pressing the button does nothing.

g4 – Assign shutter button

This option sets the Shutter Release button to either record movies or take stills. Details are as follows:

▶ **Take photos.** When this option is selected pressing the Shutter Release button fully ends movie recording and takes a still photo. The still photo is recorded in the cinematic 16:9 aspect ratio.

▶ **Record Movies.** When set to this option you press the Shutter Release halfway to engage Live View; release the button and press halfway again to focus. Fully press the button to start recording, half-press to refocus, and fully press again to end recording.

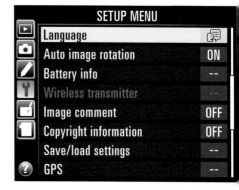

Setup Menu

This menu contains a smattering of options, most of which aren't changed very frequently. Some of these settings include the time and date. A couple of other options are the Clean image sensor and Battery info, which you may want to access from time to time.

Format memory card

This allows you to completely erase everything on your memory card. Formatting your memory card erases all of the data on the card. It's a good idea to format your card every time you download the images to your computer (just be sure all of the files are successfully transferred before formatting). Formatting the card helps protect against corrupt data. Simply erasing the images leaves the data on

3.17 The Setup Menu shown in three frames to fit it all in

the card and allows it to be overwritten; sometimes this older data can corrupt the new data as it is being written. Formatting the card gives your camera a blank slate on which to write. If two cards are present use the multi-selector to select which slot you want to format, SD or CF.

> **TIP** You can also format the card using the much more convenient two-button method (pressing and holding 🗑 and the MODE button (**MODE**) simultaneously).

Monitor brightness

This menu sets the brightness of your LCD screen. You may want to make it brighter when viewing images in bright sunlight or make it dimmer when viewing images indoors or to save battery power. You can adjust the LCD ±3 levels. The menu shows a graph with ten bars from black to gray to white. The optimal setting is where you can see a distinct change in color tone in each of the ten bars. If the last two bars on the right blend together your LCD is too bright, if the last to bars on the left side blend together your LCD is too dark.

There is also an Auto setting that uses the ambient light sensor on the back of the camera to automatically adjust the brightness.

Clean image sensor

The camera uses ultrasonic vibration to knock any dust off the filter in front of the sensor. This helps keep most of the dust off of your sensor but is not going to keep it absolutely dust free forever. You may have to have the sensor professionally cleaned periodically.

You can choose Clean now, which cleans the image sensor immediately, or you have four separate options for cleaning that you access in the Clean at startup/shutdown option. These include:

▶ **Clean at startup.** The camera goes through the cleaning process immediately upon turning the camera on. This may delay your startup time a little bit.

▶ **Clean at shutdown.** The camera cleans the sensor when the camera is switched to off. This is my preferred setting because it doesn't interfere with the startup time.

▶ **Clean at startup and shutdown.** The camera cleans the image sensor when the camera is turned on and also when it is powered down.

▶ **Cleaning off.** This disables the dust reduction function when turning the camera on and off. You can still use the Clean now option when this is set.

Lock mirror up for cleaning

This locks up the mirror to allow access to the image sensor for inspection or for additional cleaning. The sensor is also powered down to reduce any static charge that may attract dust. Although some people prefer to clean their own sensor I recommend taking your camera to an authorized Nikon service center for any sensor cleaning. Any damage caused to the sensor by improper self-cleaning will NOT be covered by warranty and can lead to a very expensive repair bill.

Image Dust Off ref photo

This option allows you to take a dust reference photo that shows any dust or debris that may be stuck to your sensor. Capture NX 2 then uses the image to automatically retouch any subsequent photos where the specks appear.

To use this feature either select Start or Clean sensor and then start. Next you will be instructed by a dialog box to take a photo of a bright featureless white object that is about 10 cm from the lens. The camera automatically sets the focus to infinity. A Dust Off reference photo can only be taken when using a CPU lens. It's recommended to use at least a 50mm lens and when using a zoom lens you should zoom all the way in to the longest focal length.

HDMI

The D800 has an HDMI (high-definition multimedia interface) output that allows you to connect your camera to a high-definition TV to review your images. There are five settings: Auto, 480p, 576p, 720p, and1080i. The Auto feature automatically selects the appropriate setting for your TV. Before plugging your camera in to an HD TV I recommend reading your TV's owner's manual for specific settings. When the camera is attached to an HDMI device the LCD monitor on the camera is automatically disabled. There's also an advanced mode. The options are:

▶ **Output range.** This detects your HDMI device's RBG output. There are three options.

- **Auto.** This option automatically detects the RGB range of your device.

- **Limited range.** This is for lower-resolution HDMI monitors with an input limited to a signal range from 16-235 brightness levels. If your shadows are too dark this is the option to choose.

- **Full range.** This option is for higher-range HDMI displays that have an input range from of 0 to 255 brightness levels. If your video seems too bright and you have loss of highlight detail, choose this option.

▶ **Output display size.** This allows you to set the output size of your image to 95 or 100 percent to fit different HDMI display sizes.

▶ **Live view on-screen display.** This allows you to turn on and off the shooting display info.

Flicker reduction

Some light sources can cause the video to flicker depending on the local AC power grid. In the United States, the frequency is 60hz; in Europe, 50hz is the standard. Auto generally takes care of the problem, but if you aren't getting good results try adjusting your shutter speed.

Time zone and date

This is where you set the camera's internal clock. There are four options:

▶ **Time zone.** Use the multi-selector to choose your time zone using the map display.

▶ **Date and time.** This is where you set the clock. It's pretty self-explanatory.

▶ **Date format.** You can set the order in which the date is displayed: Year/Month/Date, Month/Date/Year, Date/Month/Year.

▶ **Daylight saving time.** Turn this on when Daylight saving time is in effect and the time is changed by one hour.

Language

This is where you set the language that the menus and dialog boxes display.

Auto image rotation

This tells the camera to record the orientation of the camera when the photo is shot (portrait or landscape). This allows the camera and also image-editing software to show the photo in the proper orientation so you don't have to take the time in post-processing to rotate images shot in portrait orientation.

Battery info

This handy little menu allows you to view information about your batteries. It shows you the current charge of the battery as a percentage and how many shots have been taken using that battery since the last charge. This menu also shows the remaining charging life of your battery before it is no longer able to hold a charge. I find myself accessing this menu quite a bit to keep a real-time watch on my camera's power levels. Most of these info options only work with standard Nikon batteries. AA batteries cannot provide the camera with data.

▶ **Charge.** This tells you the percentage of remaining battery life from 100% - 0%. When the MB-D12 battery grip is attached and loaded with AA batteries a percentage is not shown but there is a battery indicator that shows full, 50%, and 0% power levels.

▶ **No. of shots.** This tells you how many shutter actuations the battery has had since its last charge. This option is not displayed for the MB-D12 battery grip when using AA batteries.

▶ **Calibration.** This option is only displayed when an EN-EL-18 battery is inserted into the MB-D12 battery grip. This tells you when to recalibrate the battery so that the remaining charge can be shown more accurately.

▶ **Battery age.** This is a gauge that goes from 0-4 that tells you how much working life you have left in your battery because Li-ion batteries have a finite life. This option is not shown for AA batteries. When shooting outside in temperatures below 41 degrees F (5 degrees C) this gauge may temporarily show that the battery life has lost some of its charging life. The battery will show normal when brought back to an operating temperature of about 68 degrees F.

Wireless transmitter

This option is used to change settings of the optional WT-4 wireless transmitter. You cannot access this menu option when the WT-4 is not attached. See the WT-4 wireless transmitter user's manual for more information.

Image comment

You can use this feature to attach a comment to the images taken by your D800. You can enter the text using the Input Comment menu. The comments can be viewed in Nikon's Capture NX 2 or View NX 2 software or can be viewed in the photo info on the camera. Setting the attach comment option applies the comment to all images taken until this setting is disabled.

Copyright information

This is a great feature that allows you to embed your name and copyright information directly into the EXIF data of the image as it is being recorded. Enter the information using the text entry screen. You can turn this option on or off without losing the actual information. You may want to do this when doing work for hire where you get paid to take the photos but relinquish all copyright and ownership to the person that hired you.

Save/load settings

This allows you to save the current camera settings to a memory card. You can then store this memory card somewhere or transfer the file to your computer. You can then load these settings back to your camera in case of an accidental reset or load them onto a second D800 to duplicate the settings quickly.

GPS

This menu is used to adjust the settings of an optional GPS unit, such as the Nikon GP-1, which can be used to record longitude and latitude to the image's EXIF data. Non-Nikon GPS units are connected to the camera's 10-pin remote terminal using an optional MC-35 GPS adapter.

Virtual horizon

This option has been updated from previous Nikon cameras and now includes pitch and roll (forward/backward and sideways). A sensor inside the camera allows you to completely level your camera.

Non-CPU lens data

This menu is used to input lens data from a non-CPU lens. You can save focal length and aperture values for up to nine lenses. This feature is handy because if the camera knows the focal length and aperture of the lens attached, it can apply the information to some of the automatic settings that wouldn't normally be available without the lens communicating with the camera body. Some of the automatic settings referred to include the Auto-zoom on optional Speedlights. The focal length and aperture appear in the EXIF data, flash level can be adjusted automatically for changes in aperture, and color matrix metering can be used.

To set the lens data when using a non-CPU lens, follow these steps:

1. **Select non-CPU lens data from the Setup Menu using the multi-selector, and then press ▶.**

2. **Select a lens number to set the information by pressing ◀ or ▶, choose from 1 to 9, and then press ▼.**

3. **Select the focal length of your non-CPU lens and press ▼.** You can use a lens from as wide as 6mm to as long as 4000mm.

4. **Choose the maximum aperture of your lens.** You can choose from f/1.2 to f/22.

5. **Press ▲ to highlight Done and press ⊛ to save the lens data.**

AF fine-tune

This option allows you to adjust the autofocus to fit a specific lens. Lenses are manufactured to tight specifications, but every once in a while there may be something a little off in the manufacturing process that might cause the lens to mount a little differently or perhaps one of the lens elements has shifted a few microns. These small abnormalities can cause the lens to shift its plane of focus behind or in front of the imaging sensor. I would say that this is probably a rare occurrence, but it's a possibility.

You can fine-tune the camera's AF to correct for any focusing problems. Another good thing about this feature: If you're using a CPU lens, the camera remembers the fine-tuning for that specific lens and adjusts it for you automatically.

Because there is really no simple way to determine if your lens needs an AF fine-tune adjustment unless it's so out of whack that it's completely obvious, I recommend leaving this feature alone for the most part. A little Unsharp Mask in post-processing usually cures any minor blurring issues.

I'm sure there are a few of you out there who will insist on testing out this feature so here is a very brief description on how to go about doing it:

1. **Use the multi-selector to choose AF fine-tune from the Setup menu and press ⊛.**

2. **Highlight Saved value and press ⊛.**

3. **Press ▲ and ▼ to adjust the plane of focus.** You'll have to use a little guesswork. Determine if the camera is focusing behind the subject or in front of it and if so, how far?

4. **Once it's adjusted, press ⊛.**

5. **Set the Default and press ⊛.** This should be set to 0.

The saved value stores separate tuning values for each individual lens. This is the value that will be applied when the specific lens is attached and the AF fine-tune is turned on.

NOTE When the AF fine-tune is on and a lens without a stored value is attached, the camera will use the default setting. This is why I recommend setting the default to 0 until you can determine whether the lens needs fine-tuning or not.

Each CPU lens you fine-tune is saved into the menu. To view them, select List Saved Values. From there you can assign a number to the saved values from 0-99 (although the camera only stores 20 lens values). You could use the number to denote what lens you're using for example use the number 50 for a 50mm lens, number 85 for an 85mm lens, and so on, or you could use the last two digits of the lens serial number if you happen to have two of the same lenses (for example, I have two 17-35 lenses).

The best thing to do when attempting to fine-tune your lenses is to set them up one by one and do a series of test shots. The test shots have to be done in a controlled manner so there are no variables to throw off your findings.

The first thing to do is to get an AF test chart. You can find these on the Internet or you can send me an e-mail through my website http://deadsailorproductions.com and I can send you one that you can print out. An AF test chart has a spot in the center that you focus on and series of lines or marks set at different intervals. Assuming you focus on the right spot the test chart can tell you whether your lens is spot on, back focusing, or front focusing. The test chart needs to be lit well for maximum contrast. Not only do you need the contrast for focus, but it makes it much easier to interpret the test chart. Using bright continuous lighting is best, but flash can work as well. Lighting from the front is usually best.

Next, set your camera Picture Control to ND or neutral. Ensure that all in-camera sharpening is turned off and contrast adjustments are at zero. This is to be sure that you are seeing actual lens sharpness, not sharpness created by post-processing.

Lay the AF test chart on a flat surface. This is important, there must be no bumps or high spots on the chart or your results won't be accurate. Mount the camera on a tripod and adjust the tripod head so that the camera is at a 45-degree angle. Be sure that the camera lens is just about at the minimum focus distance to ensure the narrowest depth of field. Set the camera to Single AF mode, use Single area autofocus, and use the center AF point. Focus on the spot at the center of the AF test chart. Be sure not to change the focus point or move the tripod while making your tests. Set the camera to *A* and open the aperture to its widest setting to achieve a narrow depth of field (this makes it easier to figure out where the focus is falling — in the front or the back). Use a Nikon MC-30 remote control release or the self-timer to be sure there is no blur from camera shake. The first image should be shot with no AF fine-tuning.

Look at the test chart. Decide whether the camera is focusing where it needs to be or if it's focusing behind of or in front of where it needs to be.

Next, you can make some large adjustments to the AF fine-tuning (+5, -5, +10, -10, +15, -15, +20, -20) taking a shot at each setting. Be sure to defocus and refocus after adjusting the settings to ensure accurate results. Compare these images and decide which setting brings the focus closest to the selected focus point. After comparing them you may want to do a little more fine-tuning, to -7 or +13, for example.

This can be a very tedious and time-consuming project. That being said, most lenses are already spot on and it probably isn't necessary to run a test like this on your lens unless it is extremely noticeable that the lens is consistently out of focus.

Eye-Fi upload

This option is only displayed when an Eye-Fi memory card is inserted into the camera. The Eye-Fi card allows you to wirelessly transfer your images to your computer using your wireless router.

There are a number of different types of Eye-Fi cards so it's best to check the owner's manual that comes with your specific card for more details.

Firmware version

This menu option displays which firmware version your camera is currently operating under. Firmware is a computer program that is embedded in the camera that tells it how to function. Camera manufacturers routinely update the firmware to correct for any bugs or to make improvements on the camera's functions. Nikon posts firmware updates on its website at www.nikonusa.com.

Retouch Menu

The Retouch menu (⬚) allows you to make changes and corrections to your images without the use of imaging-editing software. As a matter of fact, you don't even need to download your images to a computer. You can make all of the changes in-camera using the LCD preview (or hooked up to an HDTV if you prefer). The Retouch menu only makes *copies* of the images so you don't need to worry about doing any destructive editing to your actual files.

The first and quickest method:

1. **Press ▶ to enter Playback mode.** Your most recently taken image appears on the LCD screen.

2. **Use the multi-selector to review your images.**

3. **When you see an image you want to retouch, press ⊙ to display the Retouch menu options.**

4. **Use the multi-selector to highlight the Retouch option you want to use.** Depending on the Retouch option you choose, you may have to select additional settings.

5. **Make adjustments if necessary.**

6. **Press ⊙ to save.**

The second method:

1. **Press MENU to view menu options.**

2. **Press ▼ to move to ✍.**

3. **Press ▶ and press ▲ and ▼ to highlight the Retouch option you want to use.** Depending on the Retouch option you select, you may have to select additional settings. Once you have selected your option(s), thumbnails appear.

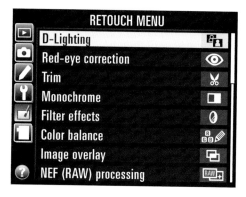

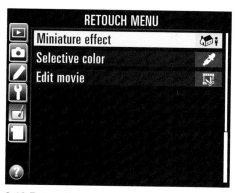

3.18 Retouch menu

4. **Use the multi-selector to select the image to retouch and then press ⊙.**

5. **Make the necessary adjustments.**

6. **Press ⊙ to save.**

D-Lighting

This allows you to adjust the image by brightening the shadows. This is not the same as Active D-lighting. D-Lighting uses a curves adjustment to help to bring out details in the shadow areas of an image. This option is for use with backlit subjects or images that may be slightly underexposed.

When the D-Lighting option is selected from ☑, you can use the multi-selector to choose a thumbnail and press 🔍 to get a closer look at the image. Press the 🆗 to choose the image to retouch, and two thumbnails are displayed; one is the original image, and the other is the image with D-Lighting applied.

You can press ▲ or ▼ to select the amount of D-Lighting: Low, Normal, or High. The results can be viewed in real time and compared with the original before saving. Press the 🆗 to save, ▶ to cancel, and 🔍 to view the full-frame image.

Red-eye correction

This option enables the camera to automatically correct for the red-eye effect that can sometimes be caused by using the flash on pictures taken of people. This option is only available on photos taken with flash. When choosing images to retouch from the Playback Menu by pressing 🆗 during preview, this option is grayed out and cannot be selected if the camera detects that a flash was not used. When attempting to choose an image directly from the Retouch Menu, a message is displayed stating that this image cannot be used.

Once the image has been selected, press 🆗; the camera then automatically corrects the red-eye and saves a copy of the image to your memory card.

If an image is selected that flash was used on but there is no red-eye present, the camera displays a message stating that red-eye is not detected in the image and no retouching will be done.

Trim

This option allows you to crop your image to remove distracting elements or to allow you to crop closer to the subject. You can also use 🔍 and ▦ to adjust the size of the crop. This allows you to crop closer in or back it out if you find that you've zoomed in too much.

Use the multi-selector to move the crop around the image so you can center the crop on the part of the image that you think is most important. When you are happy with the crop you have selected, press ⓞ to save a copy of your cropped image or press ▶ to return to the main menu without saving.

Rotating the Main Command dial allows you to choose different aspect ratios for your crop. You can choose the aspect ratio to conform to different print sizes. The options are:

▶ **3:2.** This is the default crop size. This ratio is good for prints sized 4 × 6, 8 × 12, and 12 × 18.

▶ **4:3.** This is the ratio for prints sized 6 × 8 or 12 × 16.

▶ **5:4.** This is the standard size for 8 × 10 prints.

▶ **1:1.** This gives you a square crop.

▶ **16:9.** This is what's known as a cinematic crop. This is the ratio that movie screens and widescreen televisions use.

Monochrome

This option allows you to make a copy of your color image in a monochrome format. There are three options:

▶ **Black-and-white.** This changes your image to shades of black, white, and gray.

▶ **Sepia.** This gives your image the look of a black-and-white photo that has been sepia toned. Sepia toning is a traditional photographic process that gives the photo a reddish-brown tint.

▶ **Cyanotype.** This option gives your photos a blue or cyan tint. Cyanotypes are a form of processing film-based photographic images.

When using the Sepia or Cyanotype options, you can press ▲ or ▼ to adjust the lightness or darkness of the effect. Press ⓞ to save a copy of the image or press ▶ to cancel without saving.

> **TIP** The Monochrome Picture Control offers more flexible settings than simply retouching the images using the Retouch Menu. You may want to consider shooting your images using the Picture Control rather than using this option.

Filter effects

Filter effects allow you to simulate the effects of using certain filters over your lens to subtly modify the colors of your image. There are seven filter effects available:

▶ **Skylight.** A skylight filter is used to absorb some of the UV rays emitted by the sun. The UV rays can give your image a slightly bluish tint. Using the skylight filter effect causes your image to be less blue.

▶ **Warm filter.** A warming filter adds a little orange to your image to give it a warmer hue. This filter effect can sometimes be useful when using flash because flash can sometimes cause your images to feel a little too cool.

▶ **Red intensifier.** This boosts the saturation of reds in the image. Press ▲ or ▼ to lighten or darken the effect.

▶ **Green intensifier.** This boosts the saturation of greens in the image. Press ▲ or ▼ to lighten or darken the effect.

▶ **Blue intensifier.** This boosts the saturation of blues in the image. Press ▲ or ▼ to lighten or darken the effect.

▶ **Cross screen.** This effect simulates the use of a star filter. A star filter creates a star-shaped pattern on the bright highlights in your image. If your image doesn't have any bright highlights, the effect will not be apparent. Once an image is selected for the cross screen filter, you see a submenu with a few options that you can adjust. You can choose the number of points on the stars: 4, 6, or 8. You can also choose the amount; there are three settings that give you more or fewer stars. You can choose three angle settings that control the angle at which the star is tilted. You also have three settings that control the length of the points on the stars.

▶ **Soft.** This applies a soft glow to your images. This effect is mostly used for portraiture but can also be used effectively for landscapes as well.

After choosing the desired filter effect, press ⊛ to save a copy of your image with the effect added.

Color balance

You can use the Color balance option to create a copy of an image on which you have adjusted the color balance. Using this option, you can use the multi-selector to add a color tint to your image. You can use this effect to neutralize an existing color tint or to add a color tint for artistic purposes.

Press ▲ to increase the amount of green, ▼ to increase the amount of magenta, ◀ to add blue, and ▶ to add amber.

A color chart and color histograms are displayed along with an image preview so you can see how the color balance affects your image. When you are satisfied with your image, press ⊛ to save a copy.

Image overlay

This option allows you to combine two RAW images and save them as one. This menu option can only be accessed by entering the Retouch menu using **MENU** (the longer route); you cannot access this option by pressing the ⊛ when in Playback mode.

NOTE To use this option, you must have at least two RAW images saved to your memory card. This option is not available for use with JPEG.

To use this option:

1. Press **MENU** to view the menu options and use the multi-selector to scroll down to ✍ and press ► to enter the Retouch Menu.

2. Press ▲ or ▼ to highlight Image Overlay and press ►. This displays the Image Overlay menu.

3. Press ⊛ to view RAW image thumbnails.

4. Use the multi-selector to highlight the first RAW image to be used in the overlay and press ⊛ to select it.

5. Adjust the exposure of Image 1 by pressing ▲ or ▼ and press ⊛ when the image is adjusted to your liking.

6. Press ► to switch to Image 2.

7. Press ⊛ to view RAW image thumbnails.

8. Use the multi-selector to highlight the second RAW image to be used in the overlay and press ⊛ to select it.

9. Adjust the exposure of Image 2 by pressing ▲ or ▼ and press ⊛ when the image is adjusted to your liking.

10. Press ► to highlight the Preview window.

11. Press ▲ or ▼ to highlight Overlay to preview the image, or use the multi-selector to highlight Save to save the image without previewing.

3

NEF (RAW) processing

This option allows you to do some basic editing to images saved in the RAW format without downloading them to a computer and using image-editing software. This option is limited in its function but allows you to fine-tune your image more precisely when printing straight from the camera or memory card.

You can save a copy of your image in JPEG format. You can choose the image quality and size at which the copy is saved, you can adjust the white balance settings, fine-tune the exposure compensation, and select a Picture Control setting to be applied.

To apply RAW processing:

1. **Enter the NEF (RAW) Processing Menu through** ☑️.

2. **Press ⓞ to view thumbnails of the images stored on your card.** Only images saved in RAW format are displayed.

3. **Press ◀ or ▶ to scroll through the thumbnails and press ⓞ to select the highlighted image.** This brings up a screen with the image adjustment sub-menu located to the right of the image you have selected.

4. **Press ▲ or ▼ to highlight the adjustment you want to make.** You can set image quality, image size, white balance, exposure compensation, Picture Control, Hi ISO NR, Color space, Vignette, and D-Lighting. You can also press ⚲ to view a full-screen preview.

5. When you have made your adjustments, use the multi-selector to highlight EXE and press ⓞ to save changes or ▶ to cancel without saving. EXE sets the changes and saves a copy of the image in JPEG format at the size and quality that you have selected. The camera default saves the image as a Large, Fine JPEG.

CROSS REF For more information on image size, quality, white balance, and exposure compensation, see Chapter 2.

Resize

This is a handy option that allows you to make a copy of your images that are a smaller size. These smaller pictures are more suitable for making small prints, web-sized images, and for e-mailing to friends and family.

NOTE When using two memory cards you will be asked to choose a destination for the saved copies.

The first thing you need to do when creating a resized image is to select the Choose size option from the submenu. You have four options:

▶ **2.5M.** 1920 × 1280 pixels

▶ **1.1M.** 1280 × 856 pixels

▶ **0.6M.** 960 × 640 pixels

▶ **0.3M.** 640 × 424 pixels

After you decide on what size you want your small pictures copied, go to the Select picture option. When the Select picture option is chosen, the LCD displays thumbnails of all of the images in the current folder. To scroll through your images, press ▶ or ◀. To select or deselect an image, press ▲ or ▼. You can select as many images as you have on your memory card. When all the images that you want to make a resized copy of are selected, press ⊛ to make the copies.

Quick retouch

The Quick retouch option is the easiest option. The camera automatically adjusts the contrast and saturation making your image brighter and more colorful, perfect for printing straight from the camera or memory card. In the event that your image is dark or backlit, the camera also automatically applies D-Lighting to help bring out details in the shadow areas of your picture.

Once your image has been selected for Quick retouch, you have the option to choose how much of the effect is applied. You can choose from High, Normal, or Low. The LCD monitor displays a side-by side comparison between the image as shot and the image retouched to give you a better idea of what the effect looks like.

Once you decide how much of the effect you want, press ⊛ to save a copy of the retouched image or you can press ▶ to cancel without making any changes to your picture.

Straighten

This feature allows you to fix images that may have been shot at a slight angle, which is another nice feature when printing directly from the camera. When an image is selected, press ▶ and ◀ to adjust the tilt amount. A grid overlay is displayed over the image so you can use it to align with the horizon or other straight object in the photo.

Distortion control

As discussed in Chapter 4, some lenses are prone to distortion. This retouch option allows you to correct for lens distortion right in-camera. There are two options, Auto and Manual. Auto automatically applies any needed corrections and with Manual you can apply the effect yourself using the multi-selector. Press ▶ to reduce barrel distortion (wide-angles) and press ◀ to reduce pincushion distortion (telephoto).

> **CAUTION** The Auto setting is recommended for use with Nikkor G- and D-type lenses only.

Fisheye

This option does the opposite of what distortion control does: It adds barrel distortion to the image to make it appear like it was taken using a fisheye lens. Press ◀ to add to the effect and ▶ to decrease it. To be honest, however, the effect isn't great, so use at your own peril.

Color outline

The color outline feature takes the selected image and creates an outline copy that can be opened using image-editing software, such as Photoshop or Corel Paintshop Pro, and colored in by hand. This option works best when used on an image with high contrast. It's a pretty cool effect and the image can even be used straight from the camera, which gives it the look of a drawing.

Color sketch

This option gives your image the appearance that it was drawn with colored pencils. Selecting Vividness allows you to increase the color saturation of the effect. The Outlines option allows you to change the thickness of the outlines of the "sketch."

Perspective control

This allows you to correct for problems with perspective caused by pointing the camera upward or shooting at an angle instead of shooting something straight on. Think of shooting a tall building, when you tilt the camera up at the building it causes the base to look larger than the top of the building you can correct for this using the Perspective control option. Using ▲ and ▼ you can adjust the vertical perspective; using ◀ and ▶ you can adjust the horizontal perspective.

Miniature effect

This effect is modeled after a technique that some people call (erroneously) the *tilt-shift effect* because it can be achieved optically with a tilt-shift lens. Quite simply what this effect does is simulate the shallow depth of field normally present in macro shots. This tricks the eye into seeing something large as something very tiny. The effect only works with very far-off subjects and works better when the vantage point is looking down. It's a pretty cool effect, but only works with limited subjects, so use this effect with that in mind.

3.19 An overhead shot of the I-35 freeway in Austin, Texas, with miniature effect added

Selective color

You can use this option to turn your image black and white while retaining up to three colors. After selecting the image use the multi-selector to maneuver the cursor over an object of a particular color. Once you have the cursor over the color, press the multi-selector center button to set the color. Then scroll the Main Command dial to the right to adjust highlight the color range setting. Use ▲ or ▼ to adjust the purity of the color. Lower numbers will be more specific with the color; higher numbers will select a broader range of the color selection.

Rotate the Main Command dial right to select the other color options and follow the same procedures. For more precise color selection, use 🔍 to magnify the image. To reset the image, press 🗑. Press ⊛ to save the image.

Edit movie

This option allows you to make basic edits to videos that you shoot with the D800. You have three options: choose the Start frame, choose the End frame, and grab a still image from the video. Each edit you make is saved as a new file so there's no need to worry about making any permanent changes to your original file. To edit your video:

1. **Press MENU and use the multi-selector to select the Retouch menu.**

2. **Select Edit Movie.** Press ⊛ or ▶ to view menu options.

3. **Choose the edit you want to make.** The options are Choose start point, Choose end point, or Save selected frame. Press ⊛ or ▶. This pulls up a menu with all videos that are saved to the current card.

4. **Select the video.** Use the multi-selector to scroll through the available videos. The selected video is highlighted in yellow. Press ⊛ when your video is selected.

5. **Play the video.** Press ⊛ to begin playback. Press ▲ at the moment you want to make the edit. You can press ▼ to stop playback and ◀ and ▶ to go back or forward in the video clip.

6. **Make the edit.** Press ▲ to make the cut. I prefer to actually pause the movie by pressing ▼ so I can be absolutely sure that's where I want the edit to be. I then make the edit. The movie is automatically saved.

Side-by-side comparison

This option allows you to view a side-by-side comparison of the retouched image and the original copy of the image. This option can only be accessed by selecting an image that has been retouched.

To use this option:

1. **Press ▶ and use the multi-selector to choose the retouched image to view.**

2. **Press ⊛ to display the Retouch menu.**

3. **Use the multi-selector to highlight Side-by-side comparison, and then press ⊛.**

4. **Use the multi-selector to highlight either the original or retouched image.** You can then press ⊕ to view closer.

5. **Press ▶ to exit the Side-by-side comparison and return to Playback mode.**

My Menu

The My Menu option allows you to create your own customized menu by choosing the options. You can also set the different menu options to whatever order you want. This allows you to have all of the settings you change the most right at your fingertips without having to go searching through all the menus and submenus. For example, I have the My Menu option set to display all of the menu options I frequently use, including Storage Folder, Battery info, ✎ e3, and Active D-Lighting among a few others. This saves me an untold amount of time because I don't have to go through a lot of different menus.

To set up your custom My Menu:

1. **Select My Menu, and press ⊛.**

2. **Select Add items and press ⊛.**

3. **Use the multi-selector to navigate through the menus to add specific menu options and press ⊛.**

4. **Use the multi-selector to position where you want the menu item to appear and press ⊛ to save the order.**

5. **Repeat steps 2 through 4 until you have added all of the menu items you want.**

To reorder the items in My Menu:

1. **Select My Menu and press ⊛.**

2. **Select Rank items and press ⊛.** A list of all of the menu options that you have saved to the My Menu appears.

3. **Use the multi-selector to highlight the menu option you want to move and press ⊛.**

4. **Using the multi-selector, move the yellow line to where you want to move the selected item and press ⊛ to set.** Repeat this step until you have moved all of the menu options that you want.

5. **Press MENU or tap the Shutter Release button to exit.**

To delete options from My Menu simply press 🗑 when the option is highlighted. The camera will ask for confirmation that you indeed what to delete the setting. Press 🗑 again to confirm or press **MENU** to exit without deleting the menu option.

As I mentioned earlier, you can replace the My Menu option with the Recent settings option. The Recent settings menu stores the last 20 settings you have adjusted. To switch from My Menu to Recent settings:

1. **Select My Menu from the Menu tabs and press** ⓞ **to view My Menu.**

2. **Use the multi-selector to scroll down to the Choose tab menu option and press** ⓞ.

3. **Select Recent settings and press** ⓞ **or ▶ to change the setting.**

4. **Press MENU or tap the Shutter Release button to exit.**

Information Display Settings

This display, believe it or not, is inherited from Nikon's entry-level camera, the D60. Although it's not a true menu, it allows you access to several of the most commonly changed menu items. To access the Information Display Settings press **info**. This displays the shooting info screen on the rear LCD. While the shooting info is displayed, press **info** again. This grays out the shooting info and highlights the settings shown at the bottom of the shooting info screen. Use the multi-selector directional buttons to highlight the setting you want to change then press ⓞ. This takes you straight to the specific menu options. The options are:

▶ Shooting menu bank

▶ High ISO NR

▶ Active D-Lighting

▶ Color space

▶ Assign Preview button

▶ Assign **Fn** button

▶ Assign ᴬᴱᴸ/ᴬꜰᴸ button

▶ Assign **BKT** button

▶ Long exposure NR

▶ Custom settings bank

CHAPTER 4

Selecting and Using Lenses with the Nikon D800

Lenses are the most critical accessories you can buy for your camera. The lens that you put on your camera has an enormous impact not only on image quality, but also on the end result of the image appearance. Higher-quality lenses invariably lead to superior image quality. Your photographs will appear sharper with more detail.

Perhaps the greatest thing about photography is the ability to use your lens choice to show your perception of the world around you. For example, ultrawide lenses distort spatial reality in a way that is much different than we can see, and macro lenses allow you to get up close to a subject in a way that's unique from human perspective.

A good high-quality lens is an investment that should last you throughout many dSLR camera bodies.

Deciphering Nikon's Lens Codes

When shopping for lenses, you may notice all sorts of letter designations in the lens name. So, what do all those letters mean? Here's a simple list to help you decipher them:

▶ **AI/AIS.** These are auto-indexing lenses that automatically adjust the aperture diaphragm down when the Shutter Release button is pressed. All lenses, including AF lenses, made after 1977 are auto-indexing, but when referring to AI lenses most people generally mean the older MF lenses.

▶ **E.** These lenses were Nikon's budget series lenses, made to go with the lower-end film cameras, such as the EM, FG, and FG-20. Although these lenses are compact and are often constructed with plastic parts, some of these lenses, especially the 50mm f/1.8, are of quite good quality. These lenses are also manual focus only. These are not to be confused with Nikon's PC-E perspective control lenses.

▶ **D.** Lenses with this designation convey distance information to the camera to aid in metering for exposure and flash.

▶ **G.** These are newer lenses that lack a manually adjustable aperture ring. You must set the aperture on the camera body. G lenses also convey distance information to the camera as with D lenses.

▶ **AF, AF-D, AF-I, and AF-S.** All these denote that the lens is an autofocus lens. The AF-D represents a distance encoder for distance information, the AF-I is for internal focusing motor type, and the AF-S is for an internal Silent Wave Motor.

▶ **DX.** This lets you know the lens was optimized for use with Nikon's DX-format sensor. You can use these lenses with your D800 but with reduced resolution.

> **NOTE** Full frame lenses do not carry an FX designation as they can be used effectively on DX cameras without limitation.

▶ **VR.** This code denotes the lens is equipped with Nikon's Vibration Reduction image stabilization system. Nikon's newest lenses employ a technology known as VR-II, which is capable a detecting side-to side as well as up and down motion. Both technologies are only designated as VR.

▶ **ED.** This indicates that some of the glass in the lens is Nikon's Extra-Low Dispersion glass, which means the lens is less prone to lens flare and chromatic aberrations.

Lens Compatibility

Nikon has been manufacturing lenses since about 1937 and as a company is known to make some of the most high-quality lenses in the industry. You can use almost every Nikon lens made since about 1977 on your D800, although some lenses will have limited functionality. In 1977, Nikon introduced the Auto Indexing (AI) lens. Auto-indexing allows the aperture diaphragm on the lens to stay wide open until the shutter is released; the diaphragm then closes down to the desired f-stop. This allows maximum light to enter the camera, which makes focusing easier. You can also use some of the earlier lenses, known now as pre-AI, but most need some modifications to work with the D800.

All these early lenses are manual focus and lack a CPU. When using these lenses you can enter the non-CPU lens data into the D800 to ensure that you get the most functionality out of these older lenses. The non-CPU lens data, which includes focal length and aperture size, can be entered in the Setup menu.

In the 1980s, Nikon started manufacturing autofocus or AF lenses. Many of these lenses are very high quality and can be found at a much lower cost than their 1990s counterparts, the AF-D lenses. The main difference between AF lenses and AF-D lenses is that the D lenses provide the camera with distance information based on the focus of the subject. Both types of lenses are focused by using a screw-type drive motor that's found inside the camera body.

Nikon's current line is the AF-S lenses. These lenses have a Silent Wave Motor that's built in to the lens. The AF-S motor allows the lenses to focus much more quickly than the traditional screw-type lenses and also allows the focusing to be ultraquiet. Most of these lenses are also what is known as G-type lenses. These lenses lack a manual aperture ring. The aperture is controlled by using the Sub-command dial on the camera body.

Nikon has a full complement of professional AF-S lenses available for FX cameras like the D800 ranging from the ultrawide 14-24mm f/2.8G to the super-telephoto 600mm f/4G.

4

▶ **Micro-NIKKOR.** Even though they're labeled as micro, these are Nikon's macro lenses.

▶ **IF.** IF stands for internal focus. The focusing mechanism is inside the lens, so front of the lens doesn't rotate when focusing. This feature is useful when you don't want the front of the lens element to move; for example, when you use a polarizing filter. The internal focus mechanism also allows for faster focusing.

▶ **DC.** DC stands for Defocus Control. Nikon offers only a couple of lenses with this designation. These lenses make the out-of-focus areas in the image appear softer by using special lens elements to add spherical aberration. The parts of the image that are in focus aren't affected. Currently, the only Nikon lenses with this feature are the 135mm and the 105mm f/2. Both of these are considered portrait lenses.

▶ **N.** On some of Nikon's newest professional lenses you may see a large golden N. These means the lens has Nikon's Nano-Crystal Coating, which is designed to reduce flare and ghosting.

▶ **PC-E.** This is the designation for Nikon's Perspective Control lenses. PC for perspective control and the E designating that it has an electro-magnetic Auto-Indexing aperture control instead of the typical mechanical one found on all other AI lenses.

Third-Party Lenses

Nikon is by no means the only manufacturer of lenses that fit the D800. There are quite a few companies that make lenses that work flawlessly with Nikon cameras. In the past, third-party lenses had a reputation of being, at best, cheap knock-offs of the original manufacturer's lenses. This is not the case anymore as many third-party lens makers have stepped up to the plate and started releasing lenses that rival some of the originals (usually at half the price).

Although you can't beat Nikon's professional lenses there are many excellent third-party lens choices available to you. The three most prominent third-party lens manufacturers are Sigma, Tokina, and Tamron.

Sigma is a company that has been around for over 40 years and was the first lens manufacturer to make a wide-angle zoom lens. The Sigma company makes good lenses with a great build quality. Unlike some companies, about two-thirds of Sigma's lenses are designed around the FX format and optimized for use with digital sensors. The Sigma lenses are also available with what it calls HSM or Hyper-Sonic Motor. This is an AF motor that is built inside the lens and operates in a similar fashion to Nikon's AF-S or Silent Wave Motor. It allows very fast and quiet AF. Sigma lenses have won many awards and are considered a viable and affordable alternative to Nikon's offerings.

At this time Tokina offers only three lenses that are compatible with full-frame cameras such as the D800 — the 16-35mm f/2.8, the 100mm f/2.8 Macro, and the 80-400mm f/4.5-5.6.

Zoom Lenses versus Prime Lenses

Some photographers prefer primes, and some prefer zooms. It's largely a personal choice, and there are some things to consider.

One of the main advantages of the zoom lens is its versatility. You can attach one lens to your camera and use it in a wide variety of situations, which lessens the need for changing out lenses often. This is a very good feature because every time you take the lens off your camera, the sensor is vulnerable to dust and debris.

Although today's zoom lenses can be just as sharp as a prime lens, you do have to pay for this quality. A $150 zoom lens isn't going to give you nearly the quality as a $1500 zoom lens. These days, you can easily find a fast zoom lens — one with an aperture of at least f/2.8. Because you can easily change the ISO on a digital camera and the noise created from using a high ISO is lessening, a fast zoom lens isn't a complete necessity. Some photographers prefer a zoom lens with a wider aperture — not so much for the speed of the lens but for the option of being able to achieve a shallower depth of field, which is very important in isolating subjects.

Some of the most important features of prime lenses are that they can have a faster maximum aperture, they are far lighter, and in most cases cost less (this isn't the case with Nikon's newest wide-angle super-fast f/1.4 primes though). The standard prime lenses aren't very long, so the maximum aperture can be faster than with zoom lenses. Standard primes also require fewer lens elements and moving parts, so the weight is kept down considerably. And because there are fewer elements, the overall cost of production is less; therefore, you pay less.

4

Tamron offers about ten lenses that are well regarded — the 28-75mm f/2.8 and the 90mm f/2.8 Macro lenses being the most popular. Tamron is still lagging behind on built-in focus motor technology so focusing isn't as fast or quiet as you will find with other lens manufacturers.

Wide-Angle Lenses

The focal-length range of wide-angle lenses starts out at about 12mm (ultrawide) and extends to about 35mm (wide angle). Many of the most common wide-angle lenses on the market today are zoom lenses, although there are quite a few prime lenses available. Wide-angle lenses are generally *rectilinear,* meaning that there are lens elements built in to the lens to correct the distortion that's common with wide-angle lenses; this way, the lines near the edges of the frame appear straight. Fisheye lenses, which are also a type of wide-angle lens, are *curvilinear*; the lens elements aren't corrected, resulting in severe optical distortion.

Wide-angle lenses have a short focal length, which projects an image onto the sensor that has a wider field of view, meaning it allows you to fit more of the scene into your image.

In the past, ultrawide-angle lenses were rare, prohibitively expensive, and out of reach for most non-professional photographers. These days, it's very easy to find a relatively inexpensive ultrawide-angle lens. Ultrawide-angle lenses usually run in focal length from about 12mm to 20mm. Most wide-angle zoom lenses run the gamut from ultrawide to wide angle. Some of the ones that work with the D800 include:

▶ **Nikkor 14-24mm f/2.8G.** This is one of Nikon's best lenses (see Figure 4.1). It has excellent image sharpness from corner to corner at all apertures. It has a fast constant aperture and is great for low-light shooting. It's a truly spectacular lens, but it comes at a premium cost of just about $2000. One caveat about this lens is that you can't use any filters with it due to the protruding front element.

Image courtesy of Nikon
4.1 Nikkor 14-24mm f/2.8G

▶ **Sigma 12-24mm f/4-5.6.** This is the widest lens available for FX cameras. The extra 2mm really adds some depth to the images. This lens isn't one of the top performers in its class being that it's pretty soft in the corners when shooting wide open, but if you can live with the optical shortcomings it's a well-built lens that allows you to create some truly interesting images.

▶ **Nikon 16-35mm f/4G VR.** This is a standard wide-angle zoom that is also Nikon's first wide-angle lens to incorporate VR. This lens is a full stop slower than Nikon's other pro lenses. It's nice and sharp and a bit smaller and more convenient to use than the 14-24 f/2.8G.

▶ **Sigma 17-35mm f/2.8-4.** This is a great standard wide-angle lens that Sigma has discontinued for some reason. You can still easily find them both new and used. There are three versions; however, only the EX-DG with HSM motor was designed with a digital sensor in mind. While the EX with HSM motor, and the plain EX model with aperture ring will work with your D800, the D800's high resolution shows their flaws. You'd be best to stick to the EX-DG version.

When to use a wide-angle lens

You can use wide-angle lenses for a broad variety of subjects, and they're great for creating dynamic images with interesting results. Once you get used to seeing the world through a wide-angle lens, you may find that your images start to be more creative, and you may look at your subjects differently. There are many considerations when you use a wide-angle lens. Here a few examples:

▶ **More depth of field.** Wide-angle lenses allow you to get more of the scene in focus than you can when you use a midrange or telephoto lens at the same aperture and distance from the subject.

▶ **Wider field of view.** Wide-angle lenses allow you to fit more of your subject into your images. The shorter the focal length, the more you can fit in. This can be especially beneficial when you shoot landscape photos where you want to fit an immense scene into your photo or when you shoot a large group of people.

▶ **Perspective distortion.** Using wide-angle lenses causes things that are closer to the lens to look disproportionately larger than things that are farther away. You can use perspective distortion to your advantage to emphasize objects in the foreground if you want the subject to stand out in the frame.

▶ **Handholding.** At shorter focal lengths, it's possible to hold the camera steadier than you can at longer focal lengths. At 14mm, it's entirely possible to handhold your camera at 1/15 second without worrying about camera shake.

▶ **Environmental portraits.** Although using a wide-angle lens isn't the best choice for standard close-up portraits, wide-angle lenses work great for environmental portraits where you want to show a person in his or her surroundings.

Wide-angle lenses can also help pull you into a subject. With most wide-angle lenses, you can focus very close to a subject while creating the perspective distortion that wide-angle lenses are known for (see Figure 4.2). Don't be afraid to get close to your subject to make a more dynamic image. The worst wide-angle images are the ones that have a tiny subject in the middle of an empty area.

4.2 A shot taken with a Nikon 14-24mm f/2.8G wide-angle lens at 14mm

There are a few prime lenses that fit into the wide-angle category: the 24mm, 28mm, 30mm, and 35mm are great all-around lenses. They come with apertures of f/2.8 or faster and can be found for less than $400, with the exception of the rare Nikon 28mm f/1.4, which can run up to $5000 in new condition (if you can find it) and the new 24mm and 35mm f/1.4.

Using DX Lenses

If you are upgrading to the D800 from a DX camera, such as the D300, and have many have made investments in very good lenses that are made for use with the smaller sensor DX cameras, there is good news. These DX lenses work with full functionality with the FX D800. The D800 can be set to automatically detect when a DX lens is attached to the camera and it will shoot in DX crop mode (Shooting menu→Image area). What's even better is that with the high-resolution 36MP sensor, even in DX crop mode you are getting a 15MP image, which is more than enough resolution for most standard applications.

If you have ever put a DX lens on a full frame camera you may have noticed that some lenses vignette more than others and the vignetting may change as you zoom in and out. If that is the case, you have a lens that only slightly vignettes and you can manually select the 1.2X crop option from the Image area setting which will increase the frame size and resolution more than when using the DX crop, which is a 1.5X crop factor.

When a DX lens is attached and the camera is in DX mode (or any of the other crop modes) looking through the viewfinder you see an outline of the image area. A little trick to make it easier to frame is to go to Custom Settings menu (✐) a5 – AF point illumination and set it to Off. Now when you look through the viewfinder the camera masks the unused portion of the viewfinder and it appears grayed out and blurry. The only caveat to using this is that your AF points do not light up red, so in low-light situations this may be a problem.

4

Understanding limitations

Wide-angle lenses are very distinctive when it comes to the way they portray your images and subjects, and they also have some limitations that you may not find in lenses with longer focal lengths. There are also some pitfalls that you need to be aware of when using wide-angle lenses:

▶ **Soft corners.** The most common problem that wide-angle lenses have, especially zooms, is that they soften the images in the corners. This is most prevalent at wide apertures, such as f/2.8 and f/4; the corners usually sharpen up by f/8 (depending on the lens). This problem is greatest in lower-priced lenses. The high resolution of the D800 can really magnify these flaws.

Focal Length and Depth of Field

You may have seen that focal length is a factor in depth of field, but scientifically speaking this actually isn't true. Telephoto lenses appear to have a much more shallow depth of field due to a higher magnification factor, but if the subject stays the same size in the frame, the depth of field is consistent at any given aperture no matter what focal length. What *does* change however is the distribution of the zone of acceptable sharpness. At shorter focal lengths most of the zone is behind the focal plane or subject. At longer focal lengths the zone of acceptable sharpness falls more in front of the focal plane. What this means is that, although mathematically the depth of field is consistent at all focal lengths, the distribution of the zone of sharpness is different. Wide-angle lenses have a more gradual falling off of sharpness, which makes the depth of field appear deeper. Telephoto lenses appear to have a more shallow depth of field because the zone of sharpness falls off quicker behind the focal plane. Telephoto lenses also seem to have a more shallow depth of field as well because the background is magnified due to compression distortion. This causes the background to appear much larger in relation to the subject than when using a short focal length.

▶ **Vignetting.** This is the darkening of the corners in the image. This occurs because the light that's needed to capture such a wide angle of view must come in at a very sharp angle. When the light comes in at such an angle, the aperture is effectively smaller. The aperture opening no longer appears as a circle but is shaped like a cat's eye. Stopping down the aperture reduces this effect, and reducing the aperture by 3 stops usually eliminates any vignetting.

▶ **Perspective distortion.** Perspective distortion is a double-edged sword: It can make your images look very interesting or make them look terrible. One of the reasons that a wide-angle lens isn't recommended for close-up portraits is that it distorts the face, making the nose look too big and the ears too small. This can make for a very unflattering portrait.

▶ **Barrel distortion.** Wide-angle lenses, even rectilinear lenses, are often plagued with this specific type of distortion, which causes straight lines outside the image center to appear to bend outward (similar to a barrel). This can be unwanted when doing architectural photography. Fortunately, Photoshop and other image-editing software allow you to fix this problem relatively easily.

Standard or Midrange Zoom Lenses

Midrange, or standard, zoom lenses fall in the middle of the focal-length scale. Zoom lenses of this type usually start at a moderately wide angle of around 24-28mm and zoom in to a short telephoto range between 70mm to 85mm. These lenses work great for most general photography applications and can be used successfully for everything from architectural to portrait photography. This type of lens covers the most useful focal lengths and will probably spend the most time on your camera. For this reason, I recommend buying the best quality lens you can afford.

Some of the options for midrange lenses include:

▶ **Nikkor 24-70mm f/2.8G.** This is Nikon's top-of-the-line standard zoom lens. It's a professional lens; it has a fast aperture of f/2.8 over the whole zoom range and is extremely sharp at all focal lengths and apertures. The build quality on this lens is excellent, as most of Nikon's pro lenses are. The 24-70mm f/2.8G features Nikon's super-quiet and fast-focusing Silent Wave Motor as well as ED glass elements to reduce chromatic aberration. This lens is top-notch all around and is worth every penny of the price tag.

Image courtesy of Nikon
4.3 Nikkor 24-70mm f/2.8G

▶ **Nikkor 28-70mm f/2.8D.** This lens is the precursor to the newer 24-70mm. This is a very high-quality pro lens and can be found used for much less than the newer version. This lens also features the Silent Wave Motor for fast, silent focusing. It's very sharp at all apertures. This is a great bargain pro lens.

► **Sigma 24-70mm f/2.8.** This lens is a low-cost alternative to the Nikon 24-70mm and has a fast f/2.8 aperture. You can get this lens for about one-third the cost of the Nikon version. It has a sturdy build and a fast, silent HSM motor.

There aren't a lot of full-frame options from Tamron and Tokina in this focal-length range. I recommend doing some research on the Internet to find the best lens for the best deal.

In the standard range for primes the most popular is the 50mm *normal* lenses. The term normal is because they approximate about the same field of view as the human eye. There are two Nikkor offerings: the 50mm f/1.8 and the 50mm f/1.4. The current versions are G lenses with the AF-S motor, but the D lenses are still plentiful and are a great bargain. The 50mm f/1.8D is a favorite for its sharpness and also for the fact that they can be found for about $100.

Image courtesy of Nikon

4.4 The Nikon 50mm f/1.8G is a favorite of a lot of photographers

Telephoto Lenses

Telephoto lenses have very long focal lengths that are used to get closer to distant subjects. They provide a very narrow field of view and are handy when you're trying to focus on the details of a far-off subject. Telephoto lenses have a much shallower depth of field than wide-angle and midrange lenses, and you can use them effectively to blur out background details to isolate a subject.

Telephoto lenses are commonly used for sports and wildlife photography. The shallow depth of field also makes them one of the top choices for photographing portraits.

As with wide-angle lenses, telephoto lenses also have their quirks, such as perspective distortion. As you may have guessed, telephoto perspective distortion is the opposite of the wide-angle variety. Because everything in the photo is so far away with a telephoto lens, the lens tends to *compress* the image. Compression causes the background to look too close to the foreground. Of course, you can use this effect creatively. For example, compression can flatten out the features of a model, resulting in a pleasing effect. Compression is one of the main reasons photographers often use a telephoto lens for portrait photography.

A standard telephoto zoom lens usually has a range of about 70-200mm. If you want to zoom in close to a subject that's very far away, you may need an even longer lens. These super-telephoto lenses can act like telescopes, really bringing the subject in close. They range from about 300mm up to about 800mm. Almost all super-telephoto lenses are prime lenses, and they're very heavy, bulky, and expensive. Some of these lenses are a little slower than your normal high-end telephoto zoom lens, such as the 70-200mm f/2.8G VR, and often have a maximum aperture of f/4 or smaller.

There are quite a few telephoto prime lenses available. Most of them, especially the longer ones (105mm and longer), are expensive, although you can sometimes find some older Nikon primes that are discontinued or used — and at decent prices — such as the Nikkor 300mm f/4 (shown in Figure 4.5).

Image courtesy of Nikon

4.5 Nikkor 300mm f/2.8G VR

Some of the most common telephoto lenses include:

▶ **Nikkor 70-200mm f/2.8 VR II.** This is Nikon's newest top-of-the-line standard telephoto lens. The VR makes this lens useful when photographing far-off subjects handheld. This is a great lens for sports, portraits, and wildlife photography.

Super-zooms

Most lens manufacturers, Nikon included, offer what's commonly termed a *super-zoom* or sometimes called a *hyper-zoom*. Super-zooms are lenses that encompass a very wide focal length, from a wide angle to telephoto. The most popular of the super-zooms is the Nikon 28-300mm f/3.5-5.6 VR.

These lenses have a large focal-length range that you can use in a wide variety of shooting situations without having to switch out lenses. This can come in handy if, for example, you were photographing a Himalayan mountain range using a wide-angle setting, and all of the sudden a Yeti appears on the horizon. You can quickly zoom in with the super-telephoto setting and get a good close-up shot without having to fumble around in your camera bag to grab a telephoto and switching out lenses, possibly causing you to miss the shot of a lifetime.

Super-zooms come with a price (figuratively and literally). In order to achieve the great ranges in focal length concessions must be made with regard to image quality. These lenses are usually less sharp than lenses with a shorter zoom range and are more often plagued with optical distortions and chromatic aberration. Super-zooms often show pronounced barrel distortion at the wide end and can have moderate to severe pincushion distortion at the long end of the range. Luckily, these types of distortions can be fixed in Photoshop or other image-editing software.

Another caveat to using these lenses is that they more often than not have appreciably smaller maximum apertures than zoom lenses with shorter ranges. This can be a problem, especially because larger apertures are generally needed at the long end to keep a high enough shutter speed to avoid blurring from camera shake when handholding. Of course, some manufacturers include some sort of Vibration Reduction to help control this problem.

▶ **Nikkor 80-200mm f/2.8D.** This is a great, affordable alternative to the 70-200mm VR lens. This lens is sharp and has a fast constant f/2.8 aperture. There are a few different versions of the 80-200mm. The most desirable one has the AF-S motor.

▶ **Nikkor 80-400mm f/4.5-5.6 VR.** This is a high-power, VR image stabilization zoom lens that gives you quite a bit of reach. Its very versatile zoom range makes it especially useful for wildlife photography where the subject is very far away. As with most lenses with a very broad focal-length range, you make concessions with fast apertures and a moderately lower image quality when compared to the 70-200mm or 80-200mm f/2.8 lenses.

Special-Purpose Lenses

Nikon has a few options when it comes to lenses that are designed specifically to handle a certain task. Nikon's special-purpose lenses are the Perspective Control (PC-E) and Micro-Nikkor (macro) lenses. It even has a lens that combines both of these features! These lenses, especially the PC-E lenses, aren't typically designed for every-day use and are rather specific in their applications.

Micro-Nikkor lenses

A macro lens is a special-purpose lens used in macro and close-up photography. It allows you to have a closer focusing distance than regular lenses, which in turn allows you to get more magnification of your subject, revealing small details that would oth-erwise be lost. True macro lenses offer a magnification ratio of 1:1; that is, the image projected onto the sensor through the lens is the exact same size as the object being photographed. Some lower-priced macro lenses offer a 1:2 or even a 1:4 magnifica-tion ratio, which is half to one-quarter of the size of the original object. Although lens manufacturers refer to these lenses as macro, strictly speaking they are not.

One major concern with a macro lens is the depth of field. When focusing at such a close distance, the depth of field becomes very shallow; it's often advisable to use a small aperture to maximize your depth of field and ensure everything is in focus. Of course, as with any downside, there's an upside: You can also use the shallow depth of field creatively. For example, you can use it to isolate a detail in a subject.

Macro lenses come in a variety of focal lengths, and the most common is 60mm. Some macro lenses have substantially longer focal lengths that allow more distance between the lens and the subject. This comes in handy when the subject needs to be it with an additional light source. A lens that's very close to the subject while focusing can get in the way of the light source, casting a shadow.

When buying a macro lens, you should consider a few things: How often are you going to use the lens? Can you use it for other purposes? Do you need AF? Because newer dedicated macro lenses can be pricey, you may want to consider some less expensive alternatives.

It's not absolutely necessary to have an AF lens. When shooting very close up, the depth of focus is very small, so all you need to do is move slightly closer or farther away to achieve focus. This makes an AF lens a bit unnecessary. You can find plenty of older Nikon manual focus (MF) macro lenses that are very inexpensive, and the good thing is that the lens quality and sharpness are still superb.

Nikon currently offers three focal-length macro lenses under the Micro-Nikkor designation:

► **Nikkor 60mm f/2.8.** Nikon offers two versions of this lens — one with a standard AF drive and one with an AF-S version with the Silent Wave Motor. The AF-S version also has the new Nano Crystal Coat lens coating to help eliminate ghosting and flare.

► **Nikkor 105mm f/2.8 VR.** This is a great lens that not only allows you to focus extremely close but also enables you to back off and still get a good close-up shot. This lens is equipped with VR. This can be invaluable with macro photography because it allows you to handhold at slower shutter speeds — a necessity when stopping down to maintain a good depth of field. This lens can also double as a very impressive portrait lens. This is currently the favored lens in my arsenal.

Image courtesy of Nikon
4.6 Nikon 105mm f/2.8G VR macro lens

► **Nikkor 200mm f/4.** This telephoto macro lens provides a longer working distance, which can be beneficial when photographing small animals or insects. This is a good lens for nature and wildlife photography and gives you a true 1:1 macro shot.

4.7 A macro shot taken with a 105mm f/2.8G VR at 1:1 magnification

Defocus Control lenses

Defocus Control (DC) lenses are Nikon's dedicated portrait lenses. These lenses allow you to control the spherical aberration of the lens. Spherical aberration is evident in the out-of-focus areas of the image and is the determining factor in whether the lenses' bokeh is considered pleasing or not. Bokeh is a term derived from the Japanese word *boke*, which is roughly translated as fuzzy. Bokeh refers to the out-of-focus areas of the image.

Without going into specific technical details on how this lens achieves this effect, just know that it does. It can make the out-of-focus areas, either in front of or behind the subject, appear sharper or softer and can produce ethereal soft focus effects on your subject. This lens takes some time and effort to learn how to use effectively, but once you master this lens, your portraits will look amazing.

Nikon currently offers two lenses with DC: the 105mm f/2D and the 135mm f/2D. Both of these lenses are telephoto lenses and have a wide f/2 aperture for achieving a super-shallow depth of field. These lenses are fairly expensive but well worth the cost if you shoot a lot of portraits.

Fisheye lenses

Fisheye lenses are ultrawide-angle lenses that aren't corrected for distortion like standard rectilinear wide-angle lenses. These lenses are known as *curvilinear,* meaning that straight lines in your image, especially near the edge of the frame, are curved. Fisheye lenses have extreme barrel distortion, but that's what makes them fisheye lenses.

Fisheye lenses cover a full 180-degree area allowing you to see everything that's immediately to the left and right of you in the frame. Special care has to be taken so that you don't get your feet in the frame, as often happens when you use a lens with a field of view this extreme.

Fisheye lenses aren't made for everyday shooting, but with their extreme perspective distortion, you can achieve interesting, and sometimes wacky, results. You can also *de-fish* or correct for the extreme fisheye by using image-editing software, such as Photoshop, Capture NX or NX2, and DxO Optics. The end result of de-fishing your image is that you get a reduced field of view. This is akin to using a rectilinear wide-angle lens, but will often yield a bit wider field of view than a standard wide-angle lens.

4.8 An image taken with a Nikon 16mm fisheye lens

Using Vibration Reduction Lenses

Nikon has an impressive list of lenses that offer Vibration Reduction (VR). This technology is used to combat image blur caused by camera shake, especially when handholding the camera at long focal lengths. The VR function works by detecting the motion of the lens and shifting the internal lens elements. This allows you to shoot at slower shutter speeds than you normally while still getting sharp images.

Nikon has updated the VR mechanism and refers to it as VR-II. The original VR claims you can shoot up to 3 stops slower, the newer VR-II boasts that you can shoot 4 stops slower. If you're an old hand at photography, you probably know this rule of thumb: To get a reasonably sharp photo when handholding the camera, you should use a shutter speed that corresponds to the reciprocal of the lens' focal length. In simpler terms, when shooting at a 200mm zoom setting, your shutter speed should be at least 1/200 second. When shooting with a wider setting, such as 28mm, you can safely handhold at around 1/30 second. Of course, this is just a guideline; some people are naturally steadier than others and can get sharp shots at slower speeds.

Although the VR feature is good for providing some extra latitude when shooting with low light, it's not made to replace a fast shutter speed. To get a good, sharp photo when shooting action, you need a fast shutter speed to freeze the action. No matter how good the VR is, nothing can freeze a moving subject but a fast shutter speed.

4

There are two types of fisheye lenses available: circular and full frame. A circular fisheye projects a complete 180-degree spherical image onto the frame, resulting in a circular image surrounded by black in the rest of the frame. A full-frame fisheye completely covers the frame with an image. The 16mm Nikkor fisheye is a full-frame fisheye on an FX-format dSLR. Sigma also makes a series of fisheye lenses that are both circular and full frame. There are a couple of Russian companies that also manufacture high-quality but affordable Manual focus fisheye lenses. Autofocus is not truly a necessity on fisheye lenses, given their extreme depth of field and short focusing distance.

Perspective Control lenses

Perspective lenses or *PC-E lenses* in Nikon nomenclature are used to control perspective by shift or tilting the lens elements to stop lines in the subject from converging or to control the area of focus in a way you can't with regular optical lenses. PC-E lenses are mainly used is architecture and high-end product photography. Shifting the lens in architecture allows the camera's sensor to remain parallel to the structure so that the lines are straight and the appearance of the structure isn't made to look as if it's leaning back as it would if you angle the camera back to capture the building from top to bottom.

Tilting the lens controls how the depth of field is affected. In a standard lens the depth of field is parallel to the sensor plane because the lens elements are designed to be parallel. In a PC-E lens the lens elements can be tilted so that the depth of field can be set at an angle, allowing you to keep areas of an image in focus from front to back while having a shallow depth of field on the sides of the image.

Some photographers have started experimenting with using these lenses in a more nontraditional way to add special depth-of-field effects to draw the eye to specific parts of the image in a way you can't do with a standard lens.

Nikon offers three PC-E lenses, including the 24mm f/3.5 wide-angle lens designed mostly for architecture (although most architecture photographers I know wish for a wider angle lens such as Canon's 17mm TS-E f/4L lens). The other two PC lenses are macro lenses designed more for product photography.

Image courtesy of Nikon

4.9 Nikon 24mm f/3.5D. Notice the tilt in the lens.

CHAPTER 5

Working with Light

When it comes right down to it, light is the most important aspect in photography. Not only do you need it to physically create an image, but light also impacts the end result of your image.

Light has different qualities that affect the tone of your images: It can be soft and diffused or hard and directional. The light source also plays a role in the coloring of your images.

Working with what light you have — or, to a lesser extent, controlling light — is the key to creating images as you want them and is what being a photographer is all about.

Controlling the light is the key to setting the tone of your image.

Lighting Essentials

The way the light strikes the subject can have a dramatic impact on your image. Light quality and angles can make the same subject appear differently in your photos.

In this section I cover the two main types of lighting used in photography, as well as lighting direction. Keep in mind that these light types can be used when shooting video as well as still photography.

Quality of light

Quality of light is a term photographers and filmmakers use to describe light falling on the scene. The two specific types of lighting are hard and soft. Both hard and soft light have their place in photography, and their uses span all types of photography, from portraits to landscapes and beyond.

Lighting quality is the first thing the photographer should take into consideration when coming up with a concept for an image. Planning ahead of time is a real help — for example, finding a location with good indirect light for a portrait or planning out the best time of day for a landscape shot.

Soft light

Soft light is distributed evenly across the scene, comes from a large light source, and appears to wrap around the subject. The shadows fade gradually from dark to light, which results in a subtle edge transfer. This is generally the most desirable type of light to use in most types of photography, especially in portraiture. Soft light is achieved by placing a light source close to the subject or by diffusing the light source, thereby mimicking a larger light source.

> **NOTE** The term *shadow edge transfer* is used to describe how abruptly the shadows in images go from light to dark. This is the determining factor of whether light is soft or hard. Soft light has a smooth transition and hard light has a well-defined shadow edge transfer.

Use soft light to portray your subject in a flattering way. This type of light is used to soften hard edges and smooth out the features of the subject (Figure 5.1). Soft lighting can be used effectively for almost any type of photography, although in some instances it can lack the depth that you get from using a more direct light source.

Natural soft lighting is achieved by placing the subject in a place where the light is not direct, usually someplace shady — under a porch or a tree — or by shooting on a cloudy day.

When using artificial light sources, soft lighting is usually achieved by modifying the light source in some way, by aiming the light through diffusion material or redirecting the light by bouncing it from a wall or ceiling.

Hard light

Hard light is the complete opposite of soft light; the shadow edge transfer is more defined. Hard light is very directional, and pinpointing where the light source comes from is much easier than with a soft light source. Moving the subject farther from the light source results in harder light because the light source becomes smaller relative to the subject.

Hard light isn't used extensively but can be effective in highlighting details and textures in macro subjects, flowers, and other small subjects. Oftentimes hard light in landscape shots is used to bring attention to details in natural formations.

Artificial hard light is usually achieved with a bare light source, although accessories can be used to make the light more directional, such as grids or snoots. For Figure 5.2 I used a reflector fitted with a 60-degree grid to make the mononlight directional. The bright midday sun is an excellent example of a natural hard light source.

5.1 A soft-light portrait. Taken at ISO 400, f/1.4, and 1/200 second.

5.2 The hard light in this film noir-type portrait adds an air of darkness and mystery. Taken at ISO 200, f/2.8, and 1/250 second.

5

Lighting direction

The direction from which light strikes your subject has a major impact on how your images appear. When using an artificial light source, you can easily control the direction of the lighting by moving the light source relative to the subject. When using natural lighting, moving the subject in relation to the light source is the key to controlling the lighting direction.

There are three major types of lighting direction:

▶ Frontlighting

▶ Sidelighting

▶ Backlighting

Frontlight

Frontlighting coincidentally enough comes from directly in front of the subject, which follows the old photographer's adage: Keep the sun at your back. This is a good general rule; however, frontlighting can produce rather flat results lacking in depth and dimension. You can see in Figures 5.3 and 5.4 the difference that changing the direction of the light can make in a subject. When the light is aimed straight ahead more of it reflects from the background, which brightens it significantly as well.

Frontlighting works pretty well for portraits, and a lot of fashion photographers swear by it, especially for highlighting hair and makeup. Frontlighting flattens out the facial features and hides blemishes and wrinkles very well, too.

Sidelight

Although sidelighting comes in from the side, it doesn't necessarily have to come in from a 90-degree angle. It usually comes in much shallower, such as a 45- to 60-degree angle.

Lighting the subject from the side increases the shadow contrast and causes the details to pop out and become more pronounced. This is what gives your photograph, which is a two-dimensional image, a three-dimensional feel (Figure 5.5).

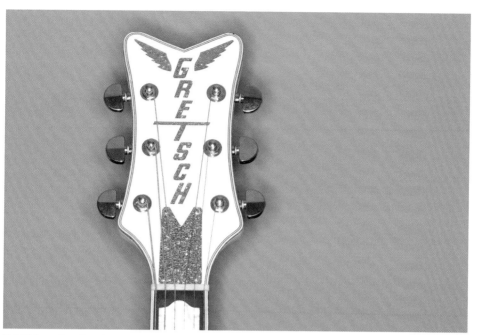

5.3 This guitar headstock was lit from the front. Notice the flat, even lighting. Taken at ISO 800, f/5.6, and 1/60 second.

5

5.4 The light was moved to the side for this shot. Notice the guitar headstock has more texture, depth, and form, giving it more dimensionality. Taken at ISO 800, f/5.6, and 1/60 second.

Sidelight is equally effective when using either hard or soft light, and works great for just about every subject.

Backlight

Backlighting is achieved by placing the light source behind the subject, and although it's the least-used lighting direction in photography, it does have its uses, especially in creating more artistic shots.

In the past backlighting had a bad name in photography, but more and more photographers are using it to add artistic flare to images. Backlight introduces things that were once perceived as undesirable in classical photography, such as lens flare and decreased contrast. Photographers these days are discovering that, when used correctly, you can create interesting images using backlight.

5.5 Sidelighting added texture and definition to this floral shot (complete with a bee ready to land and collect some pollen). Taken with a 50mm f/1.4G lens for 1/2500 second at f/2.8, ISO 100.

> **TIP** The key to making backlighting work is to spot-meter. When shooting portraits, meter on the subject; for silhouettes, meter on the brightest area in the scene.

Backlighting works great to make portraits more dynamic, bring silhouettes to landscape photos, and make translucent subjects such as flowers seem to glow, as shown in Figure 5.6.

> **TIP** Filmmakers often use backlighting to add lens flare to the shot for a classic cinematic effect, and you can do the same using the video feature of the D800.

5.6 Backlighting flowers and plants can make them seem to glow. Taken with 50mm f/1.4G lens for 1/2500 second at f/4, ISO 100.

5.7 You can even use backlighting to make action shots more interesting, as I did with this BMX rider. By metering on the brightest part of the image I caused the subject to silhouette, adding a more artistic flare to what would otherwise be a standard action shot. Taken with a Nikon 28-70mm f/2.8 lens zoomed to 28mm for 1/2500 second at f/2.8, ISO 100.

Natural Light

Natural light is by far the most abundant source of light you will find because it comes from the sun, or in some cases the moon. Although natural light is the easiest kind of light to find, it is often the most difficult to work with because it can be inconsistent and unpredictable on a partly cloudy day, or too bright and hard on a sunny day.

On the other hand, on an overcast day the light can be beautiful and soft, but may lack the depth you need to give your subject definition.

> **NOTE** Early in the morning and late in the evening when the sun is rising or setting is the best time to take photographs. This is known as the golden hour.

Natural light often benefits from some sort of modification to make it softer and a little less directional.

Here are a few examples of natural lighting techniques:

▶ **Fill flash.** You can use the flash as a secondary light source (not as your main light) to fill in the shadows and reduce contrast.

▶ **Window lighting.** One of the best ways to use natural light is to go indoors. Seating your model next to a window provides a beautiful soft light that is very flattering. A lot of professional portrait, as well as food, photographers use window light. It can be used to light almost any subject softly and evenly. This is easily the quickest and often the nicest light source you'll find.

▶ **Shade.** The shade of a tree or the overhang of an awning or porch can block the bright sunlight while still providing plenty of diffuse light with which to light your subject.

▶ **Clouds.** A cloudy day softens the light, allowing you to take portraits outside without worrying about harsh shadows and too much contrast. Even if it's only partly cloudy, you can wait for a cloud to pass over the sun before taking your shot.

▶ **Modifier.** Use a reflector to reduce the shadows or a diffusion panel to block the direct sun from your subject.

Continuous Lighting

Continuous lighting is a constant light source that gives you a "what you see is what you get" effect; therefore, it's the easiest type of light to work with. You can set up the lights and see what effect they have on your subject before you even pick up your D800.

Continuous lights are an affordable option for great photographic lighting, and the learning curve isn't steep at all.

As with other lighting systems, you have a lot of continuous light options. Here are a few of the more common ones:

▶ **Incandescent.** Incandescent, or tungsten, lights are the most common type of lights (a standard light bulb is a tungsten lamp). With tungsten lamps, an electrical current runs through a tungsten filament, heating it and causing it to emit light. This type of continuous lighting is the source of the name "hot lights."

Continuous Lights versus Flash

Incandescent lights appear to be very bright to you and your subject, but they actually produce less light than a standard flash unit. For example, a 200-watt tungsten light and a 200-watt-second strobe use the same amount of electricity per second, so they should be equally bright, right? Wrong. Because the flash discharges all 200 watts of energy in a fraction of a second, the flash is actually much, much brighter.

Why does this matter? Because when you need a fast shutter speed or a small aperture, the strobe can give you more light in a shorter time. An SB-600 Speedlight gives you about 30-watt-seconds of light at full power. To get an equivalent amount of light at the maximum sync speed of 1/250 second from a tungsten light, you would need a 7,500-watt lamp! Of course, if your subject is static, you don't need to use a fast shutter speed; in this case, you can use one 30-watt light bulb for a 1-second exposure or a 60-watt lamp for a 1/2-second exposure.

▶ **Halogen.** Halogen lights, which are much brighter than typical tungsten lights, are another type of hot light. Considered a type of incandescent light, halogen lights employ a tungsten filament, but also include a halogen vapor in the gas inside the lamp. The color temperature of halogen lamps is higher than the color temperature of standard tungsten lamps.

▶ **Fluorescent.** Fluorescent lighting is in the majority of office buildings and retail stores. In a fluorescent lamp, electrical energy changes a small amount of mercury into a gas. The electrons collide with the mercury gas atoms, causing them to release photons, which in turn cause the phosphor coating inside the lamp to glow. Because this reaction doesn't create much heat, fluorescent lamps are much cooler and more energy efficient than tungsten and halogen lamps. In the past, fluorescent lighting wasn't commonly used because of the ghastly green cast the lamps caused. These days, with color-balanced fluorescent lamps and the ability to adjust white balance, these types are lighting systems are becoming more common and are very affordable.

Some disadvantages of using incandescent lights include:

▶ **Color temperature inconsistency.** The color temperature of the lamps changes as your household current varies and as the lamps get more and more use. The color temperature may be inconsistent from manufacturer to manufacturer and may even vary within the same types of bulbs.

▶ **Light modifiers are more expensive.** Because most continuous lights are hot, modifiers such as softboxes need to be made to withstand the heat; this makes them more expensive than the standard equipment intended to be used for strobes.

▶ **Short lamp life.** Incandescent lights tend to have a shorter life than flash tubes, so you must replace them more often.

If you're really serious about lighting with continuous lights, you may want to invest in a photographic light kit. These kits are widely available from any photography or video store. They usually come with lights, light stands, and sometimes light modifiers such as umbrellas or softboxes for diffusing the light for a softer look. The kits can be relatively inexpensive, with two lights, two stands, and two umbrellas for around $100. Or you can buy much more elaborate setups ranging in price up to $2,000.

D800 Built-in Flash

The Nikon D800 has a built-in flash that pops up for quick use in low-light situations. Although this little flash is fine for snapshots, it's not always the best option for portraying your subject in a flattering light.

The best feature of the built-in flash is that it allows you to control off-camera Speedlights wirelessly, something which even Nikon's flagship camera, the D4, doesn't allow you to do. Nikon Speedlights are dedicated flash units, meaning they are built specifically for use with the Nikon camera system and offer much more functionality than a nondedicated flash. A nondedicated flash is a flash made by a third-party manufacturer; the flashes usually don't offer fully automated flash features. There are, however, some non-Nikon flashes that use Nikon's i-TTL flash metering system.

Built-in flash exposure modes

While the built-in flash is nice, if you're buying a camera of this level you shouldn't be using the built-in flash for most of your shooting. The built-in flash just doesn't make for good lighting and is best left for snapshots.

The built-in flash, however, does have a great option that can be used with great effects: the Commander mode. Nikon's most expensive cameras require an extra external Speedlight to control off-camera Speedlights. With the D800 you get this option for free, although you can control only two groups of flashes rather than three like you can with an external Commander.

i-TTL and i-TTL BL

The D800 determines the proper flash exposure automatically by using Nikon's propri-etary i-TTL (intelligent Through-the-Lens) system. The camera gets most of the meter-ing information from monitor preflashes emitted from the built-in flash. These preflashes are emitted almost simultaneously with the main flash so it almost looks as if the flash has fired only once. The camera also uses data from the lens, such as dis-tance information and f-stop values, to help determine the proper flash exposure.

Additionally, two types of i-TTL flash metering are available for the D800: Standard i-TTL flash and i-TTL Balanced Fill-Flash (BL). With Standard i-TTL flash, the camera determines the exposure for the subject only and doesn't take the background lighting into account. With i-TTL BL mode, the camera attempts to balance the light from the flash with the ambient light to produce a more natural-looking image.

When you use the built-in flash on the D800, the default mode is i-TTL BL when using Matrix or Center-weighted metering. To use the flash in Standard i-TTL, the camera must be switched to Spot metering.

Manual

The built-in flash power is set by fractions in Manual mode: 1/1 is full power. The out-put is halved for each setting (which is equal to 1 stop of light). The settings are 1/1, 1/2, 1/4, 1/8, 1/16, 1/32, 1/64, and 1/128.

The Guide Number for the built-in flash is 39 when measuring distance in feet, or 12 when using meters at full power (1/1) set to ISO 100. To determine the GN at higher ISO settings, multiply the Guide Number by 1.4 for each stop the ISO increases. For example, doubling the ISO setting to 200 increases the GN by a factor of 1.4, so GN $39 \times 1.4 = $ GN 54.6.

Similarly, when reducing the flash power by 1 stop you divide the GN by a factor of 1.4, so at 1/2 power the GN is about 28; GN 39 / 1.4 = GN 27.8.

Repeating Flash

This option allows you to set the flash to fire a set number of times while the shutter is open, producing an effect similar to that of a strobe light. This gives you an image similar to a multiple exposure. This option is useful only in low-light situations.

> **NOTE** When an SB-400 Speedlight is used with the D800 Custom Settings menu (*⌀*) e3 defaults to Optional Flash, and the Repeating Flash and Commander mode are not available.

There are three options you must set when using Repeating Flash:

► **Output.** This is the strength of the flash. The same settings are used in Manual flash mode.

► **Times.** This is where you denote how many times you want you want the flash to go off. Note that if you don't select a long enough shutter speed, you will not get the specified number of flashes.

► **Frequency.** This is expressed in Hertz (Hz) and sets the number of times per second that you want the flash to go off. The frequency and the shutter speed should be matched to get the proper effect.

Commander mode

As I mentioned previously one of the best features of the D800 is that the built-in flash can control off-camera Speedlights. To use this feature you will need at least on compatible Speedlight to be used off-camera. Compatible Speedlights with off-camera ability are the SB-600, SB-700, SB-800, SB-900, SB-910, and the SBR-200 flashes from the ring light kits. To set up the Commander mode:

1. **Press the Menu button (MENU) and the multi-selector right (▶) to navigate to the Custom Settings menu.**

2. **Use the multi-selector to highlight** ⌀ **e Bracketing/flash, and then press ▶ to enter the** ⌀ **e menu.**

3. **Use the multi-selector to highlight** ⌀ **e3 Flash cntrl for built-in flash, and then press ▶ to view flash control options.**

4. **Press the multi-selector down (▼) to choose Commander mode, and then press ▶ to view settings.**

5. **Press the multi-selector up (▲) or down (▼) to choose a flash mode for the built-in flash.** You can choose M, TTL, or --. The last option (--) allows the flash to control the remotes without adding additional exposure.

6. **Press ▶ to highlight the exposure compensation setting.** Use ▲ or ▼ to apply exposure compensation if desired. If the built-in flash is set to – this option is not available.

7. **Use the multi-selector to set the mode for Group A.** You can choose TTL, AA, M, or --. Press ▶ to highlight exposure compensation. Press ▲ or ▼ to apply exposure compensation if desired. Repeat this process for Group B.

8. **Use the multi-selector to highlight the Channel setting.** You can choose from channels 1–4. These channels can be changed if you are shooting in the

same area as another photographer using CLS. If you are both on the same channel you will trigger each other's Speedlights. If you use CLS alone it makes no difference as to what channel you choose.

9. **Press the OK button (⊛).** If this button is not pressed, no changes are applied.

CAUTION   Make sure all your Speedlights are set to the same channel or they will not fire.

Flash sync modes

Flash sync modes control how the flash operates in conjunction with your D800. These modes work with both the built-in Speedlight and accessory Speedlights, such as the SB-910, SB-700, SB-600, and so on. These modes allow you to choose when the flash fires, either at the beginning of the exposure or at the end, and they also allow you to keep the shutter open for longer periods, enabling you to capture more ambient light in low-light situations.

Before covering the sync modes, I need to talk a little about *sync speed*.

Sync speed

The sync speed is the fastest shutter speed that can be used while achieving a full flash exposure. This means if you set your shutter speed at a speed faster than the rated sync speed of the camera, you don't get a full exposure and end up with a partially underexposed image. With the D800, you can't actually set the shutter speed above the rated sync speed of 1/250 second when using a dedicated flash because the camera won't let you. This means you don't need to worry about having partially black images when using a Speedlight.

Limited sync speeds exist because of the way shutters in modern cameras work. All dSLR cameras have a *focal plane* shutter. This shutter is located directly in front of the focal plane, which is the surface of the sensor. The focal plane shutter has two shutter curtains that travel vertically in front of the sensor to control the time the light can enter through the lens. At slower shutter speeds, the front curtain covering the sensor moves away, exposing the sensor to light for a set amount of time. When the exposure has been made, the second curtain then moves in to block the light, thus ending the exposure.

To achieve shutter speeds faster than 1/250, the second curtain of the shutter starts closing before the first curtain has exposed the sensor completely. This means the sensor is actually exposed by a slit that travels the length of the sensor. This allows your camera to have extremely fast shutter speeds, but limits the flash sync speed because the entire sensor must be exposed to the flash at once to achieve a full exposure.

Front-curtain sync

Front-curtain sync mode is the default mode for your camera when you are using the built-in flash or one of Nikon's dedicated Speedlights. With Front-curtain sync, the flash is fired as soon as the shutter's front curtain fully opens. This mode works well with most general flash applications.

When the Shooting mode is set to Programmed Auto (**P**) or Aperture Priority (**A**) the shutter speed will be automatically set to between 30 seconds and 1/60 depending on your setting on CSM e2. If an external Speedlight is attached and you have one of the Auto FP settings selected in ✐ e2 when in Manual (**M**) or Standard (**S**) the shutter speed can be set up to 1/320, albeit at reduced output levels.

One thing worth mentioning about Front-curtain sync is that although it works well when you're using relatively fast shutter speeds, when using **S** and the shutter is slowed down (also known as *dragging the shutter* in flash photography), especially when you're photographing moving subjects, your images have an unnatural-looking blur in front of them. Ambient light reflecting off the moving subject creates this.

When doing flash photography your camera is actually recording two exposures: the flash exposure and the ambient light. When you're using a faster shutter speed in lower light, the ambient light usually isn't bright enough to have an effect on the image. When you slow down the shutter speed substantially, it allows the ambient light to be recorded to the sensor, causing *ghosting*. Ghosting is a partial exposure usually fairly transparent looking on the image.

Ghosting causes a trail to appear in front of the subject because the flash freezes the initial movement of the subject. Because the subject is still moving, the ambient light records it as a blur that appears in front of the subject, creating the illusion that it's moving backward. To counteract this problem, you can use a Rear-curtain sync mode, which I explain later.

Slow sync

When doing flash photography at night your subject is often lit well, but the background appears completely dark, Slow sync mode helps take care of this problem. In Slow sync mode, the camera allows you to set a longer shutter speed (up to 30 seconds) to capture some of the ambient light of the background, so the subject and the background are more evenly lit, and you can achieve a more natural-looking photograph.

Auto FP High-Speed Sync

Although the D800 has a top-rated sync speed of 1/250, Nikon has built in a convenient option in ⌀ e1 that allows you to use flash at shutter speeds faster than the rated sync speed. This is called Auto FP High-Speed Sync (the FP stands for focal plane, as in the shutter). Setting ⌀ e1 to Auto FP allows you to shoot the built-in flash at 1/320 second and other compatible Speedlights (SB-910, SB-900, SB-800, SB-700, and SB-600) to a maximum of 1/8000. Earlier I stated that the sensor must be fully exposed to receive the full flash exposure and that's limited to 1/250, so how then does Auto FP flash work?

Instead of firing one single pop, the flash fires multiple times as the shutter curtain travels across the focal plane of the sensor (hence the Auto FP). The only drawback is that your flash power, or Guide Number (GN), is diminished, so you may need to take this into consideration when doing Manual flash calculations.

Auto FP is a useful feature. It's mainly used when shooting in brightly lit scenes using fill flash. An example would be shooting a portrait outdoors at high noon; of course the light is very contrasty and you want to use fill flash, but you also require a wide aperture to blur out the background. At the sync speed 1/250, ISO 100, your aperture needs to be at f/11. If you open your aperture to f/2.8, you will then need a shutter speed of 1/8000. This is possible using Auto FP.

NOTE Slow sync mode can be used in conjunction with Red-Eye Reduction mode for night portraits.

TIP When you use Slow sync, be sure the subject stays still for the whole exposure to avoid ghosting. With longer exposures you can use ghosting creatively.

5

Red-Eye Reduction

When using on-camera flash, such as the built-in flash, you often get the red-eye effect. This is caused because the pupils are wide open in the dark, and the light from the flash is reflected off the retina and back to the camera lens. The D800 offers a Red-Eye Reduction mode. When this mode is activated, the camera either turns on the AF-assist illuminator (when using the built-in flash) or fires some preflashes (when using an accessory Speedlight), which causes the pupils of the subject's eyes to contract. This reduces the amount of light from the flash from reflecting off the retina and reduces or eliminates the red-eye effect.

Rear-curtain sync

When using Rear-curtain sync, the camera fires the flash at the end of the exposure just before the rear curtain of the shutter starts moving. This is useful when you're taking flash photographs of moving subjects. Rear-curtain sync allows you to more accurately portray the motion of the subject by causing a motion blur trail behind the subject rather in front of it, as is the case with Front-curtain sync. Rear-curtain sync mode can also be used in conjunction with Slow sync mode.

> **NOTE** Rear-curtain sync mode is available in all exposure modes (P, S, A, and M); Rear-curtain slow sync is available only when in P or 🅐.

Flash Exposure Compensation

When you photograph subjects using flash, whether you're using the built-in flash on your D800 or an external Speedlight, there may be times when the flash causes your principal subject to appear too light or too dark. This usually occurs in difficult lighting situations, especially when you use i-TTL metering. Your camera's meter can be fooled into thinking the subject needs more or less light than it actually does. This can happen when the background is very bright or very dark, or when the subject is off in the distance or very small in the frame.

Flash Exposure Compensation (FEC) allows you to manually adjust the flash output while still retaining i-TTL readings so your flash exposure is at least in the ballpark. With the D800, you can vary the output of your built-in flash's TTL setting (or your own manual setting) from –3 Exposure Value (EV) to +1 EV. This means if your flash exposure is too bright, you can adjust it down 3 full stops under the original setting. Or if the image seems underexposed or too dark, you can adjust it to be brighter by 1 full stop.

Press the Flash Exposure Compensation button (⚡️±) and rotate the Sub-command dial to apply FEC.

Creative Lighting System Basics

The Nikon Creative Lighting System (CLS) is what Nikon calls it proprietary system of Speedlights and the technology that goes into them. The best part of CLS is the ability to control Speedlights wirelessly, which Nikon refers to as Advanced Wireless Lighting or AWL.

AWL allows you to get your Speedlights off-camera so that you can control light placement like a professional photographer would do with studio type strobes.

To take advantage of AWL all you need is your D800 and at least one remote Speedlight, an SB-900, SB-800, SB-700, SB-600, or an SBR-200.

You can use the built-in flash of the D800 as a commander, also referred to as a master flash. Communications between the commander and the remote units are accomplished by using pulse modulation. *Pulse modulation* is a term that means the commanding Speedlight fires rapid bursts of light in a specific order. The pulses of light are used to convey information to the remote group, which interprets the bursts of light as coded information. The commander tells the other Speedlights in the system when and at what power to fire. You can also use an SB-700, SB-800, or SB-900 Speedlight or an SU-800 Commander as a master. This allows you to control three separate groups of remote flashes and gives you an extended range.

This is how CLS works in a nutshell:

1. **The commander unit sends out instructions to the remote groups to fire a series of monitor preflashes to determine the exposure level.** The camera's i-TTL metering sensor reads the preflashes from all the remote groups and takes a reading of the ambient light.

2. **The camera tells the commander unit the proper exposure readings for each group of remote Speedlights.** When the shutter is released, the commander, via pulse modulation, relays the information to each group of remote Speedlights.

3. **The remote units fire at the output specified by the camera's i-TTL meter, and the shutter closes.**

All these calculations happen in a fraction of a second as soon as you press the Shutter Release button. It almost appears to the naked eye as if the flash just fires once. There is little lag-time waiting for the camera and the Speedlights to do the calculations.

5

CAUTION The Nikon SB-400 cannot be used as a remote unit.

Given the ease of use and the portability of the Nikon CLS, I highly recommend purchasing at least one (if not two) Speedlights to add to your setup.

Light Modifiers

When you set up a photographic shot, you are building a scene using light. For some images, you may want a hard light that is very directional; for others, a soft, diffused light works better. Light modifiers allow you to control the light so you can direct it where you need it, give it the quality the image calls for, and even add color or texture to the image. There are many kinds of diffusers. Here's a list of the most common:

▶ **Umbrella.** The photographic umbrella is used to soften the light. You can either aim the light source through the umbrella or bounce the light from the inside of the umbrella depending on the type of umbrella you have. Umbrellas are very portable and make a great addition to any Speedlight setup.

▶ **Softbox.** These also soften the light and come in myriad sizes, from huge 8-foot softboxes to small 6-inch versions that fit right over your Speedlight mounted on the camera.

▶ **Reflector.** This is probably the handiest modifier you can have. You can use these to reflect natural light onto your subject or you can use it to bounce light from your Speedlight onto the subject making it softer. Some can act as diffusion material to soften direct sunlight. They come in a variety of sizes from 2 to 6 feet and fold up into a small portable size. I recommend that every photographer have a small reflector in his or her camera bag.

CHAPTER 6

Working with Live View and Video

Nikon has made Live View and video standard on all of its dSLRs since the D90 (which was the first dSLR to feature video). With the release of the D800, Nikon

has essentially perfected its Live View and video. It features 1080p full HD video with full-time AF and an HD output for attaching external monitors or hard drives. The D4 and the D800 are the first pro-level Nikon cameras to include these features.

Significant upgrades have been made to the way the D800 operates making it more useful to professionals and advanced shooters. No longer are you stuck with what was essentially a fully automatic point-and-shoot video camera; now you can adjust the settings without going through endless menus options. Nikon has really stepped up to the plate and added a pretty great video camera into a still camera body.

Many filmmakers are turning to dLSR cameras because of their portability and wide selection of lenses.

Live View Overview

Using Live View allows you to view a live feed of what is being projected onto the sensor from the lens. This can be used to shoot still photographs or to record a video from the direct feed. Shooting stills and videos have different options; they are similar, but they are also different. Therefore I deal with each one separately in the following sections. That being said, there are some pretty important settings that both formats share, most importantly being the Autofocus modes and the AF-area mode settings.

Focus modes

The D800 offers two different focus modes when using Live View or Movie Live View. These modes are different although similar to the ones you find when using the traditional through the viewfinder shooting method.

AF-S Single servo

This is equivalent to single AF (AF-S) when shooting stills. Use the multi-selector to move to focus point to your subject, and half-press the Shutter Release button to focus. In the still photography setting (🄾) the shutter won't release until the camera detects that the scene is in focus. In the Movie mode (Lv) you can use the AF-ON button (**AF-ON**), or half-press the Shutter Release button to bring it in focus and then press the Movie-record button to start recording video. Note that unlike in still photography, the scene doesn't have to be in focus to start recording video. You can start recording and then focus for effect. Once the camera has locked focus it will stay focused at that distance unless the Shutter Release button is half-pressed or **AF-ON** is pressed again.

For still photography, this setting is best for stationary subjects like portraits, still life, products, and landscapes.

For video you need to be sure that your subject isn't moving much, especially if you're using a wide aperture for shallow depth of field. Even the slightest change in distance can cause the subject to go out of focus. This setting is good for doing interviews or shooting scenes where there is not going to be much movement.

AF-F Full time servo

This is a feature that was introduced with the D3100 and D7000 cameras and now has made its way to the upper-echelon D4 and D800 cameras. This Focus mode allows the camera to focus continuously while in Live View and when recording video (similar to AF-C continuous AF). Even though the camera focuses continuously in still photography, the scene must be in focus before the shutter is released.

When using AF-F while recording video you should be aware that the camera often hunts for focus if the camera is being moved or panned. This can cause the video to go in and out of focus during your filming.

Full-time AF operates in conjunction with the AF-Area modes, which are covered in the next section.

AF-Area modes

To make the Live View focusing quicker and easier, Nikon gives you a few different options for AF-Area modes. These modes noticeably speed up the process of focusing as compared to previous cameras. You can change the settings in the Shooting menu under AF-area mode ➙ Live view:

> **NOTE** The AF-Area mode cannot be changed while recording video.

▶ **Face-priority AF.** Use the Face-priority AF mode (📷) for shooting portraits or snapshots of the family. You can choose the focus point but the camera uses face recognition to focus on the face rather than something in the foreground or background. This can really be an asset when shooting in a busy environment, such as when there's a lot of distracting elements in the background. When the camera detects a face in the frame, a double yellow border is displayed around the AF area. If more than one face is detected (the camera can read up to 35 faces), then the closest face is chosen as the focus point.

▶ **Wide-area AF.** The Wide-area AF mode (WIDE) makes the area where the camera determines focus from about 4X the size of the Normal-area AF mode (NORM). This is good when you don't need to be very critical about the point of focus in your image. For example, when shooting a far-off landscape you really only need to focus on the horizon line. This is a good general mode for everyday use. You can move the AF area anywhere within the image frame.

> **TIP** When using 📷, NORM, or WIDE, press the multi-selector center button to move the AF area to the center of the frame.

▶ **Normal-area AF.** The NORM has a smaller AF point and is used when you need to achieve focus on a very specific area within the frame. This is the preferred mode to use when shooting with a tripod. It's the mode I use when shooting macros, still life, and similar subjects. I also use this mode when shooting portraits instead of 📷 so I can control the AF area.

▶ **Subject-tracking AF.** The Subject-tracking AF mode (⊞) is an interesting feature especially when used in conjunction with video. Use the multi-selector to position the AF area over the top of the main subject of the image. Press the OK button (⊛) to start the tracking. The AF area follows along with the subject as it moves around within the frame. Be aware, however, that this feature works best with slow to moderately paced subjects that stand out from the background. When using this mode with very fast-moving subjects, the camera tends to lose the subject and lock on something of similar color and brightness within the frame. This mode also decreases in effectiveness as the amount of light decreases. To disable ⊞ simply press ⊛. This resets the AF area to the center. To reactivate, press ⊛ again.

When half-pressing the Shutter Release button to focus for taking a still shot, ⊞ is disabled. Releasing the button reactivates tracking.

Live View Photography

As you may already know, the image from the lens is projected to the viewfinder via a mirror that is in front of the sensor. There's a semitransparent area in the mirror that acts as a beam splitter, which is used by the camera for its normal phase detection AF. For Live View to work, the mirror must be flipped up, which makes phase-detection AF unusable, so the camera uses contrast detection directly from the sensor to determine focus. This makes focusing with Live View a bit slower than when focusing normally. In addition, when shooting, the mirror must flip down and back up, which takes some extra time. This makes Live View a challenging option to use when shooting moving subjects or events such as sports where timing is the key element in capturing an image successfully.

That being said, Live View comes in handy when shooting in a studio setting, especially when using a tripod. You can move the focus area any where in the frame. You're not limited to the 51 AF points. Live View also allows you to achieve sharper images when doing long exposures because the mirror is already raised eliminating any chance of mirror slap, which can sometimes cause images to blur slightly when shooting exposures longer than 1/2 second.

> **TIP** Keep in mind that when using Live View handheld you are holding the camera at arm's length and that increases the risk of blurry images due to added camera shake. Keep your elbows close to your sides for added stability.

Nikon has simplified the options for using Live View with still photography. Simply flip the switch on the Live View Selector switch to the Live View photography, and press the Live View button (Lv). Now you're ready to shoot. Use the multi-selector to position the focus point. When using AF-S half-press the Shutter Release button to focus or when in AF-F wait until focus is achieved, then fully press the Shutter Release button to take the picture.

The camera functions more or less the same in Live View as it does when shooting the traditional viewfinder way. There are a few exceptions though: when the Thumbnail/Zoom out button (🔍) is pressed, the monitor brightness indicator and monitor hue indicator are displayed (on the right and left respectively). While holding 🔍 use the multi-selector up button (▲) and down button (▼) to brighten the monitor and to dim the monitor. Pressing the multi-selector left button (◄) switches to the Monitor hue indicator and allows you to change the white balance setting off the monitor if it doesn't match the current setting. Pressing 🆗 displays the exposure meter on the right side of the monitor pressing it again removes it.

6.1 **Live View photography display**

The Live View photography display is a bit different than what you would see looking through the viewfinder, although some of the same information is there. The bottom of the frame looks a lot like the toolbar from the viewfinder albeit with only the essential shooting information. Here's what you find:

▶ **Metering mode**

▶ **Exposure mode**

▶ **Shutter speed**

▶ **Aperture**

▶ **ISO setting**

▶ **Remaining shots**

Displayed over the Live View feed are a number of different settings indicators, most of which should be familiar to you by now, but a few are a little different from your traditional view through the viewfinder:

▶ **Focus point.** The most obvious feature is the focus point. Move this around by using the multi-selector.

▶ **Autofocus mode.** In Live View there are only two AF modes; AF-S (Single AF) and AF-F (Full-time AF). Switch between these by press the AF mode button and rotating the Main Command dial.

▶ **AF-area mode.** Unlike in through the viewfinder shooting you aren't limited to the 51 AF points. You can move the focus point anywhere within the frame so the options for the AF area modes are different. Change these modes by rotating the sub-Command dial. The AF-area modes are covered earlier in this chapter

> **NOTE** AF mode and AF-area modes are not displayed when the camera is switched Manual focus or a manual focus non-CPU lens is attached.

▶ **Active D-Lighting.** This shows your current setting for the Active D-Lighting option, which is set in the Shooting menu (📷).

▶ **Picture Controls.** This shows your Picture control setting. Pressing the Protect button (O─┐) brings up the selection of Picture Controls on the right side of the monitor. Use ▲ and ▼ to scroll through the settings. Once you've highlighted the Picture Control you want to use press O─┐ to return to the shooting mode or press the multi-selector right (▶) to modify the setting.

Why Shoot Video with a dSLR?

Just a few years ago, when video was first introduced in dSLRs, it was good for shooting family videos and other types of noncritical video; but as the technology has advanced, dSLR videography has become a viable form of filming not only small family events but television shows and even feature-length films meant for the big screen. This is because smaller dLSR cameras have features that out-weigh some advantages of a dedicated video camera. Some of the major advan-tages are:

▶ **Price.** dSLR cameras are much cheaper than a mid- to pro-level HD video camera.

▶ **Image quality.** The D800's FX–sized sensor also allows the camera to record video with less noise at high sensitivities than most video cameras can.

▶ **Interchangeable lenses.** You can use almost every Nikon lens on the D800. And, while some HD video cameras take Nikon lenses, you need an expen-sive adapter, and you lose some resolution and the ability to get a very shal-low depth of field.

▶ **Depth of field.** You can get a much shallower depth of field than video when using a lens with a fast aperture, such as a 50mm f/1.4. Most video cameras have sensors that are much smaller than the sensor of the D800, which gives them a much deeper depth of field. A shallow depth of field gives videos a more professional, cinematic look.

▶ **White balance setting.** This is where the current white balance setting is dis-played. Change the white balance setting as normal.

▶ **Image Size/Quality.** This is where your file size and file formats are displayed, RAW, JPEG, TIFF, and the size if it applies to the file format. Change these set-tings as normal.

▶ **Image area.** These display your image area. This setting is also changed as usual.

The following settings don't appear at all times. They are called up by pressing differ-ent buttons, as described in the following bullets.

▶ **Guide.** Located just above the toolbar at the bottom of the screen is what Nikon calls the Guide. This basically gives you the information on how to adjust the brightness and the monitor hue (discussed earlier) and when using (⊞) it shows that you need to press the multi-selector center button to activate sub-ject tracking (also discussed earlier).

▶ **Time remaining.** This is a countdown timer letting you know when the Live View is going to shut down automatically. This only appears if Live View is going to end in 30 seconds.

The Info button (**Info**) is used to toggle through different options on the D800 Live View photography display. Default is information On, pressing **Info** once turns the informa-tion off leaving only the bottom toolbar, allowing you to compose your images without distraction from all of the settings icons. Press **Info** a second time and a grid is dis-played over the image area to assist in composing. A third press of **Info** brings up the Virtual horizon setting.

When viewing the exposure meter (by pressing ⊛) a live histogram option appears when scrolling through the settings by pressing **Info**.

Pressing the Playback/Zoom in button (🔍) allows you to zoom in to the image to check focus. Use the multi-selector to navigate around the image.

> **NOTE** Attaching the D800 to an HDMI video device will display the Live View as it appears in the monitor.

Movie Live View

The Live View feature of the D800 is also used to capture HD video. The Movie Live View feature operates very similarly to Live View for still photography. Simply flip the switch the Live View Selector switch to 🄻, and press 🄻. The mirror flips up and you're ready to start filming. Use the multi-selector to position the focus point. When using AF-S half-press the Shutter Release button to focus or when in AF-F wait until focus is achieved, then press the Movie Record button to start recording.

> **CAUTION** Fully depressing the Shutter Release button results in shooting a still frame and ends recording. Therefore when focusing during recording I recommend using **AF-ON**.

> **NOTE** You can set the Shutter Release button to record video in ✐ g4.

As previously mentioned, in Movie Live View the camera functions similarly to Live View except that when ⚙ is pressed the monitor brightness indicator and microphone sensitivity are displayed (on the right and left respectively). While holding ⚙ use ▲ to brighten the monitor and ▼ to dim the monitor. Pressing ◄ switches to the microphone sensitivity and use ▲ and ▼ to adjust the sensitivity (you can set it to 1-20, Auto or Off). If headphones are attached, another press of ◄ allows you to adjust the volume of the headphones (you can adjust from 1-30 or Off).

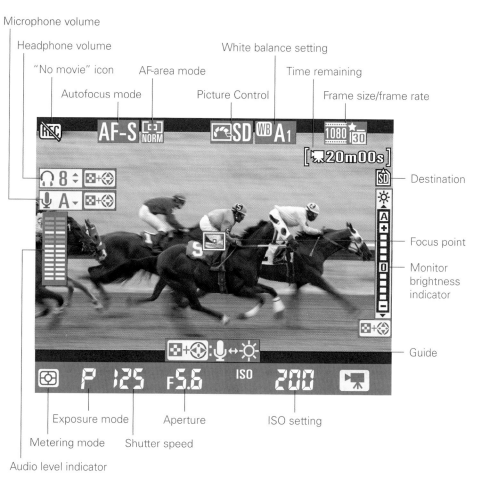

Microphone volume

Headphone volume

White balance setting

"No movie" icon   AF-area mode   Time remaining

Autofocus mode   Picture Control   Frame size/frame rate

Destination

Focus point

Monitor brightness indicator

Guide

Exposure mode   Aperture   ISO setting

Metering mode   Shutter speed

Audio level indicator

6.2 Movie Live View display

The Movie Live View display is a bit different than what you see in the Live View, but some of the same information is there. You still have the bottom toolbar with almost the same information.

► **Metering mode**

► **Exposure mode**

► **Shutter speed**

► **Aperture**

► **ISO setting**

Displayed over the Movie Live View feed are a number of different settings indicators, most of which should be familiar to you by now, but a few are a little different from your traditional through-the-viewfinder settings.

► **Focus point.** The most obvious feature is the focus point. Move this around by using the multi-selector.

► **"No movie" icon.** This icon is only shown when a movie can't be recorded, for example if the memory card is full.

► **Autofocus mode.** Just like in Live View there are two AF modes; AF-S (Single AF) and AF-F (Full-time AF). Switch between these by press the AF mode button and rotating the Main Command dial.

► **AF-area mode.** Also like in Live View, you aren't limited to the 51 AF points, you can move the focus point anywhere within the frame. The options for the AF area modes are the same as Live View (covered earlier in the chapter). Change these modes by rotating the Sub-command dial.

> **NOTE** AF mode and AF-area modes are not displayed when the camera is switched to Manual focus or a manual focus non-CPU lens is attached.

► **Picture Controls.** This shows your Picture Control setting. Pressing O━┓ brings up the selection of Picture Controls on the right side of the monitor. Use ▲ and ▼ to scroll through the settings. Once you've highlighted the Picture Control you want to use press O━┓ to return to the shooting mode or press ► to modify the setting.

► **White balance setting.** This is where the current white balance setting is displayed. Change the white balance setting as normal.

► **Frame size/frame rate.** This is where the movie size and frame rate are displayed. These can be changed in ▣ under the Movie settings sub-menu.

> **CROSS REF** See the sidebar on frame rate in this chapter to learn more about frames per second (fps).

Frame Size and Frame Rate

The D800 offers two HD video sizes: 1080p and 720p. 1080p has more resolution and therefore holds more detail and has less noise in low light. Most professionals prefer to shoot in 1080p and downsize later if necessary. There are, however, some reasons for shooting in 720p. For example, the file sizes are smaller and, if you're only shooting videos to post to the web, you don't really need the higher resolution. If you plan on making DVD's to show on an HDTV, then the extra resolution of 1080p is going make quite a bit of difference in quality. So what it boils down to is what your intended output is.

An important part of video capture is *frame rate*. This is the rate at which the still images are recorded and is expressed in terms of frames per second (fps). At the end of the resolution number (1080 or 720) there is another number in subscript (24, 25, 30, 50, or 60). This subscript number is the frame rate. Video capture is simply recording still images, linking them together, and then playing them back one after another in sequence. This allows the still images to appear as if they're moving. Most video cameras capture video at 30 or 60 fps. A rate of 30 fps is generally considered the best for smooth-looking video that doesn't appear jerky. Shooting at 24 fps is the minimum rate to fool the human eye into seeing seamless motion. This also gives videos a quality that's similar to cinema.

The Nikon D800 shoots full 1080p HD video at 30, 25, or 24fps. You can record 720p at 60, 50, 30, or 25fps. This is set in 📷 under the Movie settings option. Select 24 fps for the cinematic look or 30 fps for a smoother look. The 25 and 50 fps options are for videos that will be played back on PAL devices (the analog TV encoding system used in Europe). Shooting at 60 fps allows you to slow the video for slow motion. This allows the slow-motion effect to blend in seamlessly when combined with traditional 30 fps video.

▶ **Time Remaining.** This displays how much time remaining you have left for the video. The time can differ depending on the Movie quality and the size or remaining space on the memory card.

▶ **Destination.** This indicates what card slot the movies are being recorded to, SD or CF.

▶ **Guide.** Located just above the toolbar at the bottom of the screen is the Guide. This gives you the information on how to adjust the brightness, microphone sensitivity, headphone volume (discussed earlier), and when using ⊞ it shows that you need to press the multi-selector center button to activate it.

Video Set Up

Using the video feature on the D800 is quite simple to start with. Simply flip the Live View Selector switch to (🎥) and press (Lv), focus, and press the Movie Record button. However, there are some important settings to consider before you run off and go recording. Here are the most important things to think about before pressing that Movie Record button.

▶ **Frame size/frame rate.** Choose the image size based on your intended output and your preferred frame rate. See the previous sidebar details on frame rate and size. Your choices are:

  ▶ 1920 × 1080; 30fps (1080 🎞)

  ▶ 1920 × 1080; 25fps (1080 🎞)

  ▶ 1920 × 1080; 24fps (1080 🎞)

  ▶ 1280 × 720; 60fps (720 🎞)

  ▶ 1280 × 720; 50fps (720 🎞)

  ▶ 1280 × 720; 30fps (720 🎞)

  ▶ 1280 × 720; 25fps (720 🎞)

▶ **Movie quality.** You have two choices: High and Normal. The difference all comes down to bit rate. At higher bit rates more information is being recorded resulting in better color rendition and dynamic range, of course higher bit rates also mean more data and larger file sizes. One thing to keep in mind is that High quality movies are limited to 20 minutes and Normal quality clips can be up to 29 minute and 59 seconds. Again your choice comes down to intended output. For web using Normal quality is fine; for viewing on HDTVs stick with High quality.

▶ **Microphone.** The three settings are Auto, Manual, and Off. Auto works for most general filming, but for a more consistent sound in a controlled environment, set the microphone sensitivity manually. You can keep an eye on the levels when filming, and remember you can also adjust this setting on the Live View screen.

▶ **Picture Control.** Just like your still images, the D800 applies Picture Control settings to your movie. You can also create and use Custom Picture Controls that fit your specific application. For example, I created a Custom Picture Control called Raging Bull that uses the Monochrome Picture Control with added contrast and the yellow filter option. This gives me a black-and-white scene that's reminiscent of the Martin Scorsese film of the same name. Before you start recording your video, decide which Picture Control you want to use for your movie.

Shutter Speed

In filmmaking there's a term called the 180° shutter rule. Without getting into the technical reasons why it's named as it is, the 180° shutter rule states that your shutter speed should be about twice your frame rate for natural looking images. So 1080 ⓩ should use a shutter speed of 1/50, 30fps at 1/60, and 60 fps at 1/125. This gives the video just enough blur to make it look natural to human eyes.

Slower shutter speeds cause the video to appear smeary, although the D800 combats this by not allowing you to set the shutter speed slower than the frame rate.

On the opposite end of the spectrum, faster shutter speeds can cause the video to appear slightly jerky because just as when shooting a still the action is frozen (remember videos are just stills played in succession), as the subject moves through the frame there is no motion blur to make it look more natural to the eyes. Of course, you can use the jerky, fast shutter speed as an effect as well. Movies such as *Saving Private Ryan* and *Gladiator* made use of this effect in the action scenes.

▶ **Exposure mode.** This is a *very* important setting. The exposure mode you choose determines who chooses the settings, you or the camera.

- *P* **and** *S*.These modes leaves the camera to make all of the exposure choices for you. When you press ⌊Lv⌋ the camera sets the shutter speed, aperture, and ISO sensitivity. While you're filming, if the lighting changes, the camera adjusts the exposure by adjusting the ISO sensitivity, if the scene becomes too bright the shutter speed is raised to keep a good exposure (unless you lock the exposure using (ᴬᴱ⁻ᴸ/ᴬᶠ⁻ᴸ). The only control you have over the exposure is using exposure compensation.

- *A*. This mode allows you a little more control. You can set the aperture to control the depth of field, but the shutter speed and the ISO sensitivity are controlled automatically by the camera. You can also dial in exposure compensation to brighten or darken the image.

- *M*. If you're serious about video, this is the exposure mode you should be using. This mode lets you control the exposure by adjusting the aperture, shutter speed, and ISO setting yourself. It takes a little more time to set up, but this allows you to not only control the depth of field, but it also allows you to control the amount of noise and the shutter speed effect if so desired.

Playback

Playing back your videos is super easy. Press the Playback button (▶️) on the back of the camera and scroll through the videos and stills as normal. When the video is displayed on the LCD screen, press the multi-selector center button to start playback. Press ▲ to stop, ▼ to pause, ◄ to rewind, and ▶ to fast-forward. Use 🔍 to raise the volume and 🔍 to lower the volume.

Connecting your camera to an HDTV displays what is on the LCD on the TV and the options are the same.

In-Camera Editing

You can make simple edits to your videos in-camera; for more serious edits you need to think about using third-party software, such as iMovie for Mac or Premier Elements for PC users. In-camera, you have three options: choose the Start frame, choose the End frame, and grab a still image from the video. Each edit you make is saved as a new file so there's no need to worry about making any permanent changes to your original file. To edit the video:

1. **Press the Menu button (MENU) and use the multi-selector to select the Retouch menu (✍).**

2. **Select Edit Movie and press ⊛ or ▶ to view menu options.**

3. **Choose the edit you want to make and press ⊛ or ▶.** The options are Choose start point, Choose end point, or Save selected frame. A menu appears with all videos that are saved to the current card.

4. **Use the multi-selector to scroll through the available videos and press ⊛ when your video is selected.** The selected video is highlighted in yellow.

5. **Press ⊛ to begin playback and press ▲ at the moment you want to make the edit.** You can use ▼ to stop playback and ◄ or ▶ to go back or forward in the video clip.

6. **Press ▲ to make the edit.** I prefer to actually pause the movie by pressing ▼ so I can be absolutely sure it is where I want the edit to be. I then make the edit. The movie is automatically saved.

Using Index Points

Using ✐ g1, g2, or g3, you can assign a button to act as an index marker. This allows you to mark specific areas of the video where you may want to make a cut (you can use up to 20 index points per video). These index points are placed as you are filming when you press the specified button.

When playing back on the camera you can rotate the Main Command dial to jump to an index point and pause the video. You can then press ⊛ to make edits. Use ▲ or ▼ to choose whether you want to make the index the start or end point. Press ⊛ to select the point or ▶ to cancel the edit.

Once you select a starting and ending point, press O—┐ then ▲ to make the cut. You are then given four choices:

▶ **Save as new file.** This allows you to keep the original unedited file. I recommend using this selection.

▶ **Overwrite existing file.** This replaces your original movie with the new edited version.

▶ **Cancel.** This ends the editing session and you can start over or skip to another movie.

▶ **Preview.** This allows you to watch the newly edited clip before deciding what option to choose.

CHAPTER 7

Event Photography

E vent photography is a great way for an advanced amateur photographer to make some extra money. There are many types of events, however, and some photographers pick one — weddings, for example — and specialize in that event, or some photographers such as myself branch out and dabble in a little bit of everything from sporting events, parties, weddings, and concerts. There's no right or wrong way to approach doing events other than the fact that you must be comfortable that you can do the job sufficiently.

One of the primary concerns for a photographer that decides to take on event photography is having a responsibility to the client to produce high-quality images in a timely manner. If you don't feel that you are ready to take on an assignment, then don't do it. The best way to enter into the field of event photography is to assist a professional event photographer to help you get familiar with the process and ultimately lead you to achieving success.

The key to getting a successful event shot is knowing when to shoot at the decisive moment (as Henri Cartier Bresson would say).

Sporting Events

The key to getting the perfect action shot is timing. Capturing the athlete at the peak of the action is how you make a great action shot. Being prepared and knowing the key elements to the sport will help you figure out exactly the right moment to release the shutter. Take a few minutes to stand back and observe the action before you get out there and start shooting.

In Figure 7.1, to effectively capture this shot of BMX pro Chase Hawk doing a 360-degree back flip I had to watch carefully and snap the shot just as he was at the peak of his trick. I also had to get the timing exact — just a bit earlier and his shoulder would have been blocking his face, a bit later and he would be facing away from me.

7.1 Snapping the shot at just the right time allowed me to get the shot at the peak of the trick. ISO 280 (Auto-ISO) at f/2.8 at 1/1000 second with a 28-70mm f/2.8 lens.

When shooting unpredictable sports such as skateboard, BMX, or motocross, you need lightning-quick reflexes and you need to develop the ability to watch both the athlete and the whole composition at the same time. This takes time to perfect, but after awhile it becomes second nature.

To be successful in capturing the action you need to be in the right place at the right time. Although this may come down to luck, most sports have areas where the most action takes place. For example, in basketball almost all of the significant action takes place at the hoop. When shooting baseball, home plate and first base are the spots to see a lot of action. Once again, taking a few minutes to observe will allow you to pinpoint where most of the action occurs.

Shutter Priority (**S**) is the key to effectively capturing the action when shooting any type of sports. Your shutter speed setting controls how the motion in your image is portrayed. By using a fast shutter speed you can freeze the motion of your subject (see Figure 7.2) or conversely, you can use a slow shutter speed to capture some motion blur (see Figure 7.3), which is equally effective at showing movement in a still image.

7

In Figure 7.2, I was shooting a horse race. Horses are extremely fast animals, and in order to effectively freeze the motion of the horse a fast shutter speed is essential. Using a shutter speed of 1/800 second I was able to capture the horse just as all four hooves were off the ground. Coincidentally, in 1878, photographer Eadweard Muybridge used high-speed photography to prove that horses indeed do have all four feet off the ground at a certain point in their stride.

7.2 Using a fast shutter speed of 1/800 second was absolutely necessary to freeze the motion in this shot. ISO 1000 (Auto-ISO) at f/14 at 1/800 second with a 70-200mm f/2.8 lens zoomed to 200mm.

In contrast, I used a slow shutter speed and panning in Figure 7.3. Instead of freezing the motion this technique allows the fast-moving horses to have a blurred effect, which effectively portrays speed and motion.

7.3 A slow shutter speed allows you to show motion blur. ISO 200 at f/11 at 1/50 second with a 70-200mm f/2.8 lens at 200mm.

Concerts and Live Music

Concert and live music photography is quickly growing in popularity, and although one shouldn't expect to make much money from this type of photography there are opportunities for small monetary gain. Just so you don't set yourself of for disappointment, don't expect to start out shooting Madonna or the Rolling Stones. Access to the most famous acts is severely restricted. In order to shoot top performers, affiliation with a publication or agency is a necessity and the only way to get there is to work your way up.

CAUTION The D800 is not necessarily the best camera for this type of photography, but can be used effectively. The D4 is much better suited for low-light work.

If you're looking to start making money from music photography right away, try looking at your local craigslist. Often there are bands looking for promotional or live shots and are willing to pay a little bit of money, but the best way to get started if you're really serious about doing this type of photography is to start in the clubs (see Figure 7.4). Go to small venues, shoot pictures of bands you like, and offer them low-res copies to use on their websites. Later on the band is likely come back to you when it needs a photographer for another gig, CD cover, or press kit.

7.4 More often than not you will start out taking pictures in tiny crowded venues such as this one, so bring a wide, fast zoom. This photo was taken of local Austin, Texas, rock and rollers, the Nouns. ISO 2000 at f/2.8 at 1/100 second with a 17-35mm f/2.8 lens at 17mm.

TIP You can use Photoshop to mark your images with your name and website (also known as a watermark). Consider these images as advertising.

Settings

When shooting live music, I have typical settings that I generally stick with and modify if need be. Here's a list of the settings that I start out with:

▶ **Manual exposure.** Generally, I start at 1/125 second at f/2.8. If the subject is slower I may slow down the exposure a bit. If the subject is faster or I'm using a longer lens I speed up the shutter a bit, usually up to 1/250 second, but almost never higher than 1/320 second unless I'm shooting outside. If I need to get more than one performer in focus I will stop down a bit.

▶ **Auto ISO.** This is a great setting for making sure your images have as little noise as possible. As the lighting changes the camera automatically adjusts the ISO exposure resulting in the cleanest images.

▶ **AF-C.** I almost always set my AF to continuous because the performers are generally moving quite a bit. In rare circumstances when a performer is seated I may switch to AF-S.

▶ **Single point AF.** Using the multi-selector, I place the focus point exactly where I want the focus to be. 3D-tracking is just too unpredictable for this type of photography.

▶ **Spot meter.** Spot metering allows you get the exposure from the focus point of the image. Although you may be using Manual exposure you should keep your eye on the meter to make sure you're getting proper exposures, and if you're using Auto-ISO this will help the camera with choosing the proper ISO setting for your exposure settings.

7.5 Sometimes if you're lucky you'll catch a rock star in action. While I was shooting local Austin, Texas, legend singer/songwriter Alejandro Escovedo, Bruce Springsteen came out for a surprise duet. I stopped down a bit for this shot to make sure both performers were in focus. ISO 3200 at f/4.5 at 1/200 second with a 24-70mm f/2.8 lens at 70mm.

Equipment

Photographers often have differing opinions of lens choice, but it usually comes down to primes or zooms. The general consensus among most amateurs is a fast prime, but from being a professional in the live music photography business I can tell you a fast zoom is the best way to go. A zoom offers you more freedom for composition than a prime lens does, and with the way newer cameras like the D800 operate in low light there's absolutely no need to use a lens faster than f/2.8 unless you are in the most extremely dark venue.

My preferred lens choices for the D800 when shooting live music are the following:

► **Nikon 24-70mm f/2.8G.** This is my go-to lens for most shots. It's Nikon's best wide to short telephoto and is the perfect focal length for most venues.

► **Nikon 17-35mm f/2.8D.** This is an older lens that still boasts AF-S for fast and silent focusing and has replaced my 14-24mm f/2.8G as my wide-angle lens of choice for concerts. I find the focal length to be much more usable than the ultrawide 14-24mm and the extra stop over the newer 16-35mm f/4G VR gives me better low-light performance.

► **Nikon 70-200mm f/2.8G VR.** I usually only bring this lens to larger venues with high stages or to concerts that I know will have to shoot from the crowd or the soundboard.

Weddings

In the opinions of many aspiring photographers weddings are the key to making a good living as a photographer. This may be the case in some instances for a few photographers but it's the exception rather than the rule. A wedding is an extremely special day for a couple and shooting a wedding is a serious responsibility and should be treated as such. If you plan on taking up wedding photography as your main profession I highly suggest assisting or acting as a second shooter for an established wedding photographer for at least a few months before actually attempting to shoot a wedding on your own.

Wedding photography is a very challenging profession and a very nerve-wracking type of photography. At a wedding there are numerous things happening at once and you can't be everywhere at the same time. You only have one chance to get it right. Becoming a competent wedding photographer is a very complicated journey and there isn't enough room in this book to cover all of the different facets so I'm only touching on the most basic tenets that you'll need to know to get started. There are many great books out there dedicated solely to wedding photography and I suggest you do some research into some of these books for more detailed information.

7.6 The recessional is a classic shot. In this shot I managed to get some great lens flare to give the shot a cinematic look. The couple was very pleased with this. ISO 400 at f/5.6 at 1/890 second with a 24-70mm f/2.8 lens at 28mm.

Wedding photography involves more than just showing up during the wedding day and shooting. There's quite a bit of planning involved. Sit down and have a meeting with the bride and groom, or at the very least the bride, and have a conversation about their expectations. Be sure that they are aware of your shooting style, be it traditional or photojournalistic, and make sure they know what to expect of your work. Find out what kinds of shots they are expecting, establish a time frame for delivery of the images, discuss whether they want an album or just a disc with the images, and discuss payment.

One of the main things you should go over with the couple is the shot list. To capture a wedding successfully, you must find out what shots they want. As the professional, you should make up a list of all possible shots and present the list to them so that they have an idea of what the key shots for most weddings are. I specialize in nontraditional weddings so when I present a typical shot list many of my clients are not interested in "standard" shots such as selective color shots, but *your* clients may expect these things. You must know *exactly* what your clients want before you show up. Here's a short list of some of the key shots you should get:

▶ **Bride getting ready.** This can include shots such as the bride applying makeup, the bridesmaids helping her into the dress, and her mom adjusting the veil, among other things.

▶ **Groom getting ready.** Some shots include putting on the tie and boutonniére, groomsmen hanging around, and so on.

▶ **Bridal party portraits.** This should include pictures of the bride with her parents, grandparents, and siblings, as well as portraits of the bride with her bridesmaids. Don't forget to get portraits of the bride alone, including headshots, 3/4 length, and full length.

7.7 Don't forget detail shots. Brides love shots of the dress before it's on. I used the window for natural backlighting to bring out the details of the dress, which can be difficult to discern once the dress is on. ISO 400 at f/4 at 1/80 second with a Nikon 24-70mm f/2.8 lens at 38mm and spot metering.

▶ **Leaving for the venue.** These are optional but it's nice to get some candid photojournalistic-type shots of the bride and groom (hopefully separately) getting into the vehicle to depart.

▶ **The ceremony.** This is where it starts getting hectic, but you should get pictures of the mothers of the bride and groom being escorted down the aisle as well as each bridesmaid and the maid of honor, and, of course, the bride being led down the aisle and given away. The exchange of the rings and the kiss should are an absolute must. Also, don't forget to photograph the recessional or the bride and groom leaving.

▶ **Formal portraits.** This can be one of the most frustrating aspects of the whole wedding. Everyone will be running around trying to get ready for the reception and congratulating the bride and groom. You will need to be assertive to get everyone together that you need for the shots. Here's a short list of some of the shots you might need.

- Entire bridal party

- Bride and groom

- Groom and groomsmen

- Groom and best man

- Groom alone

- Groom with parents

- Bride and groom with groom's parents

- Bride and groom with bride's parents

▶ **The reception.** The reception is where you can relax and start having a little more fun and being a little more creative. Some of the shots should include the first dance, the toasts, the cake cutting, and the bouquet and garter toss, and, candid shots of the guests dancing and having fun.

Even with a shot list don't overlook small details. You should photograph things such as the rings, the bride's shoes, minute details of the dress, the table settings, the bouquet, and the cake (before it's cut).

Some other very important things to think about:

▶ **Scout the location.** Check out the location ahead of time to help you figure out what equipment you may need or what settings you might have to use. If you know that the ceremony is going to be in a dark church you may want to bring a faster lens such as a 24, 35, or 50mm f/1.4. If you can, attend the rehearsal to get an idea of some of the angles you may want to shoot from. This can also help as a dry run to get an idea of the lighting and some of the settings you may want to use or some pitfalls to avoid.

▶ **Be prepared.** Although remembering these items may seem like a no-brainer be sure that you have enough spare formatted memory cards, extra batteries, and a lens cloth.

Using Flash

Using flash during the ceremony is generally not allowed. It's pretty much an unspoken rule. A flash going off every couple of seconds is going to be a distraction to the couple's big moment. Before the ceremony and at the reception don't be afraid to use flash if you need to, but use a diffuser and bounce flash so as to not get that standard on-camera flash snapshot look.

Another consideration to make is when to use flash and when *not* to use flash. I program the Function button (**Fn**) on my D800 to cancel the flash when I press it. (The Preview button can also perform the same operation.) Oftentimes I'll see a shot that looks better in natural light and rather than fumbling to turn off my Speedlight, I simply press a button. You can set this in either Custom Settings menu (✐) f4 or f5.

Using a slower shutter speed, or *dragging the shutter*, is another good effect, as shown in the image here. This allows some of the ambient light to add to the exposure. This makes your images more natural looking. Be careful not to slow the shutter speed down too much or you will end up with *ghosting*, although this can be a creative effect as well.

▶ **Have a backup.** One of the most important things to have is a backup camera. Whether you buy, borrow, or rent one, you should have one. Cameras, as with any electronic equipment, can fail at any time. You could drop it, the shutter could fail, any number of things could happen. You only get one try at a wedding and if you're camera is inoperable, you're sunk.

> TIP Turn off the sound on your camera. You don't want your camera beeping all during the ceremony. You're there to record the event as unobtrusively as possible. The sound can be turned off using ✎ d1.

CHAPTER 8

Landscape and Nature Photography

Wandering around outdoors affords you the simple opportunity to make some truly inspirational photography. The natural world is filled with many diverse subjects to photograph. Plants, flowers, rock formations, and coastlines are just a few of the many types of subjects you can discover. The great thing about landscape and nature photography is that you don't need a lot of specialized gear to do it. Your D800 and almost any type of lens will suffice, and you can use the sun to light your subject.

You can use photography to capture images of places you've visited.

Photographing Landscapes

Simply put, landscape photography is recording a scene exactly as it exists in nature. For the most part, people and animals aren't included in the scene and the focus is placed upon the formations of the land.

Landscape photography can encompass almost any type of natural environments, from coastlines and the sea to desert scenes, mountains, forests, and lakes. Although exotic scenes make for interesting images, you don't necessarily have to travel far and wide to capture a great landscape scene — you can take a quick trip to the local park and find a suitable subject.

You can also return to the same scene numerous times and capture a completely different image. Returning at different times of the day, in different seasons, and in different types of weather all have an effect on the scene.

There are three distinct styles of landscape photography:

▶ **Representational.** This is a straight landscape; the "what you see is what you get" approach. This is not to say that this is a simple snapshot; it requires great attention to details such as composition, lighting, and weather.

▶ **Impressionistic.** With this type of landscape photo, the image looks less real due to filters or special photographic techniques such as long exposures. These techniques can give the image a mysterious or otherworldly quality.

▶ **Abstract.** With this type of landscape photo, the image may or may not resemble the actual subject. The compositional elements of shape and form are more important than an actual representation of the scene.

Capturing a great landscape image has a lot to do with *quality of light*. Quality of light is the way that the light interacts with the subject. Photographers have many terms to describe the quality of light, including hard, diffused, mixed, and more. The key to getting great landscape lighting is to know how the light looks at different times of day.

Most photographers agree that the best time to photograph a landscape is just after the sun rises and right before the sun sets. The sunlight at those times of day is refracted by the atmosphere and bounces off of low-lying clouds, resulting in a sunlight color that is different and more pleasing to the eye than it is at high noon. This time of day is often referred to as the *golden hour* by photographers due to the rich golden color and soft quality of the light at this time.

Figure 8.1 is a representational landscape image that I shot at twilight. I used Spot metering and metered the brightest part of the scene to underexpose the shot to give the sky rich, deep color and to allow the palm tree to silhouette. Traditionally, landscape images are framed horizontally, hence the term landscape orientation, but I composed this image vertically (portrait orientation) to play up the striking cloud formations. Bending the rules sometimes adds interest to your composition.

In Figure 8.2, I used a Lensbaby 2.0 lens, which allowed me to bend the lens to create a sweet spot of focus while blurring and distorting the rest of the frame. The blurred edges and sharp center give this impressionistic landscape shot a *dream sequence* quality that you often see in films.

8

8.1 This landscape was shot just at twilight at sunset in Hermosa Beach, California. However, you don't necessarily need to leave the city to get a great landscape shot. Nikon 28-70mm f/2.8 lens for 1/125 second at f/2.8 ISO 200.

8.2 This landscape shot is more of an impressionistic shot due to the use of the Lensbaby selective focus lens. Lensbaby 2.0 for 1/400 second at f/2.0, ISO 400.

High Dynamic Range

High Dynamic Range, or as it's more commonly known, HDR is a terrific tool to use when shooting landscape. I'm not referring to the overly processed surreal-looking HDR photography, but using HDR to balance out the highlights, mid-tones, and shadows giving the image more dynamic range resulting in a more believable and true-to-life photograph. (See Chapter 3 for more information on using the D800's HDR feature.) The D800 has an automatic HDR feature that can easily be set to the BKT button if you use this feature frequently. You can also create HDR images by bracketing at least two exposures and combining them using software. For this image of Sunset Cliffs in California I combined seven images using Photoshop CS5 Merge to HDR Pro feature.

Paying close attention to the foreground is key when using a wide-angle lens for landscape shooting. Wide-angle lenses allow you to fit a vast amount of the scene into your image, which can lead to an image with lots of empty space in the composition, which is something you want to avoid. Make an effort to add interest to the foreground by including patterns, textures, and leading lines.

In Figure 8.3, I used a wide-angle lens to exaggerate the landscape. To add some interest to the image I used the lines on the highway as leading lines to draw the viewer's eye up through the image.

While wide-angle lenses are generally your best bet for landscapes you can use telephotos with great success as well. The use of a telephoto achieves compression perspective; distortion flattens the image.

8.3 This landscape was shot with a wide-angle lens and uses leading lines to draw the eye in. Nikon 14-24mm f/2.8G lens for 1/125 second at f/11 ISO 400.

Here are a few other landscape tips:

▶ **Maximize your depth of field.** Using a small aperture allows you to get everything in focus, which is generally the goal in landscape photography.

▶ **Use a tripod.** When using smaller apertures your shutter speed will be slower by necessity. Using a tripod helps to ensure that your images are sharp.

▶ **Pay attention to the horizon.** Be sure your horizons are straight. Nothing ruins a great landscape shot quicker than a wonky horizon.

Architecture

Although strictly speaking, architecture photography doesn't fall into the realm of landscape photograph; however, outdoor architecture photography does incorporate some of the same skills. Using leading lines, texture, and patterns all apply, as well as keeping a nice straight horizon and using a tripod are all tricks of the trade in both types of photography. In this image of the Long Center for Performing Arts, I applied all of these techniques as well as the D800 HDR feature.

Nature

There are no real hard and fast rules about what nature photography is. Ask ten photographers and you might get ten different answers, but most can agree that nature photography is done outdoors. Your subjects can be a diverse group: plants and flowers, animals, insects, and more.

The techniques of nature photography can be as diverse as the subjects. Nature photography can be many types of photography rolled into one, from landscapes to macros and even action if shooting moving animals. You can use different types of lenses to get different effects; the options are varied.

A good idea when heading out to take general nature shots is to bring two lenses: a wide to normal zoom, such as a 24-70mm, and a longer lens like a 105mm macro lens. If there is a chance that you may run into some wildlife, bring a long telephoto zoom. Another great option is to bring a multipurpose lens. Sigma's recently discontinued 24-70mm f/2.8 macro is a great lens and can be found used relatively cheap. Another option is a super-zoom like the Nikon 28-300mm f/3.5-5.6.

Flowers and plants are by far the easiest subjects to photograph for nature shots. Many artists throughout the centuries have turned to flora for inspiration because of the simplicity and beauty. Flowers and plants have an amazing array of colors and textures, from reds and greens to purples and yellows; the color combinations are endless.

8

8.4 Flowers are easy subjects for nature shots. The complementary colors of green and purple really help the flower to pop from the background. Nikon 105mm f/2.8G VR Macro lens for 1/8000 second at f/3, ISO 200.

A few tips on photographing plants and flowers in nature:

▶ **Look very closely.** Look for interesting patterns or features. Pay attention to the way the light interacts with the foliage. Light coming through a transparent flower petal can add a wonderful glow.

▶ **Use complementary colors can give your images an added boost.** Pay attention to the color scheme of the background and subject. Try to avoid a subject and background with similar colors. Use a wide aperture to achieve a shallow depth of field to separate the subject from the background.

CROSS REF See Chapter 2 for more information regarding the D800's HDR feature.

Wildlife

Wildlife photography is another type of nature photography. Wildlife can be found at many places — wildlife preserves, animal sanctuaries, and even zoos, as well as out in the wild. One of the easiest ways to capture wildlife photos is to be where you know the animals are.

Opportunities to take wildlife pictures can occur while you're hiking or even when you're sitting on your back porch enjoying the sunset. With a little perseverance and luck, you can get some great wildlife images, just like the ones you see in *National Geographic*.

A multipurpose zoom lens like a 28-300mm will help you be ready for anything. The most important thing to remember about wildlife photography is to be careful. Wild animals can be unpredictable and aggressive when confronted by humans.

CHAPTER 9

Portrait Photography

A portrait is nothing but a photo of a person, quite simply. But, in order to make a great portrait you should be able to capture or at least evoke a bit of the personality of the person of whom you are taking a portrait. Candid portraits will show the personality of the person you are capturing, but a good model, like an actor, can *portray* different personalities. This is something to keep in mind.

Portrait photography is simple to explain, but not necessarily the easiest type of photography to accomplish correctly. You can simply point a camera at a person and create a great candid portrait, or you can create an elaborate lighting setup to create a more stylized portrait. Neither type of portrait is better than the other, but I will say that the D800 excels in a studio environment when shooting portraits because the higher resolution looks better better under controlled lighting. That's not to say that you can't do natural-light portraits with the D800, because you absolutely can.

"Some will not recognize the truthfulness of my mirror. Let them remember that I am not here to reflect the surface... but must penetrate inside. My mirror probes down to the heart. I write words on the forehead and around the corners of the mouth. My human faces are truer than the real ones." – Paul Klee

Studio Portraits

With studio portraits the lighting and background are controlled to a much greater extent. They set the tone of the image. The most important part of a studio setting is the lighting setup. Directionality and tone are a big part of studio lighting, and you need to pay close attention to both. You have quite a few things to keep in mind when setting up for a studio portrait, such as:

▶ **What kind of tone are you looking for?** Do you want the portrait to be bright and playful or somber and moody? Consider these elements, and set up the appropriate lighting and background.

▶ **Do you want to use props?** Sometimes having a prop in the shot can add interest to an otherwise bland portrait.

▶ **What kind of background is best for your shot?** The background is crucial to the mood and/or setting of the shot. For example, when shooting a *high-key* or brightly lit portrait, you must have a bright, colored background. You can also use props in the background to evoke a feeling or specific place.

▶ **What type of lighting will achieve your mood?** Decide which lighting pattern (discussed in the next section) you are going to use, and light the background if needed.

Lighting Patterns

In this age of digital photography, classical portrait has almost been forgotten because most photographers these days aren't trained in the classic techniques of the great portrait photographers like Irving Penn, Cecil Beaton, and especially George Hurrell. These photographers used light to create amazing portraits instead of taking snapshots. Candid portraits have their time and place, but with the resolution of the D800, meticulous studio portraiture should make a comeback.

As a studio portrait photographer your job is to control where the shadows fall on the face of the subject. If you don't control the shadows it can make your subject's face look less than flattering, with shadows falling in strange places. Another thing you need to consider when shooting studio portraits is controlling how soft or hard the light is. Types of lighting were covered in Chapter 5; here we are going to deal with lighting specifically for portraits, but most of the lighting essentials still apply.

There are two main types of lighting — broad lighting and short lighting. Broad lighting occurs when your main light is illuminating the side of the subject that is facing toward you. Short lighting occurs when your main light is illuminating the side of the subject that is facing away from you.

Whether you use broad lighting or short lighting depends on the subject's facial structure. Broad lighting tends to make facial structures look wider and short lighting can make the subject's face look thinner. Again, it's specific to each person, so I suggest when shooting portraits that you try finding the best fit for his or her face.

In Figure 9.1 on the left side, Amber is lit with broad lighting and on the right side I used short lighting. In my opinion, broad lighting works better with Amber's facial structure.

9

9.1 The left side of the picture shows broad lighting and the right side is an example of short lighting. Taken with a Nikon 28-70mm f/2.8D lens zoomed to 70mm for 1/200 seconds at f/10, ISO 400.

In addition to broad and short lighting, there are five major lighting patterns in portrait photography and each of them can be used with a short or broad lighting technique with the exception of shadowless and butterfly, which are straight-on lighting approaches.

▶ **Shadowless.** This is when your main light and your fill light are at equal ratios. Set up a light at 45 degrees on both sides of your model. This type of light can be very flattering, although it can lack moodiness and drama. You can also use one large light source pointed directly at the model.

▶ **Butterfly or Hollywood glamour.** This type of lighting is mostly used in glamour photography. The name is derived from the butterfly shape of the shadow that the nose casts on the upper lip. You achieve this type of lighting by positioning the main light directly above and in front of your model.

9.2 Shadowless lighting. Taken with a 50mm f/1.4 lens for 1/60 second at f/16, ISO 640.

9.3 Butterfly lighting. Taken with a 28-70mm f/2.8 lens zoomed to 56mm for 1/200 second at f/10, ISO 400.

▶ **Loop or Paramount.** This is one of the most commonly used lighting techniques for portraits. Paramount Studios used this pattern so extensively in Hollywood's golden age that this lighting pattern became synonymous with the studio's name. This lighting pattern is achieved by placing the main light at a 15-degree angle to the face, making sure to keep the light high enough that the shadow cast by the nose is at a downward angle and not horizontal.

▶ **Rembrandt.** The famous painter Rembrandt van Rijn used this dramatic lighting pattern extensively. It's a moody pattern achieved from using less fill light. The light is placed at a 45-degree angle and aimed a little bit down at the subject. Again, I emphasize using little or no fill light. This pattern is epitomized by a small triangle of light underneath one eye of the subject.

9

9.4 Loop, or Paramount, lighting. Taken with a 28-70mm f/2.8 lens zoomed to 70mm for 1/200 second at f/8, ISO 200.

9.5 Rembrandt lighting. Taken with a 28-70mm f/2.8 lens zoomed to 70mm for 1/200 second at f/8, ISO 200.

▶ **Split.** This is another dramatic pattern that benefits from little or no fill light. You can do this by simply placing the main light at a 90-degree angle to the model.

9.6 Split lighting. Taken with a 28-70mm f/2.8 lens zoomed to 70mm for 1/200 second at f/10, ISO 400.

Indoor Portraits

As opposed to a studio setting, sometimes you may be called to do a standard indoor shoot. This happens a lot if you work with busy clients who don't have time to come to your studio or for you to set up a lot of lighting equipment. I often get these types of shoots when shooting executives. Often, the light inside offices is dim and lifeless. To get a great portrait you need to add some depth.

The easiest and quickest way to set up a shoot like this is to get the subject next to a window. Windows are the best and most accessible light source available in a pinch. The window acts as a diffuser and gives a great soft light that's perfect for portraits. Having a reflector also helps to add a little fill light if you need it. Having an assistant helps, but I generally use a Photoflex light disc holder.

For example, in Figure 9.7, I simply placed Amber next to a window, had a reflector set up to add some fill and snapped off this shot. One shot and we were done. Quick and easy with about a 5-minute setup.

If you're on a tight schedule and there are no windows available, bounce flash works in a pinch. You can use a shoe-mounted Speedlight and bounce it off the wall or the ceiling, I prefer to stand the subject next to a wall and bounce off that if possible. Or you can use the built-in flash as a commander and take the Speedlight off-camera holding it in your hand and aiming the light where you want it. This works best when using a diffuser if you are pointing the flash straight at the subject, but I still prefer to bounce it. Just be aware, holding the flash in one hand and camera in the other hand, will make your camera a little shakier.

For Figure 9.8, I simply used my SB-910 with the head tilted up to 60 degrees with the bounce card pulled out to help fill in the eyes and provide a bit of a catchlight in the eyes.

When the light is poor and no window is available, the best option is to use the built-in flash as a commander and use an off-camera remote Speedlight on a stand with a diffuser such as an umbrella. This is a quick setup and is about as close to a studio setting as you can get while being on location.

9.7 Window lighting. Taken with a 50mm f/1.4 lens for 1/60 second at f/1.4, ISO 400.

9.8 Bounce flash portrait. Taken with a 28-70mm f/2.8 lens zoomed to 70mm for 1/60 second at f/2.8, ISO 200.

Backlighting

An old adage in photography is to keep the sun to your back. While in general this is a good idea when photographing most subjects, sometimes backlighting adds an interesting twist on portraits — it can introduce lens flare, reduced contrast, and other special effects. This is a technique that a lot of editorial fashion photographers have been using lately.

It's much more interesting than your standard frontlighting portrait and can give outstanding results if done correctly. The key to shooting backlit portraits is spot metering. Here I spot metered on Doa's face and allowed the sun to shine in at her right shoulder adding a bit of softness and reducing the contrast.

Outdoor Portraits

When you shoot portraits outdoors, the problems that you encounter are usually the exact opposite of the problems you have when you shoot indoors. The light tends to be too bright, causing the shadows on your subject to be too dark. This results in an image with too much contrast.

In order to combat this contrast problem, you can use your flash. I know that this sounds counterintuitive; you're probably thinking, "If I have too much light, why should I add more?" Using the flash in the bright sunlight fills in the dark shadows, resulting in a more evenly exposed image. This technique, shown in Figure 9.9, is known as fill flash.

Another way to combat images that have too much contrast when you're shooting outdoors is to have someone hold a diffusion panel over your model or move your model into a shaded area, such as under a tree or a porch. This helps block the direct sunlight, providing you with a nice, soft light for your portrait.

9.9 In this figure you can see what a little fill flash can do to improve the shadow detail. I simply used the built-in flash set to TTL-BL to add the fill light.

In Figure 9.10, I simply placed Erick in the shade of a building and used some palmetto trees to add a bit of interest in the background. Always remember to keep an eye on the background when shooting on location. You never know when a person might wander into the scene or a car may drive through the background. Be conscious of everything in the frame before tripping the shutter.

9.10 Diffuse light portrait. Taken with an 85mm f/1.8 lens for 1/500 second at f/1.8, ISO 100.

CHAPTER 10

Product Photography

Product photography is a huge genre and can encompass almost anything — from the tiniest microchip to something as large as an automobile. The light scenarios are vast and can include available light all the way up to elaborate lighting setups with dozens of strobes, reflectors, gobos, and scrims.

Professional product photographers are paid enormous amounts of money because companies need their images to look flawless in magazines and billboards. Of course, although most readers of this book aren't going to be photographing a Mercedes Benz advertisement, you can still benefit from knowing about the most basic techniques to get started.

Even a well-used guitar can make for great product photography.

Studio and Advertising

This type of photography is meant to showcase a product to make it look its best. The images must be flawless and almost always require a lighting setup. Advertising images are almost always shot on a clean seamless backdrop. This leaves the scene uncluttered and ensures that the product isn't in competition with anything else in the shot.

Commercial advertising photographers generally use a shooting table with translucent white or clear Plexiglas that fits into the table and sweeps up for a seamless appearance. The translucent Plexiglas allows you to shoot through it so you can get a soft backlight or underlight that is especially useful for shooting glass, crystal, or clear objects, although you can use traditional lighting methods for almost any type of subject.

A shooting table is necessary if you plan on doing a lot of high-end product photography. A small to medium shooting table can cost from $300-$1000, but is definitely worth it.

Figure 10.1 shows what is called a *black-line glass* shot. The bottle was photographed using Speedlight shot through the translucent white Plexiglas providing backlighting. A white reflector was used to add some highlights. The bottle itself was spot-metered and 1 stop of exposure compensation was added to ensure that the background was totally blown out to white.

On the opposite end of the spectrum you can also use what's called *white-line glass* in which you use a dark background and two lights bounced from white reflectors on each side to highlight the edges of the glass.

10.1 This figure shows a black-line glass studio shot. ISO 200 f/8 at 1/30 sec. using a 70-200mm f/2.8 lens zoomed to 100mm.

Of course, not everyone is going to go into the high-end advertising photography business so it's not necessary to have a shooting table and Plexiglas. You can make a similar setup using seamless paper and a regular table. Seamless backdrops are available in hundreds of colors and can work for almost any product.

> **TIP** A cheaper alternative to buying a roll of seamless paper is to use poster board available at any local art supply store.

You can usually pack a few small Speedlights and a couple of stands, umbrellas, and a reflector and you'll be set.

> **TIP** Using a small piece of Plexiglas underneath your subject can add a nice reflection and is an inexpensive way to mimic a Plexiglas sweep.

Using simple backgrounds is usually best: whites, blacks, and grays work great. Figure 10.2 is a shot of my old Contax Quartz 135 with Zeiss lens (and cool red faux snake-skin) on a simple white background. Starting out, you'll often be shooting simple products like these. For example, one of my first professional jobs was shooting small products such as key chains, hats, and other sports paraphernalia on white backgrounds for online websites.

There are a few easy ways to get a shot like this. For Figure 10.2, I simply used an SB-910 Speedlight placed camera right and bounced it from an umbrella onto the Contax. At camera left I placed a silver reflector to fill in the shadows a bit. The side-lighting allowed the texture of the faux snakeskin to show with more depth. I controlled the off-camera flash using the Commander mode of the built-in flash. I also set the SB-910 to TTL +1.3EV to keep the white background from being underexposed.

For a softer light, some photographers like to place one larger light directly above the product and shoot through a softbox or diffusion panel. This is a great approach for subjects that don't need a lot of contrast, such as clothing or food.

Shooting metallic objects and things such as jewelry you must be very aware of your lighting placement. Metal reflects a lot more than you may realize so keeping an eye on reflections is very important. Sometimes *adding* reflections to metallic objects is what you need to do to give them a 3-D effect. Having an assistant hold a strip of white or black in a strategic position can add specular highlights or dark shadows to add depth. Shooting *tethered* (connected directly to your computer) and previewing your images closely helps.

Another alternative is to use a light tent, which is essentially a box made of translucent nylon. One of the nice things about a light tent is that the translucent material softens the light so you can use a Speedlight without an umbrella or softbox as you would have to do when shooting with seamless paper. These types of setups are great for shooting small products.

10

10.2 This figure shows a standard product shot on white seamless background. ISO 400, f/16 at 1/125 sec. with a 70-200mm f/2.8 lens zoomed to 200mm.

Sometimes shooting in a studio requires building a set or adding things to the background so that the subject appears as if it's in a relevant place. Usually the background is out of the focus plane but still gives the subject somewhere to *live*, so to speak. In Figure 10.3, I simply placed this pack of candy cigarettes on a table in the office of my studio. Everything in the background was existing décor except for the ice cream sign in the foreground, which I borrowed from my neighbor who specializes in re-creating vintage-style signs. I used two lights for this setup: an SB-600 with a tungsten filter shot through an umbrella to light the background at camera left just behind the subject, and an SB-800 at camera right with no filter and a grid screen to focus the light on the subject. This is known as mixed lighting, and in some cases is frowned upon but it often works in product photography to make the subject stand out.

One thing you need to know about the D800 and especially the D800E is that with the high amount of resolution, focus is unforgiving. You need to check, double-check, triple-check that your focus is spot on. When shooting in a studio situation a tripod is highly recommended, as is being aware of the diffraction limits of your lenses. Using an aperture somewhere between f/8 and f/11 is recommended for most lenses although at times you my need to stop down more to achieve a deeper depth of field

10.3 **This shot was set up in the office of my studio, which I used as a set. ISO 200 at f/2, 1/250 second with a 35mm f/1.4 lens.**

Food

Food photography is a type of photography that can be shot using an elaborate setup, or it can be photographed just as effectively using nothing more than simple window light.

When you see advertising shots of food for major restaurants, what you are generally looking at are highly planned shots with lots of lighting, art directors, and food stylists. As it is unlikely you are going to be working in that kind of situation as you are getting started with this type of photography, I am going to focus on how to make food look great without having a food stylist, a team of people, and a large budget to pull off.

While a commercially shot food product may look fresh, it's often not because the shoot takes place over a number of hours. A food stylist is a person that is paid to make the food look fresh. Personally, I recommend shooting the food while it's actually fresh. Window light is my preferred method; when shooting food on location (at the restaurant, for example), I almost always use window light and a fast aperture lens. However, sometimes I've been caught in a bind and used a Speedlight.

The shot in Figure 10.4 of venison meatloaf with garlic mashed potatoes and asparagus was shot using only window light. When I was hired by a local food magazine doing a feature on the lunch menu of a new restaurant, I made sure to ask to be seated next to a window. As previously noted, window light is amazing — soft yet directional, which is perfect for showing off food, and still allows the texture to show through.

10.4 This was a shot taken for a local food magazine. ISO 1600 at f/2 at 1/15 second with a 35mm f/1.4 lens.

TIP Bring along a small reflector to add a little fill light if needed.

Sometimes when you're on an assignment, you get requests for certain shots after you are already onsite. For Figure 10.5, I was sent to cover a party and got a request to shoot some of the food. Window light wasn't available (in any case it was dark outside), and all I had was an SB-900 and my camera. I used the SB-900 on-camera and bounced the flash off of the wall to soften the light. Bounce flash is one of the easiest and best ways to get usable low-light images in a pinch. Remember that you will not always be prepared when sent on assignment, and the key is to be able to get the shot in less-than-ideal circumstances. I do, however, always carry a flash diffuser, which is indispensable in all kinds of situations.

10.5 I used bounce flash to capture this photo of the sushi being served at a party event I was covering. ISO 800 at f/5.6 at 1/80 second with a 24-120mm f/4 lens zoomed to 105mm.

Small Products/Macro

Oftentimes you may have to shoot extremely small products such as coins, stamps, jewelry, or the like. When shooting extremely small products you may have to resort to macro or close-up photography.

A macro shot is determined by the ratio at which the lens projects the image onto the sensor. The relative size of the magnification of the subject is defined as a ratio. The true definition of a macro shot is when the ratio is 1:1, which means that the image projected onto the sensor is the same size as the subject.

Most true macro lenses allow you to focus close enough to get a 1:1 ratio, but some lens manufacturers use the term macro loosely and designate a lens as macro when it can focus down to 1:2 (half-size) or even 1:4 (quarter-size) on some of the longer lenses. That being said, a lens that focuses down to 1:2 isn't too bad and can get you some decent close-ups. In the strictest terms any thing less than 1:1 is actually termed close-up photography.

The most difficult aspect of macro photography is dealing with the reduced depth of field. The closer you focus on the subject and the higher the magnification ratio the less depth of field you get at any given aperture. This shallow depth of field is a double-edged sword so to speak. On one hand, the extreme shallow depth of field allows you to isolate your subject from the background and use selective focus. On the other hand, the shallow depth of field can also make it difficult to maintain focus when handholding so a tripod is a necessity. The shallow depth of field can also make it difficult to get everything you need in focus, so keep in mind that you may need to use a smaller aperture and use the depth-of-field preview to check the depth of focus before shooting.

You must also consider lighting when shooting small objects. When focusing very close, it's hard to get directional light without the camera and/or lens blocking it. You may need to use a ring flash to get on-axis lighting to really highlight the details.

Figure 10.6 shows two shots of the same coin. The shot on the left was taken with available light, and although you can see some details the coin has relatively low contrast. The image on the right was shot with a ring flash. The on-axis lighting really highlights the fine details of the coin. Putting the flash around the lens allows the light to surround the optical axis of the lens.

The settings I used for the flash were very simple. I used Matrix metering and set the flash to TTL. After a couple of test shots I decided to dial down the flash exposure –1EV. You will often find that when photographing up close with a ring flash you will need to reduce the output a bit to avoid overexposure.

For the camera settings, I chose to use Aperture Priority when shooting with the available light as shown in the image on the left of Figure 10.6. I set the aperture to f/5.6. For a shot like this, using a small aperture isn't absolutely necessary. The camera was on a tripod pointed at a 90-degree angle to the coin. Because coins are thin a deep depth of field isn't required. When shooting something with a lot of depth at an angle, you want to maximize your depth of field.

10.6 These two images show the difference on-axis lighting can make in a small product macro shot. ISO 400 at f/5.6 at 1/80 second with a Nikon 1-5mm f/2.8G VR lens.

If you don't have (or don't want to buy) a ring flash and you have an additional Speedlight such as the SB-400, SB-600, SB-800, or SB-900, you can get your light on-axis by using an inexpensive off-camera TTL flash cord such as the Nikon SC-27 or the Commander mode of the built-in flash. This cord allows you to hold the Speedlight next to the lens. I often use this technique because the one-sided light adds nice depth to some images allowing textures to be highlighted.

10

CHAPTER 11

Stock Photography

If you've invested a substantial amount of money in a professional camera like the D800 you're probably interested in making a little income to recoup some of your expenditure. Not everyone who buys a D800 is going to be interested in becoming a full-time professional photographer, but there are ways to make a little cash on the side to help your hobby pay for your equipment. One of the easiest ways is by selling stock photography.

Stock photography comes in many different forms including food.

Stock Photography Overview

Stock photography is a collection of images that are used by photo buyers, art directors, web designers, advertising agencies, and the like for all kinds of uses: magazines, books, ads, brochures both electronically and in print, or even TV. So, as you can imagine, it can include almost any type of photography conceivable. These images can be bought for a one-time fee and used over and over however the buyer see fit. This is called royalty-free, or the image can be leased for a usage fee wherein the photographer retains the rights and the buyer uses the image for a specific time and usage.

There are two types of uses for stock photography: creative and editorial. Creative stock photography is generally used for advertising campaigns and almost anything that has to do with business from mailers, pamphlets, billboards, packaging, or any number of things. Editorial stock photography generally deals with current events, entertainment, documentary, and even archival photographs. Editorial stock is used for mostly magazines, books, and sometimes television or film documentaries.

Creative stock

Creative stock is more conceptual in form. The photographer thinks of an idea or concept of images and sets out to make these images a reality. These can be still-life images or lifestyle images. Lifestyle photography is about the hottest type of stock these days. It's very lucrative because the images can be set up for almost anything. The core goal of creative stock photography is to brand and sell a product.

Lifestyle photography

Lifestyle photography is a loosely interpreted term that can mean almost anything. Lifestyle photography shows a brand style or attitude. It features people or groups of people in settings involved in some sort of staged action (which is usually supposed to appear as if it was not staged). Think of the ads that you see for pharmaceuticals or medical products. They often feature vague settings of people enjoying themselves, implying the medicine makes them feel good, or models portraying medical personnel, which implies that you can trust that product. Lifestyle photography can feature families, medical personnel, or even extreme sports types. Basically, this form of photography uses imagery that groups of people can identify with and may or may not feature a product of some sort.

> **TIP** Be sure to get model releases for any stock images with people in them.

Basically, this is how it works:

▶ **Conceive a concept.** This is basically where you conceive an idea. Think of things like a trip to the beach, renovating a house, gardening, and so on.

▶ **Create a shot list.** Take the idea and think of things that would be happening for the concept. For example, unpacking moving boxes, painting, and putting up shelves when moving into a new house. A shot list should consist of a various number of different shots and you should also list what kind of angles you want, the depth-of-field effect you're after, and whether you want a wide-angle or tele-photo shot.

▶ **Setup the location.** Get your pieces into place. This consists of finding or build-ing a set and hiring models and putting together wardrobe and props.

▶ **Execute the shot.** Exactly what you'd expect: Shoot the photos.

▶ **Edit the images.** Edit out the weakest images and post-processing for the ones that you have selected as keepers.

Lifestyle photography is an ambitious endeavor and can get very expensive if you want to make a serious go of it. Of course, you can make it much simpler and do smaller shoots, but the more variety you have of different styles the more likely you will be to sell your images.

Figure 11.1 shows a typical lifestyle shot. This shot was basically a simple setup con-sisting of a model enjoying a glass of wine. This shot is intended to portray a poetic and evocative feeling or it can be used to convey an artistic feeling. Using the Rule of Thirds also allows plenty of space for text to be added to the image.

Product

Lifestyle photography, more often than not, has people in it, but you don't necessarily need people to portray a lifestyle. You can portray a lifestyle simply by making a still-life setup that evokes a feeling or an attitude. Figure 11.2 is a stock photography-type shot that evokes a feeling of the Southwest by portraying a cold margarita on a bartop and a cowboy hat in the background blurred by the shallow depth of field but still recognizable.

Although probably less lucrative than traditional lifestyle photography, this type of pho-tography is often much more accessible for most people. All you really need is a good concept and a few props.

11

11.1 This figure shows a typical lifestyle shot. Shot with 50mm f/1.4 lens at f/2, 1/10 second at ISO 1600.

11.2 This figure shows a still-life-type of stock photography shot. Shot with a Sigma 17-35mm f/2.8-4 lens zoomed to 28mm at f/3.5. 1/20 second at ISO 640.

Animals

There are quite a few stock agencies that deal with pet and animal photography. More often than not these are clean pet portraits — the types done on a plain background to allow ad agencies to drop in text or to easily drop in another background if desired.

Figure 11.3 is a stock-type shot of my dog Henrietta. This shot was very easy to execute, and when setting up this type of shot you can get a variety of different shots by adding props or different poses. I've seen some shots similar to this at stock photo websites that feature dogs with party hats, wigs, bones, or many other types of props.

11.3 A stock shot of a Boston terrier. The model is my dog Henrietta. Shot with a Nikon 50mm f/1.4 at f/5.6. 1/500 second at ISO 100.

Editorial stock

This type of photography is used for books, magazines, newspapers, and so on. Editorial stock isn't necessarily used for selling a product, but is more likely to be used to illustrating a story or simply to show a current event. This type of photography can also be conceptual or in laymen's terms, "art photography" which may or may not make a point, but serves as eye candy to interest a person enough to take a look at the accompanying material.

Documentary

Documentary photography consists of a multitude of subjects. Food, travel, nature and wildlife, and science and technology are some of the types of images covered. These images are often used in feature stories of magazines and newspapers when it's not considered news or current events. I've sold many documentary stock images ranging from a shot of a crowd at a concert hall to a photo of a chilidog I took at a famous hot dog shop in Pittsburgh, Pennsylvania.

11

11.4 This image was licensed by a food magazine featuring famous restaurants in Pittsburgh, Pennsylvania. Taken with a Sigma 17-35mm f/2.8-4 lens at f/4 zoomed to 35mm. 1/320 second at ISO 400.

Current events and entertainment

This type of photography can include everything from newsworthy events, such as politicians giving speeches, to movie premiers, sporting events, concerts, and more.

Figure 11.5 is a shot of two famous guitar players from Austin attending the same event: Ray Benson from Asleep at the Wheel, and Gary Clark Jr. I happened to run into them while they were chatting about guitars and asked to snap a photo. This is a good example of the type of image that when placed with a stock agency, may be picked up by trade magazines or movie or celebrity websites.

Stock Photography Licensing

There are two distinct types of licensing available to the purchasers of stock images: royalty-free and rights-managed. What does licensing mean exactly? It means that you own your images and you grant the right to use them to a buyer for specific applications and time limits. The price is usually determined by a number of factors that are explained in the following sections.

11.5 . Ray Benson and Gary Clark Jr. attending a benefit for a local Austin musician. Taken with a Sigma 17-35mm f/2.8-4 lens at f/5.6 zoomed to 35mm. 1/4 second at ISO 400.

Royalty-free

This is the cheapest way for someone to obtain a stock image. Royalty-free doesn't mean that anyone is free to use the image as they see fit. The buyer must pay for the image. The payment is a one-time fee that allows the purchaser of the image to use it multiple times without paying additional royalties to the copyright owner.

One of the most attractive things about royalty-free images to buyers is that the price is generally based on file size, meaning that if the buyer wants to use it on a blog at 72 dpi the image is usually very cheap, and a buyer who wants to use it on the web for 1000 blogs doesn't need to pay additional fees.

11

One of the downsides to royalty-free images (for the buyer at least) is that the images are usually licensed under what's known as a *nonexclusive license*, meaning that same image could be licensed to a competitor and used for the same application. This is an upside to the photographer because multiple small fees for an image can make almost as much (sometimes more) money than a one-time fee for exclusive licensing that is more expensive.

Rights-managed

These types of images get more bang for the buck for both the photographer and the buyer than royalty-free images. Licensing these types of images costs more than the royalty-free photos. The price is determined by quite a few factors, which usually include, but aren't limited to:

▶ **Usage.** What is the image going to be used for? It could be advertising as in a billboard or print ad in a magazine; corporate, for example, an image for a company newsletter or website; or, editorial, as in a newspaper article.

▶ **Size.** What size with the image appear? A billboard sized-image is worth more than a postage stamp-sized image buried in the back pages of the Sunday paper.

▶ **Print run.** How many times is the photo going to be used for the specific usage? For example, a small local paper will have a print run of a few thousand whereas a national magazine will print a million or more. Of course, the larger the print run, the larger the fee.

▶ **Duration.** How long will the image be displayed? It could be a daily paper, a bimonthly magazine, and so on.

▶ **Geographical location.** In what area will the image be used? This can refer to the specific country the image is to be used in or can be broken down into smaller areas. For example, if the image is to be used nationwide it will be worth more than if it's going to be used in a small town.

▶ **Exclusivity.** How exclusive will the buyer's usage be? Rights-managed images aren't necessarily exclusive. The buyer is usually guaranteed that the image won't be used by a competitor or in the same geographical location. This really all depends on the contract.

There are other factors that go into determining the price including the number of images, whether the buyer has purchased your images previously, if the buyer has a contract with the agency, and the current market rate.

Breaking into the Market

Right about now you're probably thinking, "Stock photography sounds like an easy way to make a little money with my photography. How do I get started?" One easy way is to start your own website, post your images there, and hope a photo buyer sees them. The problem is that photo buyers need to know about you. You need marketing.

Probably the easiest way to start marketing yourself is to get a Flickr account. Flickr has made a deal with Getty Images that allows members to opt into a Request for License option through Getty Images. Getty also has a team of editors that looks through images on Flickr and selects them to be featured in the Flickr Collection by Getty Images.

You don't need to opt in to the Getty Request for License. I've had many requests to license my images from Flickr and I'm not signed up to the Getty program. Figure 11.4 was found on Flickr, and I recently sold an image found on Flickr to HBO that appears at the end of the opening credits to the TV show *Luck*. Be wary though. Most of the e-mails I get from Flickr are people wanting to use my images for free. Personally, I don't allow my images to be used unless I'm compensated. I've spent a lot of money on my gear and I can't pay the rent with a photo credit.

Stock photography used to be a thriving business that had many agencies representing the work of a select amount of professional photographers. But the advent of digital photography and the subsequent affordability of pro-level digital SLR cameras has turned the industry upside-down. In the 1990s as digital photography boomed and the Internet made it easy to browse images online larger companies began buying out the smaller companies to create a few huge stock photography agencies. These two companies are Getty Images and Corbis (which is owned by Microsoft's Bill Gates). My work is licensed through Corbis, which has helped me place images in many national and international outlets.

Along with marketing, these agencies also handle the negotiations of the sale of the image leaving you free to create your photos. This comes at a cost. First, the agency usually sets the price of your images. Second, the agency takes a cut, usually to the tune of a little bit more than 50 percent. That's a pretty small price to pay for national exposure, though.

The best thing would be to get on with one of the super agencies. This is where the national magazines and ad agencies shop. It's pretty simple to apply to them, but you need to have a top-notch portfolio and usually many, many years of experience behind you. That's not say you don't have a chance at getting on with one of them, but it's probably best to start small. There are a number of agencies known as micro-stock agencies (these agencies are often subsidiaries of the big two, so it's a good way to get your foot in the door). Micro-stock agencies are different than the big guys in that most of their images are culled from the Internet, they accept small amounts of stock photography from a large amount of photographers including amateurs, and they sell royalty-free images at very low prices.

> **NOTE** Micro-stock agencies generally keep between 60 to 80 percent of the royalty fees of each image sold.

Micro-stock agencies work on the premise that small businesses and people wanting to buy images for personal use don't want to pay the larger rates of the bigger agencies and don't need to worry about exclusivity. They just want good images at fair prices.

Most micro-stock agencies don't accept all photographers that submit. They review the work, but they don't expect you to have a huge portfolio. Here's a list of a few of the most popular micro-stock sites:

- ▶ **istockphoto.** This is one of the largest micro-stock agencies with more 5 million images for sale. This company was purchased by Getty in 2006. You must apply with three sample images and take a short quiz before you can start to submit stock.

- ▶ **shutterstock.** This is another large micro-stock agency boasting almost 8 million images for sale. Shutterstock pays a flat fee of 25 cents per image with an increase of 5 cents per image once you reach $500 in sales. You must fill out a questionnaire before you're allowed to submit. Images are reviewed before they are posted to the site.

- ▶ **fotolia.** This micro-stock agency operates a little differently than the others. It pays 50 percent and allows the photographer to set the price. You must become a member to submit photos.

Essential Photography Concepts

This appendix offers a quick refresher course on a few of the most important concepts of photography. This section is meant for people relatively new to dSLR cameras. Although advanced users may be familiar with these concepts, there still may be some new information here for you as well. For example, having a grasp on concepts such as depth of field and composition are the building blocks of creating great images.

Exposure

By definition, exposure as it relates to digital photography is the total amount of light collected by the camera's sensor during a single *shutter cycle*. A shutter cycle occurs when the Shutter Release button is pressed, the shutter opens, closes, and resets. One shutter cycle occurs for each image (with the exception of multiple exposures, of course). An exposure is made of three elements that are interrelated. Each depends on the others to create a proper exposure. If one of the elements changes, the others must increase or decrease proportionally or you will no longer have an equivalent exposure. The following are the elements you need to consider:

▶ **Shutter speed.** The shutter speed determines the length of time the sensor is exposed to light.

▶ **ISO sensitivity.** The ISO setting you choose influences your camera's sensitivity to light.

▶ **Aperture/f-stop.** How much light reaches the sensor of your camera is controlled by the aperture, or f-stop. Each camera has an adjustable opening on the lens. As you change the aperture (the opening), you allow more or less light to reach the sensor.

Shutter speed

Shutter speed is the amount of time light entering from the lens is allowed to expose the image sensor. Obviously, if the shutter is open longer, more light can reach the sensor. The shutter speed can also affect the sharpness of your images. When hand-holding the camera and using a longer focal-length lens, a faster shutter speed is often required to counteract camera shake from hand movement, which can cause blur (this is the effect that VR lenses were made to combat). When taking photographs in low light, a slow shutter speed is often required, which will also cause blur from camera shake and/or fast-moving subjects.

The shutter speed can also be used to effectively show motion in photography. Panning, or moving the camera horizontally with a moving subject while using a slower shutter speed, can cause the background to blur while keeping the subject in focus. This is an effective way to portray motion in a still image. On the opposite end, using a fast shutter speed can freeze action such as the splash of the wave of a surfer, which can also give the illusion of motion in a still photograph.

Shutter speeds are indicated in seconds, long shutter speeds in whole seconds and short shutter speeds in fractions of seconds. Common shutter speeds (from slow to fast) in 1-stop increments are: 1 second, 1/2, 1/4, 1/8, 1/15, 1/30, 1/60, 1/125, 1/500, 1/1000, and so on. Increasing or decreasing shutter speed by one setting doubles or halves the exposure, respectively. The D800 allows you to adjust the shutter speed in 1/3 stops.

ISO

The ISO sensitivity number also tells how sensitive to light the medium is — in this case the CMOS sensor. The higher the ISO number, the more sensitive it is and the less light you need to take a photograph. For example, you might choose an ISO setting of 100 on a bright, sunny day when you are photographing outside because you have plenty of light. However, on a cloudy day you may want to consider an ISO of 400 or higher to make sure your camera captures all the available light. This allows you to use a faster shutter speed should it be appropriate to the subject you are photographing.

It is helpful to know that each ISO setting is twice as sensitive to light as the previous setting. For example, at ISO 400, your camera is twice as sensitive to light as it is at ISO 200. This means it needs only half the light at ISO 400 that it needs at ISO 200 to achieve the same exposure.

As with shutter speeds, the D800 allows you to adjust the ISO in 1/3-stop increments (100, 125, 160, 200...), which enables you to fine-tune your ISO to reduce the noise inherent with higher ISO settings.

Aperture

Aperture is the size of the opening in the lens that determines the amount of light that reaches the image sensor. The aperture is controlled by a metal diaphragm that operates in a similar fashion to the iris of your eye. Aperture is expressed as f-stop numbers, such as f/2.8, f/5.6, and f/8. Here are a couple of important things to know about aperture:

▶ **Smaller f-numbers equal wider apertures.** A small f-stop such as f/2.8 opens the lens so more light reaches the sensor. If you have a wide aperture (opening), the amount of time the shutter needs to stay open to let light into the camera decreases.

▶ **Larger f-numbers equal narrower apertures.** A large f-stop such as f/11 closes the lens so less light reaches the sensor. If you have a narrow aperture (opening), the amount of time the shutter needs to stay open to let light into the camera increases.

I am often asked why the numbers of the aperture seem to be counterintuitive. The answer is relatively simple: The numbers are actually derived from ratios that translate into fractions. The f-number is defined by the focal length of the lens divided by the actual diameter of the aperture opening. The simplest way to look at it is to put a 1 on top of the f-number as the numerator. For the simplest example, take a 50mm f/2 lens (okay, Nikon doesn't actually make a 50mm f/2 anymore, but pretend for a minute). Take the aperture number, f/2. If you add the 1 as numerator you get 1/2. This indicates that the aperture opening is half the diameter of the focal length, 25mm. So at f/4 the effective diameter of the aperture is 12.5mm. It's a pretty simple concept once you break it down.

NOTE The terms aperture and f-stop are interchangeable.

As with ISO and shutter speed there are standard settings for aperture, each of which is 1 stop difference from the other. The standard f-numbers are f/1.4, f/2, f/2.8, f/4, f/5.6, f/8, f/11, f/16, and f/22. At first glance these may appear to be a random assortment of numbers, but they aren't. Upon closer inspection you will notice that every other number is a multiple of 2. Broken down even further you will find that each stop is a multiple of 1.4. This is where the standard f-stop numbers are derived from. Starting out with f/1, multiply by 1.4 and you get f/1.4, again multiply by 1.4 you get 2, multiply by 1.4 you get 2.8, and so on.

Fine-Tuning Your Exposure

Your camera's meter may not always be completely accurate. There are many variables in most scenes, and large bright or dark areas can trick the meter into thinking a scene is brighter or darker than it really is, causing the image to be over- or underexposed. One example of this is in a really bright situation such as the beach on a sunny day or a snowy scene in winter. The camera's meter sees all of the brightness in the scene and underexposes to try to preserve detail in the highlights causing the main subject and most of the image to be dark and lacking in contrast. Snowy scenes present a special problem because the snow appears gray and dingy. The general rule of thumb in this situation is to add 1 to 2 stops of exposure compensation.

Similar to the ISO and shutter speed settings the Nikon D800 also allows you to set the aperture in 1/3-stop increments.

TIP In photographic vernacular, *opening up* refers to going from a smaller to a larger aperture, and *stopping down* refers to going from a larger to a smaller aperture.

The most common reason why a certain aperture is selected is to control the depth of field or how much of the image is in focus. Using a wider aperture (f/1.4 to f/4) gives you a shallow depth of field that allows you to exercise *selective focus;* this allows you to focus on a certain subject in the image while allowing the rest to fall out of focus. Conversely, using a small aperture (f/11 to f/32) maximizes your depth of field allowing you to get everything in focus. Using a wider aperture is generally preferable when shooting portraits to blur out the background and draw attention to the subject and a smaller aperture is generally used when photographing landscapes to ensure that the whole scene is in focus.

Another way that the aperture setting is used, oddly enough, is to control the shutter speed. You can select a wide aperture to allow in a lot of light so that you can use a faster shutter speed to freeze action. On the opposite end of the spectrum you can use a smaller aperture to be sure that your shutter speed is slower.

Exposure compensation

Exposure compensation is a feature of the D800 that allows you to fine-tune the amount of exposure to vary from what is set by the camera's exposure meter. Although you can usually adjust the exposure of the image in your image-editing software (especially if you shoot RAW), it's best to get the exposure right in the camera. This ensures that you have the highest image quality, and it also saves you time in post-processing. If, after taking the photograph, you review it and it's too dark or too light, you can adjust the exposure compensation and retake the picture to get a better exposure. Exposure compensation is adjusted in EV (Exposure Value); 1 EV is equal to 1 stop of light. You adjust exposure compensation by pressing the Exposure Compensation (⊞) button, next to the Shutter Release button, and rotating the Main Command dial to the left for more exposure (+EV) or to the right for less exposure (-EV). Depending on your settings, the exposure compensation is adjusted in 1/3, 1/2, or 1 stop of light. You can change this setting in the Custom Settings menu (✐) b3.

You can adjust the exposure compensation up to +5 EV and down to -5 EV, which is a wide range of 10 stops. To remind you that exposure compensation has been set, the Exposure Compensation indicator is displayed on the top LCD control panel and the viewfinder display. It also appears on the rear LCD screen when the shooting info is being displayed.

> **CAUTION** Be sure to reset the exposure compensation to 0 after you finish to avoid unwanted over- or underexposure.

There are a few ways to get the exact exposure that you want. You can use the histogram to determine whether you need to add or subtract from your exposure. You can also use bracketing to take a number of exposures and choose the one that you think is best, or you can combine the bracketed images with different exposures to create one image using post-processing software.

Histograms

The easiest way to determine if you need to adjust the exposure compensation is to simply review your image. If it looks too dark, add some exposure compensation; if it's too bright, adjust the exposure compensation down. This, however, is not the most accurate method of determining how much exposure compensation to use. To accurately determine how much exposure compensation to add or subtract, look at the *histogram*. A histogram is a visual representation of the tonal values in your image. Think of it as a bar graph that charts the lights, darks, and midtones in your picture.

This range is broken down into 256 brightness levels from 0 (absolute black) to 255 (absolute white), with 128 coming in at middle or 18 percent gray. The more pixels there are at any given brightness value, the higher the bar. If there are no bars, then the image has no pixels in that brightness range.

NOTE The histogram displayed on the LCD screen is based on an 8-bit image. When working with 12- or 14-bit files using editing software, the histogram may be displayed with 4096 brightness levels for 12-bit or 16, 384 brightness levels for 14-bit.

The D800 offers four histogram views: the luminance histogram, which shows the brightness levels of the entire image; and separate histograms for each color channel — Red, Green, and Blue.

The most useful histogram for determining if your exposure needs adjusting is the luminance histogram. To display the luminance histogram, simply press the multi-selector up while viewing the image on the LCD screen. This displays a thumbnail of the current image, the shooting info, and a small luminance histogram. You can also view a larger version of the luminance histogram directly overlaid on the current image. You can set this up in the CSM f2 assigning this function to the multi-selector center button when in Playback mode.

To view the luminance histogram using the multi-selector center button, follow these steps:

1. **Press the Menu button (MENU) .**
2. **Use the multi-selector to select ✐ .**
3. **Use the multi-selector to highlight CSM f2, Controls.** Press the OK button (⊙) or the multi-selector right (▶) to view CSM f options.
4. **Use the multi-selector to highlight menu option f2 multi-selector center button and press ⊙ or ▶.**
5. **Choose Playback mode from the menu options by pressing the multi-selector down (▼), and then press ⊙ or ▶.**
6. **Choose Playback mode from the menu options and press ▶ to view options.**
7. **Select View histograms and press ⊙ or the multi-selector center button to save the setting.**

Once you've followed these steps, press the Playback button 🔍 to view an image and press the multi-selector center button to view the histogram.

Ideally, you want to expose your subject so that it falls right about in the middle of the tonal range, which is why your camera's meter exposes for 18 percent gray. If your histogram graph has most of the information bunched up on the left side, then your image is probably underexposed; if it's bunched up on the right side, then your image is probably overexposed. Ideally, with most average subjects that aren't bright white or extremely dark, you want to try to get your histogram to look sort of like a bell curve, with most of the tones in the middle range, tapering off as they get to the dark and light ends of the graph. But this is only for most average types of images. As with almost everything in photography, there are exceptions to the rule. If you take a photo of a dark subject on a dark background (a low-key image), then naturally your histogram will have most of the tones bunched up on the left side of the graph. Conversely, when you take a photograph of a light subject on a light background (a high-key image), the histogram will have most of the tones bunched up to the right.

The most important thing to remember is that there is no such thing as a perfect histogram. A histogram is just a factual representation of the tones in the image. The other important thing to remember is that although it's okay for the graph to be near one side or the other, you usually don't want your histogram to have spikes bumping up against the edge of the graph; this indicates your image has blown-out highlights (completely white, with no detail) or blocked-up shadow areas (completely black, with no detail).

Depth of Field

Depth of field is used in photography to control what the viewer sees. A shallow depth of field is used to isolate the subject from the background so that the viewer only focuses on the most important part of the image. Deep depth of field is used when you want the viewer to take in the entire scene as the subject.

When your lens focuses on a point, everything at that specific distance perpendicular to the camera lens is in focus. Everything behind and in front of that point is technically out of focus. The point where everything is in focus is called the focal plane. Because the acuity of human vision is limited we can't discern the minor blur that occurs directly in front of and behind the focal plane so to our way of seeing it is still sharp. This is what we call the *zone of acceptable sharpness,* or depth of field.

Depth of field is the distance range in a photograph in which all included portions of an image are acceptably sharp. There are few different factors that go into determining the depth of field; aperture and focus distance are the two predominant factors, and background distance also comes into play.

This zone of acceptable sharpness is based on the *circle of confusion*. The circle of confusion explained simply is the *largest blurred circle that is perceived by the human eye as acceptably sharp.*

> **NOTE** A few factors go into determining the size of the circle of confusion, such as visual acuity, viewing distance, and enlargement size.

The following list explains how each factor affects depth of field:

▶ **Aperture.** Circles of confusion are formed by light passing through the body of a lens. Changing the size of the circle of confusion is as easy as opening up or closing down your aperture. Therefore, when you open up the aperture, the circle of confusion is larger, resulting in decreased depth of field and a softer, more blurred background (and foreground). When the aperture is closed down, the circle of confusion is smaller, resulting in increased depth of field and causing everything in the image to appear sharp.

▶ **Focus distance.** When focusing on your subject the closer you get the larger the circle of confusion gets therefore the depth of field decreases. This is due to the way the rays of light converge through the lens elements.

Depth of field is usually referred to in two ways:

▶ **Shallow depth of field.** This results in an image where the subject is in sharp focus, but the background has a soft blur. You likely have seen it used frequently in portraits. Using a wide aperture, such as f/2.8, results in a subject that is sharp with a softer background. Using a shallow depth of field is a great way to get rid of distracting elements in the background of an image.

▶ **Deep depth of field.** This results in an image that is reasonably sharp from the foreground to the background. Using a narrow aperture, such as f/11, is ideal to keep photographs of landscapes or groups in focus throughout.

> **TIP** Remember, for a deep depth of field, you want a large f-number; for shallow depth of field, you want a small f-number.

A

A.1 An image with a shallow depth of field only has some of the image in focus. Taken at f/3.5 for 1/800 second at ISO 200.

A.2 An image with a deep depth of field has most of the image in focus. Taken at f/40 for 1/50 second at ISO 1600.

Rules of Composition

Photography, like any artistic discipline, has general rules. This isn't to say you need to follow all of the rules every time you take a photograph. These are really just general guidelines that when followed can make your images more powerful and interesting.

However, when you start out in photography, pay attention to the rules of composition. Eventually, you become accustomed to following the guidelines and it becomes second nature. At that point you no longer need to consult the rules of composition; you just inherently follow them.

One piece of advice that I was given while attending school was that it's important to know the rules of photography because when you know the rules it makes it easier to recognize when you can break them.

Keep it simple

Simplicity is invariably the key to creating a compelling image. If the viewer can't readily identify what the intended subject is, the image is confusing to the eye and it will wander off. The viewer will get bored and move on. Having too many competing elements in an image is distracting to the viewer.

Probably the most common technique for achieving simplicity in a photograph is using a shallow depth of field to isolate the subject from a background that may be busy. By causing the background to go out of focus the subject stands out better.

Changing your perspective is sometimes an easy way to change the background of your subject from busy to plain. Shooting from up high or down low can completely change the background of the same subject.

A.3 There's no question as to what the subject is in this photograph. Taken at f/3 for 1/160 second at ISO 800.

Simplicity in an image can speak volumes. Try to concentrate on removing any unnecessary elements to achieve simplicity.

Rule of Thirds

Beginners and snapshot photographers usually take the subject and place it right in the middle. This may seem like the obvious thing to do, but placing the subject off-center can make your images more interesting.

The Rule of Thirds is a compositional guideline that has been in use for centuries and has been followed by artists throughout history. Using the Rule of Thirds, you divide the image into nine equal parts using two equally spaced horizontal and vertical lines, kind of like a tic-tac-toe pattern. You want to place the main subject of the image at an intersection, as illustrated in Figure A.4 The subject doesn't necessarily have to be right on the intersection of the line, but merely close enough to it to take advantage of the Rule of Thirds.

A.4 The star on top of this fencepost, which is the main subject of this photograph, is placed to the right of the frame according to the Rule of Thirds. Taken at f/1.8 for 1/800 second at ISO 200.

When using the Rule of Thirds with a moving subject, you want to be sure to keep most of the frame in front of the subject to present the illusion that the subject has someplace to go within the frame.

Helpful Hints

Here are a few tips that you can follow that will make your images more interesting:

► **Use leading lines.** Using lines and curves helps draw your viewer's eye through the image thus creating interest and movement.

► **Frame the subject.** Use elements of the foreground to make a frame around the subject, which keeps the viewer's eye on the subject.

► **Avoid having the subject looking directly out of the side of the frame he or she is closest to.** Having the subject looking out of the photograph can be distracting to the viewer. For example, if your subject is on the left side of the composition having him or her face the right is better, and vice versa.

► **Avoid *mergers*.** A merger is when an element from the background appears to be a part of the subject, like the snapshot of granny at the park that looks like she has a tree growing out of the top of her head.

► **Try not to cut through the joint of a limb.** When composing or cropping your picture, it's best not to end the frame on a joint, such as an elbow or a knee and if the hands are included in the photo keep all of the fingers in the frame.

► **Avoid having bright spots or unnecessary details near the edge.** Anything bright or detailed near the edge of the frame draws the viewer's eye away from the subject and out of the image.

► **Fill the frame.** Try to make the subject the most dominant part of the image. Avoid lots of empty space around the subject unless it's essential to make the photograph work.

► **Use odd numbers.** When photographing multiple subjects, odd numbers seem to work best.

Accessories

There are an overwhelming number of accessories for the D800 for all different kinds of purposes. Nikon makes some of them and third party manufacturers make some. This is just a short list of some of the accessories that Nikon has available for the D800.

Nikon MB-D12 Battery grip

While not absolutely necessary this accessory is one that I find the most useful. Not only does it allow you to add an extra battery for extended shooting time, it also provides you with a full set of controls for handling the camera vertically. In addition to that, if you use the Nikon EN-EL-18 battery (the D4 battery) or AA batteries it allows you to increase the frame rate from 4 frames per second (fps) in FX up to 6 fps in DX mode (without the grip the D800 shoots at 5 fps). This isn't a great improvement like the D700, which allowed a jump from 5 fps to 8 fps in FX mode, a great increase in speed if you're a sports or photojournalist.

> **NOTE** If you're looking for a speedier frame rate you need the D4, which shoots at 10 fps in continuous AF and 11 fps with AF locked. The D4 is also half the resolution and twice the price.

The vertical controls allow you to hold the camera at a normal angle, which helps prevent the *elbow up in the air* shooting style and allows you to shoot in the more comfortable traditional style all while providing you with all of the controls that you have while shooting in the traditional style including a Shutter Release button (which can be switched off to prevent accidental shutter releases), both Main and Sub-command dials, a multi-selector, and a programmable AF-ON button.

Image courtesy Nikon USA

B.1 The D800 with the attached MB-D12 battery grip

One of the downfalls of the MB-D12 is the price. Nikon's list price is $616. I've found them online for $529, which I still consider extravagant considering I only paid $259 for the MB-D10 for the D700 and D300s and it does exactly the same job.

The good news is that just like the MB-D10, the MB-D12 is made from magnesium alloy and is weather sealed, just like the D800 camera body.

Speedlights

A Nikon Speedlight is, in my opinion, one of the most important accessories you can buy for your D800. Speedlights aren't just simply used on-camera for shooting in low light, but they give you the power and flexibility of professional lighting for a much more affordable price. They're much smaller, and they can be controlled wirelessly from the D800 straight out of the box.

Nikon Speedlights operate as a system of what Nikon terms Advanced Wireless Lighting (AWL) and are part of what is known as the Nikon Creative Lighting System (CLS). AWL allows you to wirelessly control multiple Speedlights and groups of Speedlights while using Nikon's proprietary i-TTL flash metering system. This allows you to achieve professional lighting results with a much smaller budget and a much smaller gear bag.

As I discussed in Chapter 5, the D800 allows you to control up to two groups of additional Speedlights using the built-in flash, and up to three groups of flashes when using an external commander such as an SU-800, SB-800, SB-900, or SB-910. The SB-700 is also limited to controlling two groups of Speedlights as well.

> **NOTE** The SB-600, SB-800, and SB-900 are discontinued, but still work perfectly with the D800.

The SB-600, SB-700, SB-800, SB-900, SB-910 can all be used as remote flashes.

You can find SB-600, SB-800, and SB-900 units used (and sometimes new), so don't hesitate so snag one if you find one at a good price. They provide full functionality with all current Nikon dSLRs and will likely continue to work with Nikon dSLRs into the future.

Nikon's current lineup of available Speedlights is the SB-910 flagship model, The SB-700, and the SB-400, as well as the SU-800 Commander and the R1 and R1-C1 Close-up flash system.

Image courtesy Nikon USA
B.2 The SB-910

Nikon GP-1 GPS Unit

For traveling photographers, the Nikon GP-1 GPS unit automatically geotags your images with latitude, longitude, and specific time information acquired from GPS satellites. The GP-1 is connected directly to the D800 to the 10-pin accessory port using the included GP1-CA10 connector.

The GP-1 can be attached via the hot shoe or can be attached to the strap with an included adapter.

You can also use Nikon's free ViewNX2 software to correlate the images with a map.

Nikon ME-1 Stereo Microphone

If you're serious about video, an external microphone is an essential accessory. The Nikon ME-1 is a small stereo microphone that fits into the D800's hot shoe. This external microphone allows you to record sound much more clearly than the internal microphone. And because it is located farther away from the lens, it also helps minimize the noise created by the autofocusing mechanism.

The ME-1 also comes with a windscreen to reduce wind noise when shooting outdoors and also features a low-cut filter to reduce other unwanted low-frequency noises.

Image courtesy Nikon USA

B.3 The Nikon ME-1 stereo microphone

WT-4A Wireless Transmitter

This handy little device allows you to transmit your images straight to your computer without the need for any wires using a wireless LAN connection or a peer-to-peer connection and a computer or FTP server.

While shooting tethered in the studio is great, being able to shoot wireless is even better because it removes the constraints of a cord and allows you to move about freely.

Remote Releases

When shooting tethered, doing timed exposures or long shutter speeds, or doing any type of photography while using a tripod, a remote release is a very handy tool. This allows you to release the shutter without actually touching the camera so you don't cause the camera to move during the exposure. This is important because even slight movement can cause motion blur.

Nikon has a few releases that work with the D800.

▶ **MC-30 remote trigger release.** This is just a basic release. Press the button, the camera focuses, and the shutter releases. You can also use Manual focus, which is what I'd recommend. This release can also be locked so you can use it in the Bulb mode to do timed exposures.

▶ **MC-36 multi-function remote cord.** This remote has a few more features. It can activate the Bulb function, it can be set to release the shutter at a certain time, and it can be programmed as an intervalometer. However, because the D800 already has a built-in intervalometer that can be programmed to shoot at a certain time, MC-30 is a less expensive choice.

▶ **ML-3 compact modulite remote.** Unfortunately, unlike the entry-level cameras, the D800 doesn't have built-in IR receiver so it can't be used with the inexpensive ML-L3 infrared remote. If you want to trigger your camera wirelessly you need to spend an extra $230 for this remote. It comes with an IR receiver that fits in the camera hot shoe. The modulite remote does have some pretty cool features though. You can use it as a standard wireless release, choose from single or continuous release, and it can also be programmed to release the shutter automatically when something comes between the remote and the receiver.

How to Use the Gray Card and Color Checker

Have you ever wondered how some photographers are able to consistently produce photos with such accurate color and exposure? It's often because they use gray cards and color checkers. Knowing how to use these tools helps you take some of the guesswork out of capturing photos with great color and correct exposures every time.

The Gray Card

Because the color of light changes depending on the light source, what you might decide is neutral in your photograph, isn't neutral at all. This is where a gray card comes in very handy. A gray card is designed to reflect the color spectrum neutrally in all sorts of lighting conditions, providing a standard from which to measure for later color corrections or to set a custom white balance.

By taking a test shot that includes the gray card, you guarantee that you have a neutral item to adjust colors against later if you need to. Make sure that the card is placed in the same light that the subject is for the first photo, and then remove the gray card and continue shooting.

> TIP When taking a photo of a gray card, de-focus your lens a little; this ensures that you capture a more even color.

Because many software programs enable you to address color correction issues by choosing something that should be white or neutral in an image, having the gray card in the first of a series of photos allows you to select the gray card as the neutral point. Your software resets red, green, and blue to be the same value, creating a neutral midtone. Depending on the capabilities of your software, you might be able to save the adjustment you've made and apply it to all other photos shot in the same series.

If you'd prefer to made adjustments on the spot, for example, and if the lighting conditions will remain mostly consistent while you shoot a large number of images, it is advisable to use the gray card to set a custom white balance in your camera. You can do this by taking a photo of the gray card filling as much of the frame as possible. Then, use that photo to set the custom white balance.

The Color Checker

A color checker contains 24 swatches which represent colors found in everyday scenes, including skin tones, sky, foliage, etc. It also contains red, green, blue, cyan, magenta, and yellow, which are used in all printing devices. Finally, and perhaps most importantly, it has six shades of gray.

Using a color checker is a very similar process to using a gray card. You place it in the scene so that it is illuminated in the same way as the subject. Photograph the scene once with the reference in place, then remove it and continue shooting. You should create a reference photo each time you shoot in a new lighting environment.

Later on in software, open the image containing the color checker. Measure the values of the gray, black, and white swatches. The red, green, and blue values in the gray swatch should each measure around 128, in the black swatch around 10, and in the white swatch around 245. If your camera's white balance was set correctly for the scene, your measurements should fall into the range (and deviate by no more than 7 either way) and you can rest easy knowing your colors are true.

If your readings are more than 7 points out of range either way, use software to correct it. But now you also have black and white reference points to help. Use the levels adjustment tool to bring the known values back to where they should be measuring (gray around 128, black around 10, and white around 245).

If your camera offers any kind of custom styles, you can also use the color checker to set or adjust any of the custom styles by taking a sample photo and evaluating it using the on-screen histogram, preferably the RGB histogram if your camera offers one. You can then choose that custom style for your shoot, perhaps even adjusting that custom style to better match your expectations for color.

Glossary

Active D-Lighting A camera setting that preserves highlight and shadow details in a high-contrast scene with a wide dynamic range.

AE (Autoexposure) A function of a camera where the camera selects the aperture and/or shutter speed according to the camera's built-in light meter. See also *Aperture Priority, Shutter Priority, and Programmed Auto.*

AE/AF (Autoexposure/Autofocus) Lock A camera control that lets you lock the current metered exposure and/or autofocus setting prior to taking a photo. This allows you to meter an off-center subject and then recompose the shot while retaining the proper exposure for the subject. The function of this button can be altered in the setup menu under the Buttons heading.

Autofocus A feature of the camera that allows it to focus on the subject automatically using electronics. Commonly referred to as AF.

AF-assist illuminator An LED light that's emitted in low-light or low-contrast situations. The AF-assist illuminator provides enough light for the camera's AF to work in low light.

ambient lighting Lighting that naturally exists in a scene.

angle of view The area of a scene that a lens can capture, which is determined by the focal length of the lens. Lenses with a shorter focal length have a wider angle of view than lenses with a longer focal length.

aperture The opening of the lens similar to the iris of an eye. The designation for each step in the aperture is called the f-stop. The smaller the f-stop (or f-number), the larger the actual opening of the aperture; and the higher-numbered f-stops designate smaller apertures, letting in less light. The f-number is the ratio of the focal length to the aperture diameter.

Aperture Priority An exposure mode setting where you choose the aperture and the camera automatically adjusts the shutter speed according to the camera's metered readings. Aperture Priority is often used by a photographer to control depth of field.

aspect ratio The ratio of the long edge of an image to the short edge as printed, displayed on a monitor, or captured by a digital camera.

autofocus The capability of a camera to determine the proper focus of the subject automatically.

backlighting A lighting effect produced when the main light source is located behind the subject. Backlighting can be used to create a silhouette effect or to illuminate translucent objects. See also *frontlighting* and *sidelighting*.

barrel distortion An aberration in a lens in which the lines at the edges and sides of the image are bowed outward. This distortion is usually found in shorter focal-length (wide-angle) lenses.

bokeh A term that refers to the out of focus areas of an image. It's derived from the Japanese word *boke,* which is loosely translated as fuzziness.

bounce flash Pointing the flash head in an upward position or toward a wall so that it bounces off another surface before reaching the subject, which softens the light reaching the subject. This often eliminates shadows and provides smoother light for portraits.

bracketing A photographic technique in which you vary the exposure over two or more frames. Doing this ensures a proper exposure in difficult lighting situations where your camera's meter can be fooled.

camera shake Camera movement, usually at slower shutter speeds, which produces a blurred image.

catchlight Highlights that appear in the subject's eyes.

center-weighted metering A light-measuring device that emphasizes the area in the middle of the frame when you're calculating the correct exposure for an image.

chromatic aberration A flaw of lens design where the lens doesn't focus all of the wavelengths of light on the same plane. This is typified by color fringing at the edges of high contrast areas of the image.

colored gel filters Colored translucent filters that are placed over a flash head or light to change the color of the light emitted on the subject. Colored gels can be used to create a colored hue of an image. Gels are often used to match the flash output with the ambient light as well as to change the color of a background when shooting portraits or still lifes by placing the gel over the flash head and then firing the flash at the background.

compression Reducing the size of a file by digital encoding, which uses fewer bits of information to represent the original subject. Some compression types, such as JPEG, actually discard some image information, while others, such as RAW (NEF), preserve all the details in the original.

Continuous Autofocus (AF-C) A camera setting that allows the camera to continually focus on a moving subject.

contrast The range between the lightest and darkest tones in an image. In a high-contrast image, the shades fall at the extremes of the range between white and black. In a low-contrast image, the tones are closer together.

curvilinear A lens that does not adjust for the curvature of the lens elements which results in an image that appears curved, especially at the edges. Fish-eye lenses are curvilinear.

dedicated flash An electronic flash unit, such as the Nikon SB-910, Nikon SB-900, SB-800, SB-700, SB-600, or SB-400, designed to work with the autoexposure features of a specific camera.

depth of field (DOF) The portion of a scene from foreground to background that appears sharp in the image.

diffuse lighting A soft, low-contrast lighting.

D-Lighting A function within the camera that can fix the underexposure that often happens to images that are backlit or in deep shadow. This is accomplished by adjusting the levels of the image after it's been captured. Not to be confused with Active D-Lighting.

DX Nikon's designation for digital single-lens reflex cameras (dSLRs) that use an APS-C–sized (23.6mm × 15.8mm) sensor.

equivalent focal length A DX-format digital camera's focal length, which is translated into the corresponding values for 35mm film or the FX format.

exposure The amount of light allowed to reach the sensor, which is determined by the ISO setting, the amount admitted by the aperture of the lens, and the length of time determined by the shutter speed.

exposure compensation A technique for adjusting the exposure indicated by a photographic exposure meter, in consideration of factors that may cause the indicated exposure to result in a less-than-optimal image.

exposure mode Camera settings that control how the exposure settings are determined. See also *Aperture Priority*, *Shutter Priority*, and *Programmed Auto*.

FX Nikon's designation for digital single-lens reflex cameras (dSLRs) that use a 35mm-sized (36mm × 24mm) sensor.

fps (frames per second) This is a term that describes how many images are being recorded per second.

GL

fill flash A lighting technique where the Speedlight provides enough light to illuminate the subject to eliminate shadows. Using a flash for outdoor portraits often brightens the subject in conditions where the camera meters light from a broader scene.

fill lighting The lighting used to illuminate shadows. Reflectors or additional incandescent lighting or electronic flash can be used to brighten shadows. One common outdoor technique is to use the camera's flash as a fill.

flash An external light source that produces an almost instant flash of light to illuminate a scene. Also known as electronic flash.

Flash Exposure Compensation (FEC) Adjusting the flash output. If images are too dark (underexposed), you can use FEC to increase the flash output. If images are too bright (overexposed), you can use FEC to reduce the flash output.

flash modes Modes that enable you to control the output of the flash by using different parameters. Some of these modes include Red-Eye Reduction and Slow Sync.

flash output level The output level of the flash as determined by one of the Flash modes used.

focal plane The point at which the lens focuses the image. In a dSLR the focal planer is where the sensor lies.

Front-curtain sync Front-curtain sync causes the flash to fire at the beginning of the period when the shutter is completely open in the instant that the first curtain of the focal plane shutter finishes its movement across the film or sensor plane. This is the default setting. See also *Rear-curtain sync*.

frontlighting The illumination coming from the direction of the camera. See also *backlighting* and *sidelighting*.

f-stop See *aperture*.

histogram A graphic representation of the range of tones in an image.

hot shoe The slot located on the top of the camera where the flash connects. The hot shoe is considered hot because it has electronic contacts that allow communication between the flash and the camera.

ISO sensitivity The ISO (International Organization for Standardization) setting on the camera indicates the light sensitivity. In digital cameras, lower ISO settings provide better-quality images with less image noise; however, a lower ISO setting requires more exposure time.

JPEG (Joint Photographic Experts Group) This is an image format that compresses the image data from the camera to achieve a smaller file size. The compression algorithm discards some of the detail when closing the image. The degree of compression can be adjusted, allowing a selectable trade-off between storage size and image quality. JPEG is the most common image format used by digital cameras and other photographic image-capture devices.

Kelvin A unit of measurement of color temperature based on a theoretical black body that glows a specific color when heated to a certain temperature. The sun is approximately 5500 K.

lag time The length of time between when the Shutter Release button is pressed and the shutter is actually released; the lag time on the D800 is so short, it's almost imperceptible. Compact digital cameras are notorious for having long lag times, which can cause you to miss important shots.

leading line An element in a composition that leads a viewer's eye toward the subject.

lens flare An effect caused by stray light reflecting off the many glass elements of a lens. Lens shades typically prevent lens glare, but sometimes you can choose to use it creatively by purposely introducing flare into your image.

macro lens A lens with the capability to focus at a very close range, enabling extreme close-up photographs.

manual exposure Bypassing the camera's internal light meter settings in favor of setting the shutter and aperture manually. Manual exposure is beneficial in difficult lighting situations where the camera's meter doesn't provide correct results. When you switch to manual settings, you may need to review a series of photos on the digital camera's LCD screen to determine the correct exposure.

Matrix metering The Matrix meter (Nikon exclusive) reads the brightness and contrast throughout the entire frame and matches those readings against a database of images (over 30,000 in most Nikon cameras) to determine the best metering pattern to be used to calculate the exposure value.

metering Measuring the amount of light by using a light meter.

NEF (Nikon Electronic File) The name of Nikon's RAW file format.

noise Pixels with randomly distributed color values in a digital image. Noise in digital photographs tends to be more pronounced with low-light conditions and long exposures, particularly when you set your camera to a higher ISO setting.

Noise Reduction (NR) A technology used to decrease the amount of random information in a digital image, often caused by long exposures and/or high ISO settings.

pincushion distortion A lens aberration in which the lines at the edges and sides of the image are bowed inward. It is usually found in longer focal-length (telephoto) lenses.

Programmed Auto (P) A camera setting where shutter speed and aperture are set automatically.

GL

RAW An image file format that contains the unprocessed camera data as it was captured. Using this format allows you to change image parameters, such as white balance saturation and sharpening. Although you can process RAW files in-camera, the preferred method requires special software, such as Adobe Camera Raw (available in Photoshop), Adobe Lightroom, or Nikon's Capture NX2 or View NX 2. See also *NEF*.

Rear-curtain sync Rear-curtain sync causes the flash to fire at the end of the exposure an instant before the second, or rear, curtain of the focal plane shutter begins to move. With slow shutter speeds, this feature can create a blur effect from the ambient light, showing as patterns that follow a moving subject, with the subject shown sharply frozen at the end of the blur trail. This setting is usually used in conjunction with longer shutter speeds. See also *Front-curtain sync*.

rectilinear A lens design feature that corrects for the curvature distortion than is found in wide-angle lenses. Most wide lenses are rectilinear whereas a fish-eye lens is not and retains the field curvature.

red-eye An effect from flash photography that appears to make a person's eyes glow red or an animal's yellow or green caused by light bouncing from the retina of the eye. It is most noticeable in dimly lit situations (when the irises are wide open) as well as when the electronic flash is close to the lens and, therefore, prone to reflect the light directly back.

Red-Eye Reduction A Flash mode controlled by a camera setting that's used to prevent the subject's eyes from appearing red in color. The Speedlight fires multiple flashes just before the shutter is opened, with the intention of causing the subject's iris to contract, therefore reflecting less light from the retina to the camera.

selective focus Using shallow depth of field to isolate the subject and make it more prominent by blurring out the rest of the image.

self-timer A mechanism that delays the opening of the shutter for several seconds after the Shutter Release button has been pressed.

short lighting When your main light is illuminating the side of the subject that's facing away from you.

shutter A mechanism that allows light to pass to the sensor for a specified amount of time.

Shutter Priority In this camera mode, you set the desired shutter speed and the camera automatically sets the aperture for you. It's best used when you're shooting action shots to freeze the subject's motion by using fast shutter speeds.

shutter speed The length of time the shutter is open to allow light to fall onto the imaging sensor. The shutter speed is measured in seconds or, more commonly, fractions of seconds.

sidelighting Lighting that comes directly from the left or the right of the subject. See also *frontlighting* and *backlighting*.

Single Autofocus (AF-S) A focus setting that locks the focus on the subject when the Shutter Release button is half-pressed. This allows you to focus on the subject and then recompose the image without losing focus as long as the Shutter Release button is half-pressed.

Slow Sync A Flash mode that allows the camera's shutter to stay open for a longer time to allow the ambient light to be recorded. The background receives more exposure, which gives the image a more natural appearance.

Speedlight A Nikon-specific term for its accessory flashes.

spherical aberration A problem with lens design that causes the light coming through the lens not to converge at a single point resulting in soft or unfocused images. Most lenses on the market today include an aspherical lens element that corrects this problem.

spot meter A metering system in which the exposure is based on a small area of the image. On the D800 the spot is linked to the AF point.

TTL (Through-the-Lens) A metering system where the light is measured directly through the lens.

vanishing point The point at which parallel lines converge and seem to disappear.

Vibration Reduction (VR) A function of the lens in which the lens elements are shifted by a mechanism in the lens to reduce the effects of camera shake.

white balance A setting used to compensate for the differences in color temperature from different light sources. For example, a typical tungsten light bulb is very yellow-orange, so the camera adds blue to the image to ensure that the light looks like standard white light.

GL

Index

Guides to go

Digital Field Guides are packed with essential information about your camera, plus great techniques for everyday shooting. Colorful and easily portable, they go where you go.

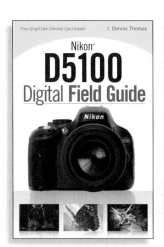

978-0-470-63352-6

978-0-470-64864-3

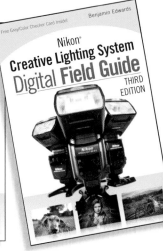

978-1-118-02223-8

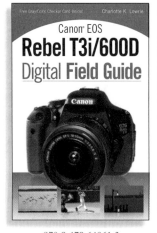

978-0-470-64861-2

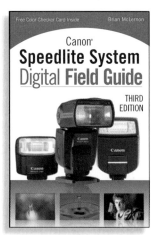

978-1-118-11289-2

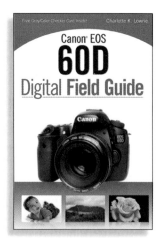

978-0-470-64862-9